ETHICS AND THE ELDERLY

ETHICS AND THE ELDERLY

The Challenge of Long-Term Care

SARAH M. MOSES

ORBIS BOOKS

Maryknoll, New York 10545

ORBIS BOOKS
Maryknoll, New York 10545

Fathers and Brothers
MARYKNOLL™

Founded in 1970, Orbis Books endeavors to publish works that enlighten the mind, nourish the spirit, and challenge the conscience. The publishing arm of the Maryknoll Fathers and Brothers, Orbis seeks to explore the global dimensions of the Christian faith and mission, to invite dialogue with diverse cultures and religious traditions, and to serve the cause of reconciliation and peace. The books published reflect the views of their authors and do not represent the official position of the Maryknoll Society. To learn more about Maryknoll and Orbis Books, please visit our website at www.maryknollsociety.org.

Copyright © 2015 by Sarah M. Moses

Published by Orbis Books, Box 302, Maryknoll, NY 10545-0302.

Biblical quotations in this volume are taken from *The New Oxford Annotated Bible with the Apocrypha* (New Revised Standard Version).

Manufactured in the United States of America

Library of Congress Cataloging-in-Publication Data

Moses, Sarah M.
    Ethics and the elderly : the challenge of long-term care / Sarah M. Moses.
       pages cm
    Includes bibliographical references and index.
    ISBN 978-1-62698-131-7 (pbk.)
       1. Older people—Long-term care—Moral and ethical aspects. 2. Older people—Long-term care—Religious aspects—Catholic Church. I. Title.
RC954.3.M67 2015
362.16—dc23
                                                              2014045882

In loving memory of
Betty Touhey

Contents

Acknowledgments

My research into ethics and aging began during my graduate work in the Department of Theology at Boston College. During my years there my thinking about contemporary aging was enriched and challenged by fellow grad students such as Kathryn Getek, Laurie Johnston, and Autumn Ridenour. And I owe a special debt of gratitude to the professors who served as mentors and friends—Lisa Cahill, David Hollenbach, and Steve Pope. The final research and writing that went into this book happened thanks to the generous support of the University of Mississippi through summer research grants. And I would like to thank my department chairs—Bill Lawhead and Steven Skultety—who have supported and encouraged me throughout this process. I would also like to heartily thank my editor, Jim Keane, and all the folks at Orbis Books who made the publication of this book possible.

On a personal note, I would like to thank my grandparents, Hayden and Harbert Thornton and Mary and John Moses. Long before I began reflecting on issues of aging in an academic context, they showed me the beauty and dignity of old age. A special word of gratitude is also due my parents and my husband and two children. Without their concrete support and encouragement this book would have never been finished!

Finally, in addition to Betty Touhey, to whom this book is dedicated, I would like to thank all of my elderly friends whom I came to know through the work of the Community of Sant'Egidio in Boston. There are too many to name here, but each in his or her own way contributed to my thinking about long-term care. It is through these concrete experiences that I discovered the potential and dignity of older people and came to see that our society could do so much better at providing care in a way that honors and enables the participation of the elderly in our communities. Beyond contributing to my understanding of contemporary aging, they have also enriched my life immeasurably with their friendship, and for this I am forever grateful.

CHAPTER ONE

Introduction

I begin with the story of a seventy-three-year-old woman named Kate who participated in the elderly outreach program of the Community of Sant'Egidio, a lay association of the Roman Catholic Church. Kate was divorced and lived alone in a one-bedroom apartment in a public housing development for seniors and disabled adults. Kate's income was almost entirely based on a Social Security benefit check, and she received medical insurance through the state Medicaid program. Although her income was meager, Kate was able to pay her bills, including extras such as cable TV and telephone, and purchase groceries, which were augmented by a daily delivery from Meals on Wheels. While Kate maintained contact with her two adult children, they lived too far from the city to be involved with her care on a daily or weekly basis. But despite minor frailty and limited mobility, she had been able to maintain her independence through various elder services. For instance, Kate had a subsidized "home-maker" service that sent someone once a week to help with housecleaning and laundry. And she was able to get to the grocery store through a weekly bus service operated by the public housing management. For other transportation needs such as doctor's appointments, Kate used a car service run through the city's public transportation system, which allows seniors and disabled adults to schedule rides as an alternative to city buses and the subway.

Kate also maintained many friendships in her building and helped to organize various social occasions for fellow residents. For instance, she helped to coordinate a weekly coffee hour held in the building's community room and organized rummage sales several times a year to raise money for special events such as holiday parties. When members of the Community of Sant'Egidio began their outreach at her building, Kate became one of their first friends. She received weekly visits from Sant'Egidio members, and they also occasionally helped her with transportation needs and minor house projects. Kate also began to participate in their outreach to a nursing home in another part of the city. With members of Sant'Egidio, she would visit once a month and bring snacks and gifts for residents.

During a holiday party at that nursing home, Kate noticed that the piano was in very poor shape. And so she decided to take out an ad in the local town paper asking for the donation of a piano for this facility. Within a week she received a phone call from someone who wanted to donate a piano. Through a series of phone calls, Kate found a moving company that would transport the piano for free. Her Sant'Egidio friends then coordinated the delivery and met the movers at the nursing home. When Sant'Egidio members came to see her to report the safe delivery of the new piano, she said to them, "I can do a lot if I have others to help me."

This brief story provides a window into one of the most remarkable developments of the past century: more of us than ever before are reaching old age, and we are living longer than ever before. But as Kate's story also illustrates, more of us are reaching ages at which we begin to experience various care needs, ranging from help with basic daily tasks to more serious health issues. And, as Kate's statement reflects, these care needs are not merely medical or economic issues, but also impact one's sense of ongoing purpose and dignity. One of the major arguments in this book is that whether the new old age is experienced as a blessing or a burden will largely depend on our response as individuals and as a society. Thus, I seek to contribute to that response in a way that would allow the elderly and our society to experience these added years as an opportunity for ongoing meaning and participation, just as Kate did.

Over forty years ago, the Second Vatican Council of the Roman Catholic Church published *Gaudium et spes*, a document that set forth an understanding of "the presence and function of the Church in the world of today" (163). This document declared that the Christian church is called in every age to listen to and engage with the larger society about the defining social questions of the day. Specifically the council affirmed, "In every age, the church carries the responsibility of reading the signs of the times and of interpreting them in the light of the Gospel.... We must be aware of and understand the aspirations, the yearnings, and the often dramatic features of the world in which we live" (165). In our own present day, aging and the elderly are recognized as a dramatic feature of our world by virtually all sectors of society. Trends that marked the last century, and now follow us into the twenty-first, literally place us in a new moment in human history: the elderly have become a social and common question for our time. As the United States Conference of Catholic Bishops stated in 1999, in light of the demographics of aging populations and life expectancy, "The current situation is unprecedented" (1999).

Guided by the framework of *Gaudium et spes*, I understand the following as primary tasks of Christian ethics: (1) to identify the pressing moral challenges of our day and (2) to inform the church's response to those challenges. The reality of aging and the elderly today presents multiple challenges, from issues of age-based discrimination to adequate retirement funding. This book specifically focuses on what is now widely recognized as one of America's most pressing challenges in the new millennium: long-term care for our growing elderly population. Drawing on concrete models and biblical and theological resources, I seek to contribute to the church's engagement in social dialogue concerning a fundamental ethical question: how can our society meet the challenge of long-term care in a just manner so that the dignity of older persons is promoted and protected? Thus, while this book is about aging, it also represents a model of Christian ethics able to engage the public sphere in critical dialogue.

The chapters that follow present what I consider a Christian ethical vision adequate to guiding the church's internal response and external engagement on the challenge of long-term care today. In order to reflect on this ethical challenge, I start from the insight of *Gaudium et spes* that we must first recognize and understand the world in which we live. Or, as ethicist William Schweiker has argued, religious ethics must attend to the basic question: "What is going on?" (2004, 6). As Schweiker explains, answering this question is the important "descriptive" task of ethics, which is "to describe and analyze a situation in terms of its moral meaning." Thus, Chapter 2 sketches the significant features of the dramatic characteristic that is aging today, particularly those features that relate to understanding the moral challenge of long-term care. First, I present an understanding of aging today as encompassing two salient aspects: we are living longer, healthier, and better overall; and at the same time, we are facing increasing long-term care needs that arise from the disease and disability of late old age. Second, I will argue that the ethical challenge of long-term care today involves not only the distribution of economic and human resources but the preservation of dignity in late life.

As *Gaudium et spes* argued, it is imperative to gain an adequate understanding of aging today because of the church's responsibility to engage the wider society on important social issues. In the document, the Second Vatican Council articulated the need for Christians to embrace a profound solidarity with the world in which they live: "The joys and hopes, the grief and anguish of the people of our time, especially of those who are poor or afflicted, are the joys and hopes, the grief and anguish of the followers of Christ as well. Nothing that is genuinely human fails to find an echo in their hearts" (163). Further, the council suggested that by entering into dialogue about these hopes and anxieties the church provides the clearest expression of its "solidarity, respect and love for the whole human family, of which it forms part" (164). Likewise, *Gaudium et spes* warned against the withdrawal of Christians from society and affirmed the responsibility that comes from their inextricable involvement in earthly societies: "The council exhorts Christians, as citizens of both [heavenly and earthly] cities, to perform their duties faithfully in the spirit of the Gospel. It is a mistake to think that, because we have here no lasting city . . . we are entitled to evade our earthly responsibilities" (211). The council goes on to state that the church should actively seek those sources from society that help it to better understand the contemporary world. The perspective of *Gaudium et spes* actually reflects a long-accepted use in Christian ethics of nontheological sources, particularly where those sources illuminate an area of applied ethics. Chapter 2 thus lays out a descriptive analysis of contemporary aging drawing on diverse resources, including gerontology, the social sciences, medicine, and Christian ethics.

Chapters 3, 4, and 5 then move to what Schweiker calls the "normative dimension" of religious ethics (2004, 6). This aspect of the ethical task seeks to answer the question: what norms and values ought to guide human life and what are the authoritative sources of those norms and values? The Christian ethical tradition has long recognized human experience as a source of moral insight, and Chapter 3 begins the normative task with two concrete models of long-term care programs: The Community of Sant'Egidio and The Green House Project. The Community of Sant'Egidio is an international, ecumenical lay association in which friendship to and care of the elderly is a fundamental aspect of its outreach ministry.[1] The Green House Project is a U.S.-based, nonprofit initiative that promotes a small scale, family-style, long-term care model for the elderly as an alternative to existing institutional care models such as assisted living facilities and nursing homes. While this model has been adapted in several states by religiously affiliated health-care and senior-service organizations, it is also used by for-profit and secular nonprofit groups. I will analyze each of these programs as regards the way in which they challenge Christian ethics and society to approach long-term care in a manner that preserves and promotes the dignity of older persons.

I have chosen to begin with these two concrete models for several reasons. First, the experiences of these two programs stimulate the moral imagination to envision practical possibilities beyond the standard ways in which long-term elder care has been provided to the elderly in the past. Second, individual and communal experience itself can serve as a source of ethical norms. For instance, Protestant theologian Ronald Thiemann has suggested that the church contributes to public life not only through its theological traditions but also by being communities that embody ethical values in their own *practices*, what he calls "schools of public virtue" or "communities of hope" (1991, 43, 123). Likewise, *Gaudium et spes* argues that the church is not only a source of ideas but also, through the actions of its members,

---

1. The analysis of Sant'Egidio provided in this book is based partially on my first-hand involvement with the organization's elderly outreach programs starting in 2000. That involvement included exposure to Sant'Egidio's work in various U.S. cities such as Boston, MA, and in Rome, Italy.

a potential source of virtues for the world (213). And though not a faith-based organization like Sant'Egidio, The Green House Project is intentional about shaping its practices to embody specific moral ideals. Thus, analyzing the vision and action of these two models yields important ethical norms that contribute to the construction of a Christian ethic of long-term care. Finally, employing experience as a primary source for Christian ethics contributes to the potential for dialogue with nonreligious entities in the public sphere.

Drawing on the ethical insights gained from the two concrete models, Chapters 4 and 5 turn to the particular resources of the Christian tradition to further shape a normative framework. Chapter 4 presents the biblical building blocks of my ethic of long-term care. Material from the Hebrew Bible and New Testament will be analyzed to show that the biblical injunctions calling for familial and societal care of older people are set within a theological vision of the elderly as subjects who continue to have purpose before God and within the community of faith. I will also show that the biblical material presents faithful older people in a realistic manner, acknowledging the onset of age-related weakness and disability and that elderly people do not possess automatic wisdom but struggle with vice and disappointment as at other stages of life. The chapter seeks to go beyond a method typical of Christian ethics in which the Bible is read only in order to identify injunctions, obligations, or principles; in fact, because of a dominant interest in establishing familial duties in the care of the elderly, such a method has often limited moral inquiry into the relation of the Bible to aging. Instead, I will also concentrate on stories of elderly persons as the narratives present these figures responding to God's calling. By doing so, Chapter 4 expands the usefulness of the biblical text in providing a vision of old age that can guide and animate a Christian ethical response to long-term care in our own context.

Use of the biblical text as a primary source for Christian ethics is based partially on a concern to construct a long-term care ethic that is ecumenical in its appeal. In his essay "The Status of Scripture in the Church," Catholic theologian Roger Haight notes that the Bible has been a normative source for Christian life and practice throughout the history of Christian thought, including Roman Catholic and

Protestant thought (1990, 89). In addition, Haight observes that the Bible has been a source of reform not only in the Protestant tradition but also in the reforms of the Second Vatican Council (89). Though the Bible is more often associated with Protestant ethical traditions, Vatican II brought about a revival of interest in the Bible as important to the development of Catholic social ethics. For example, *Gaudium et spes* states the church should respond to the pressing issues of contemporary society by "throwing the light of the Gospel on them and supplying humanity with the saving resources which the church has received . . ." (164). Thus, the approach of Chapter 4 is shaped by the ecumenical relevance of Scripture. As Haight has observed, "Today the ecumenical context for theology demands in a new way the normativity of scriptures" (89).

Chapter 5 moves to a second resource of the Christian tradition: the theological vision of the church as a community of disciples in which persons live in mutual love and support. From this theological perspective, the dignity of older persons is affirmed because, as disciples who are called by God throughout their lives, they remain equal participants in the mutuality of Christian fellowship. Here I draw on Karl Barth's approach to discipleship and Christian fellowship, Paul Wadell's writings on the church as a community of friendship, and Protestant and Catholic theological writings that demonstrate the significance of discipleship and Christian fellowship for elderly persons today. My argument is that the church's response to long-term care should be guided by a Christian ethic of care rooted in the agency of older persons as ongoing disciples who remain equal, participating members in the mutual fellowship and service of the church.

Though particular to the Christian tradition, the explicit use of biblical and theological sources need not hinder Christian ethics from dialogue in the public sphere. While some contemporary Christian ethicists have emphasized the distinctiveness and nonintelligibility of specifically religious sources, my approach is in line with others who have argued for the possibility of bringing these sources into engagement with the larger society. For instance, in *Constructing a Public Theology: The Church in a Pluralistic Age*, Thiemann states, "Our challenge is to develop a public theology that remains based in the particularities of the Christian faith while genuinely addressing issues of public significance" (1991, 19).[2] He argues that this approach allows the church to maintain its prophetic voice and its ability to make substantive contributions to public debate. In this regard Thiemann calls for contemporary theologians to "engage the world of culture from within an integral vision of reality as formed by the Christian gospel" (1991, 92). Thiemann's interest is not in establishing a "new Christendom," but rather in making available the resources of Christian theology and practice for the betterment of public policy and increased justice in our society. From this perspective Christians are able to contribute to the public sphere not *in spite* of the particularity of faith, but rather *because* of it.

The ecumenical relevance of this approach is evident in the parallels found in *Gaudium et spes*, the Catholic Church's defining statement on church–world relations in the twentieth century. For *Gaudium et spes* reflected a renewed emphasis on theology and Scripture as primary resources for the church's engagement with social issues. For example, ethicist David Hollenbach concludes that "the document makes a major new contribution to modern Catholic social teaching by presenting more explicitly developed theological grounds for the Church's social engagement than are found in the earlier social encyclicals." As Hollenbach notes, the structure of the document itself reflects this approach: for each major topic addressed, the council offered comments based on "central religious convictions of the Christian tradition" along with nonreligious sources. In contrast, Hollenbach notes that the social encyclicals prior to Vatican II "relied almost exclusively on a natural law approach based on philosophical rather than biblical and theological categories" (2005, 266-75). Thus, in a way similar to Thiemann's approach, *Gaudium et spes* suggests that Christians

---

2. Thiemann defines public theology as "faith seeking to understand the relation between Christian convictions and the broader social and cultural context within which the Christian community lives" (1991, 21). For Thiemann's more extensive analysis of democratic pluralism in American political thought and institutions and the public role of religious faith, see Thiemann 1996.

should not abandon the particular language and practices of faith and Scripture in the public sphere, but that in fact it is precisely this that provides their most substantive contribution.

Having laid out the normative framework for a Christian ethic of long-term care, I move on in Chapter 6 to explore the implications of this ethic for the church's internal practices and its dialogue and cooperation with the wider society on practical issues of public policy. This section of the book addresses what Schweiker calls the "practical dimension" of religious ethics: "what ought I or we to do?" (2004, 7). In relation to the practical task, Chapter 6 will illustrate that an adequate Christian ethic of long-term care must address not only personalized, direct care provided in the context of families and the church's ministry, but also the sphere of social justice. Thus I will suggest ways for the church to actively cooperate with wider initiatives to enhance dignity and participation in old age, such as increased funding for community-based care and new models of congregate living such as the Green House. In its engagement with the public sphere, the Christian ethical vision outlined here also finds common cause with secular concepts of justice as participation, such as United Nations' advocacy on the rights of the elderly. And finally, based on the prophetic capacity of Christian practices and resources, I will discuss how a Christian ethic of long-term care rooted in the agency of older persons enables the church to prophetically critique aspects of contemporary society and public policy that marginalize older persons and diminish their participation in society.

The approach to public engagement taken in Chapter 6 envisions the relationship between the church and wider society as defined by a free dialogue of mutual enrichment and challenge. Here again Thiemann's work and *Gaudium et spes* are complementary resources. In his approach to public theology Thiemann asserts that effective and genuine public theology is carried out through a respectful, free back and forth between the church and other entities in the wider society. While the church serves the world by bringing a voice of prophetic criticism where necessary, it also allows the voices of genuine truth in culture and society to challenge its thought and practices. As Thiemann writes, "Public theology is a genuine risk-taking venture. By opening the Christian tradition to conversation with those in the public sphere, public theology opens Christian belief and practice to the critique that inevitably emerges from those conversation partners" (1996, 23). Likewise, Thiemann suggests that through this dialogue the church is able to identify "some common ground between Christian faith and secular culture and for some common good in which all persons can share" (1996, 92). However, Thiemann warns against any fixed identification of Christian faith with particular voices or entities in wider society, such as economic theories or political parties. Instead, Thiemann suggests that the church maintain a sense of freedom, which allows it to be open to new possibilities of interaction between Christian faith and the wider culture and to seek alliances where that interaction can promote greater justice in the world. For Thiemann this involves not only alliances of thought and ethical values, but also "joint action for the common good" (1996, 123).

In a similar manner, *Gaudium et spes* insisted that the nature of the church's interaction with society is one of two-way dialogue. As Hollenbach observes, the council provided "an approach to dialogue in which the Christian community begins from its own distinctive beliefs but goes on to engage those who are different" (2005, 287). *Gaudium et spes* reflected this approach in the explicit statement that its proposals were addressed to "all people," Christian and non-Christian. And like Thiemann's approach, the document affirmed that this dialogue involves not only the contribution of the church to society, but the church's openness to contributions from society. Hollenbach describes the two-way exchange envisioned by the council: "[A commitment to dialogue] will lead both to a transformation of the world by its encounter with the gospel and to transformation of the Church by Christian encounter with diverse societies and cultures" (2005, 278). In a subsection of *Gaudium et spes* entitled "What the Church Receives from the Modern World," the council declared its awareness of ways the church has been enriched by human experience, the sciences, and the diversity of cultures it has encountered. Not only does *Gaudium et spes* encourage mutual enrichment based on a dialogue of ideas and values, but it also puts forth the possibility of concrete cooperation with institutions and entities where "truth, goodness, and justice" are found and that are "compatible with its mission" (210).

Finally, like Thiemann's approach, *Gaudium et spes* insists that dialogue and engagement occur in the freedom proper to the church and to the society. For instance, the document insists that "By its nature and mission the church is universal in that it is not committed to any one culture or to any political, economic or social system" (210). This approach is helpfully summarized by Hollenbach: "The relation of Church to society is neither oppositional nor one of identity; it is a relation of mutual interaction and dialogue" (2005, 275). Chapter 6 shows through practical application of ethical norms the possibility of a free, mutually enriching, and challenging relationship between church and society in relation to the issue of long-term elder care.

To conclude the introduction to this project, I offer a brief word on my use of the terms agency and subject/subjectivity throughout this book. For instance, we will see in Chapter 2 that some long-term-care reform experts prefer to use the language of autonomy as a way of discussing the importance of self-determination and self-direction for older people. However, partially because of its long history of usage in medical ethics and its association with notions of personal independence, I prefer to use the language of agency and the elderly as participating subjects. In this book, my use of these terms should be understood as reflecting concepts articulated by the various authors we will discuss: the elderly as possessing the capacity for ongoing development and contribution, as having preferences and desires that correspond with one's self-identity and life goals, and as capable of interpersonal relationships and exchange of affection and support. It should also be noted that I use agency with the understanding that, as at other stages of life, though perhaps less visibly, older people's exercise of these qualities of agency is done in relation to and in partial dependence on others rather than in isolation.

While the term subject or subjectivity has its own history in fields such as philosophy, I have chosen to use this term here to indicate the very plain sense of the opposite of being an object, particularly as that relates to correcting notions of older people merely as the object of the care of others. While the provision of care by others to the elderly is vital, I will also insist that such care can be given in a way that promotes the dignity of older people only when they are also recognized as subjects, as persons capable of mutuality. Thus, part of the argument of this book is related to these key terms in that the manner in which we provide long-term care in the United States must reflect the fact that these qualities of the human agent and subject do not disappear with the onset of disability and dependence in late old age. A clearer picture of the way the dignity and agency of older people is threatened is the focus of our next chapter.

CHAPTER TWO

Aging Today: Understanding a Dramatic Feature of Our World

As I noted in Chapter 1, *Gaudium et spes* argued that the church has a responsibility to "be aware of and understand" the "dramatic features" of the world and historical context in which it exists. Towards the task of understanding the issue of aging in contemporary society, this chapter thus focuses on what William Schweiker calls the descriptive task of ethics, that is identifying "what is going on" both in terms of relevant facts and in terms of the ethical dimensions of particular situations. Schweiker observes that the descriptive task is a challenging one because all situations are complex and are open to multiple interpretations (2004, 6-7). However, this is a crucial task in ethics, because the way in which we conceptualize a particular social issue will impact our understanding of the proper action to take in response. Certainly the dramatic feature of aging and the elderly today is a vastly complex reality with multiple aspects and, as evidenced by current public debates, is seen from many different perspectives. While not claiming to cover every relevant aspect of this reality, the purpose of this chapter is first to present two demographic trends crucial to understanding contemporary aging and why elder care is now a major social and personal issue. Second, this chapter will identify some specific ethical dimensions of long-term care today that help us to appreciate the need for a response.

The Demographics of Contemporary Aging:
Population Aging and Human Longevity

As the President's Council on Bioethics stated in a 2005 report on caregiving in the United States, "In the years ahead, the age structure of most advanced industrial societies will be unlike anything seen in human history, with both the average age of the population and the absolute number of old people increasing dramatically" (2005, 5). Thus, the first aspect of current aging trends to consider is the aging of populations. As gerontologist Harry Moody describes, the aging of a population points to the dynamic whereby, due to various causes, there is a "shifting balance of age-groups in the population: a larger proportion of old people, a smaller proportion of children" (1988, 1).[1] In visual terms, it has been said that "the age pyramid that existed less than half a century ago has literally been turned upside down" (Pontifical Council for the Laity 1998). Stated in numerical terms, British aging expert Sarah Harper observes, "By 2050, more people globally will be over age 50 than under age 15" (2006, 20).

The United States is not immune to this demographic trend: in the United States in 1900, there were three million people aged sixty-five or older, accounting for 4 percent of the population; in 2011, there were approximately forty-one million people aged sixty-five or older, making up 13 percent of the population; by 2040, the group of those sixty-five and older is expected to reach about seventy-nine million, representing 21 percent of the population ("A Profile of Older Americans 2013," 2-3). In fact, it is significant to note that the projected elderly population in 2040 reflects a *doubling* of the number of people age sixty-five and older in the United States in a mere thirty years. Thus, while the United States still remains a "young" country relative to its European counterparts, it is nonetheless increasingly marked by the realities of an aging population. For instance, the 2010 U.S. Census reported that from 2000 to 2010, the population of those sixty-five and older grew faster than the general population (15.1 percent compared to 9.7 percent respectively), making the sixty-five-plus

---

1. Causes include lower fertility rates, improved health care, eliminating early death, and social programs that meet basic needs throughout the lifespan. See Bureau of the Census 1999; Harper 2006, 21.

population the largest in census history (Werner 2011, 4). Furthermore, Harper makes the important point that this trend is not merely a short-term effect of the Baby Boom generation hitting sixty-five; rather, this "demographic maturing" indicates a long-term, global trend (2006, 20). Summarizing the significance of the moment in which we find ourselves, European demographer Chris Wilson states, "The twentieth century was, above all else, a century of population growth; the twenty first century will be a century of aging" (2006, 5).

The second demographic aspect of contemporary aging for us to consider is the enormous increase in human longevity. Concerning general life expectancy trends, researcher on aging Paul B. Baltes writes, "In industrialized countries over the last century, we have witnessed truly astonishing increases in average life expectancy, from about forty-five years in 1900 to close to eighty years in 2000" (2006, 33). Federal agencies provided the following figures on current life expectancy as of 2013: on average, persons who live to age sixty-five can anticipate living about nineteen additional years, and those reaching eighty-five can expect to live close to six and seven years more for men and women respectively ("A Profile of Older Americans 2013," 2). Baltes provides a historical perspective on the increased life expectancy among the very old: "Thirty years ago, an 80-year-old would live, on average, another four years; today, an 80-year-old can expect to live longer for double that time" (2006, 33). Furthermore, statistics show that more and more people in the United States will reach sixty-five: a recent report stated that 69 percent of those born in 1925 lived past their sixty-fifth birthday, while it is estimated that 80 percent of those born in 1955 will live past that age (President's Council 2005, 6).

In fact, U.S. census data shows that those aged eighty-five and older are the fastest growing segment of the elderly population, and current demographic projections suggest that by 2050 the elderly population age eighty-five and older will reach 5 percent of the general population or nineteen million people, up from 2 percent in 2000 (Federal Interagency Forum 2012, 4). This increase in life expectancy has led experts to say that, for the first time, we are reaching a place in which the "normal" lifespan of most people converges with what scientists consider to be the current "maximum" lifespan encoded in the genetic make-up of the human species (Harper 2006, 21).

The significance of the increase in average life expectancy can also be seen in shifting cultural notions of the life cycle. As Moody observes, "For the first time in history, most people can expect to live out the full course of the human life cycle from childhood through old age (1988, 1). Or, as another article states, "The way old age is experienced today is quite different from yesteryear. The difference lies in the increased life and health expectancy, and in their higher educational achievement level. This has contributed a new segment of the life course—the third age" (Dickerson and Watkins 2003, 204). Underlying the concept of the "third age" is the understanding that various factors have created a full and significant life stage at a time of life that used to be considered a "short epilogue" to one's life. The cultural "surprise" of this new life stage is humorously and yet accurately illustrated by the Allstate Insurance Company advertisement.

As gerontologist Robert Rubinstein explains, "The term 'Third Age' has come to mean this portion of the life span: post-career and post-familial responsibility.... Its characteristics have been made possible by increased longevity, better health, and an increased level of financial well-being among the cohort of newly old" (2002, 31). Given the increases in the length of this stage of life and distinguishing features of those eighty and older, some experts now speak of a "Fourth Age" in the life cycle. For instance, Baltes suggests, "Currently, in developed countries, the Third Age begins, on average, at about age 60; the Fourth Age generally starts around 80" (2006, 32). Another way in which experts refer to distinct phases in the latter years of life is with the terms "young old," starting at sixty-five, and the "oldest old," starting at eighty-five (President's Council 2005, 5).

A further significant implication of increased life expectancy for cultural notions of the life cycle is the association of mortality and dying with the Third and Fourth Ages of life. As Aaron explains in his examination of the history of longer life spans, prior to the Industrial Revolution, the majority of people died young, and few survived to old age (2006, 10). Thus, while mortality is not a "condition" one acquires in old age, it is true that, as Moody states, gains in human longevity during the last century have "displaced death more and more into later life" (1992, 23). Today more than two-thirds of all deaths in the United States occur in persons sixty-five and older (Moody 1992,

The generation that wouldn't trust anyone over 30

— ⚙ —

NEVER PLANNED ON A 30-YEAR RETIREMENT.

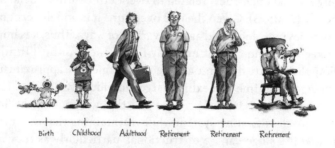

| Birth | Childhood | Adulthood | Retirement | Retirement | Retirement |

Average life expectancy in the U.S. has risen to an all-time high. Great news, except that the amount of money people put away for retirement isn't rising at all. How is our nation going to make sure its citizens have the money to retire? Allstate has a few ideas:

1. EXAMINE SOCIAL SECURITY
Americans will not be able to rely solely on Social Security for a comfortable retirement. In the future, it's projected to cover an increasingly smaller percentage of the average retirement. There's debate as to whether it should be repaired or replaced. But what's clear is we need to reform Social Security *now*.

2. BOOST RETIREMENT PLAN ENROLLMENT
Companies should continue looking for ways to encourage employee participation in 401(k) plans. One proven method to increase retirement savings is through company matches. Another is automatic enrollment—employees are signed up for savings plans when they join the company, unless they specifically opt out.

3. INCREASE PERSONAL SAVINGS
Ultimately, everyone is responsible for their own retirement. It's why we support laws that reward people for saving. Tax-advantaged savings vehicles, like annuities and IRAs, are two examples of products that can help allay Baby Boomers' biggest fear: living to see the well run dry.

Let's save retirement by saving for retirement.
THAT'S ALLSTATE'S STAND

Allstate.
You're in good hands.

Auto   Home   Life   Retirement

The New Yorker 83.2, March 5, 2007

20). Because of this alteration in the structure of death, it is not seen as a part of the condition of youth and adulthood but rather something that distinguishes the later stage of life. Gerontologists Fahey and Holstein summarize this cultural mentality: "In the third age, we are inexorably closer to death than at other times in our life" (1993, 243).

Of course, any attempt at neat categorization of life stages by chronological age immediately confronts the reality of enormous diversity within age cohorts and diverse cultural constructions of "old age." For instance, the President's Council on Bioethics notes that the significance of age sixty-five in the American cultural imagination is "largely a social construct" related to twentieth-century Social Security policy (2005, 5). Given the role of culture, it is widely recognized that societies may define old age in a variety of ways. Thus, it is important to keep in mind a point made by Baltes and Smith: "[Third Age and Fourth Age] are dynamic and heuristic concepts, approximations that change with time and exhibit large individual variations" (2003, 32). Throughout this book, I proceed with the awareness of the limitations of any classification system while maintaining that distinctions of age and life stage can be instructional, particularly as they relate to understanding pressing ethical issues arising from contemporary aging. For, as Fahey and Holstein also argue, "At whatever point it begins—often gradually and unremarked, noted by others before ourselves and frequently denied—we would still suggest that most people at some point in their lives—perhaps their late 60s or early 70s and beyond—share some significant characteristics that define them as entering their third age" (1993, 243).[2] And, as the President's Council on Bioethics suggests, despite the fluidity of cultural constructions, "the outlines of growth and decline still hold in our lives, as does the sense that life has a shape, with different phases, each with

---

2. For instance, Fahey and Holstein offer the following as "unique features that mark old age": chronological age does mark persons as closer to death than at earlier times and thus creates a more tangible awareness of finitude, a time for coming to terms with who one has been, a time of fewer socially expected roles, a time in which cumulative effects of various socioeconomic variables constrain us more clearly, and the experience of physical decline and loss (1993, 244-45).

different qualities" (2005, 33). Similarly, Henry Simmons, a scholar in the field of gerontology and religion, has suggested that regardless of chronological age, it is possible to look for "recurring life situations" that represent "shared themes and patterns of change in the last third of life" (1998, 82).

It is these dramatic features of an aging population and increased longevity that define the historic significance of our current moment. Furthermore, these historic demographics of contemporary aging are becoming a worldwide reality, despite previous assumptions that these trends were confined primarily to the wealthy Western world. Demographer Wilson writes, "While rich countries still lead in life expectancy, the gap between these leaders and most developing countries has shrunk substantially" (2006, 7).[3] For instance, in April 2002 at the Second World Assembly on Ageing, the United Nations reported that the world population of persons sixty or older is likely to triple to two billion by 2050, with one in five persons worldwide sixty or older ("U.N. Offers Action Plan" 2002, A4). Furthermore, Harper notes that it is projected that by this time, "three-quarters of the 2 billion elderly people in the world will live in developing countries" (2006, 25). Similarly, a report of the United Nations Department of Economic and Social Affairs Population Division confirms that, by 2050, many countries in Latin American, Africa, and Asia will see the percentage of their population aged sixty or older grow to 20 to 25 percent (2003, 23-26). Such statistics led one UN official at the Second World Assembly on Aging in 2002 to highlight the international significance of aging today, "If the demographic focus of the 20th century was on education and employment for the young, then the theme for the 21st century will be the elderly" ("U.N. Offers Action Plan" 2002, A4).

In order to maintain a reasonable scope, this book focuses on the United States as its primary context. However, it is also written within the larger horizon of a world increasingly united in its shared experience of the ethical challenges posed by contemporary aging. Furthermore, in poorer countries the elderly face particular problems related

---

3. There are major exceptions to this trend: for instance, the post-Communist states and AIDS-ravaged Sub-Saharan Africa, which have seen a *decrease* in life expectancy in the past fifty years (Wilson 2006, 7).

to lower economic status. Harper explains, "With the lowest levels of income, education, and literacy, they lack savings, assets, and land; have few skills or capital to invest in productive activity; and have very limited access to jobs, pensions, or other benefits. In fact, many developing countries have yet to establish even minimal social insurance schemes" (2006, 25). Thus, I hope that the insights offered here may be relevant in other contexts in which people must reflect on the ethically just way to approach long-term care for the elderly.

In this brief introduction to the demographics of contemporary aging, I have sought to explain two important aspects of the phenomenon. Noting the historical significance of our current situation, Harry Moody observed, "Astonishingly, two thirds of all the gains in life expectancy since the emergence of the human species have occurred in the twentieth century. . . . These advances in longevity will certainly be remembered as an achievement of world-historical importance in our time" (1988, 1). This is not to say that no one grew old prior to the twentieth century; ancient sources testify to the fact that old age in and of itself is not "new." Nonetheless, the aging of populations and the advances in longevity mean that the *experience* of old age today in much of the world *is* new—at both the individual and societal levels. However, recognizing a dramatic feature of our time does not necessarily entail the language of "crisis." In fact, I wish to avoid the tone of social fear and negativity toward current aging demographics that dominates public rhetoric in the United States—what Harper describes as the "demographic burden hypothesis" (2006, 21). Despite the "crisis" language accompanying public discussion of these demographic and societal changes, current shifts related to aging are not *in and of themselves* problematic; as a contrasting illustration of the effect of changing demographics, we might think of the situation of exploding fertility after World War II, when the need was for increased construction of new schools. Furthermore, while scientists continue to explore the genetics of longevity, Harper explains that the increases in life expectancy seen during the twentieth century were the direct result of "advances in living standards, education, public health, and medicine" (2006, 21). Or, as social scientist Matilda Riley and her colleagues point out, "We are the beneficiaries of great gains in economic productivity and public health as well as advances in science and education" (1994, 1-2).

Thus, in fulfilling the descriptive task of ethics, I argue that the aging trends that follow us into the twenty-first century should first be seen as the inheritance of remarkable successes in the twentieth century in the areas of economics, education, and health policies. In fact, in the United States, the economic security and health of today's elderly can also be tied to the success of age-based, twentieth-century public policies such as Medicare and Social Security. Therefore, the determination as to whether we are in a crisis depends upon our *response* to this inheritance, not the demographic trends themselves. As noted in relation to the opening story about Kate, it is true that the question articulated by Moody concerning our understanding of this new reality is still before us: "Is the new abundance of life now produced by gains in longevity to be seen as a problem or an opportunity?" (1988, 265). Furthermore, a 2003 report by the United Nations Department of Economic and Social Affairs put the burden of proof where it belongs, that is, on the creativity and timeliness of our social response and not on the aged per se: "Society has some time to adapt to the projected changes, especially as savings can be accrued because of the slow growth and eventual reduction of the number of children. However, in historical terms, the time available is short and successful adaptation requires that we embark early in the path of societal change" (UN Department of Economic and Social Affairs 2003, 25). This successful adaptation is based on our response to several different ethical questions raised by the dramatic feature of aging today. One of the key questions we have to respond to, and the specific focus of this work, is the ethical challenge of long-term care.

The Ethical Challenge of Care

Contrary to popular negative images of old age, the increased life expectancy discussed above has also been accompanied by increased health and well-being. Given the visible gains in health for many older people, the President's Council on Bioethics states, "By historical standards, it is a wonderful time to be old" (2005, xviii). Noting that the experience of a long period of retirement spent in good health was extremely rare in the nineteenth century, Matilda Riley and her colleagues write, "Today, by contrast, survival into old age is commonplace and many years of vigorous postretirement life are a realistic expectation" (1994, 1-2). Thus, despite persistently negative ideas about aging and disease, it is important to first understand that research now shows people are not only living longer, but they are living *healthier* longer.

An important medical concept in regard to this dynamic is that of "compressed morbidity," first proposed in the 1980s by Dr. James F. Fries. The basic thesis, as explained by Fries, is that "the lifetime burden of illness could be reduced if the onset of chronic illness could be postponed and if this postponement could be greater than increases in life expectancy" (2003, 455). This hypothesis ran counter to the theory that the months and years gained by increased longevity would be experienced in poor health and thus increase an individual's lifetime burden of illness. Research by Fries and others over the past two decades has vindicated the compression of morbidity theory, proving that it is occurring at the population level and thus contributing to a healthier old age. As Baltes reports concerning the scientific data, there have been proven gains in "compressing major events of illness into the few years preceding natural 'biological' death" (2006, 38).[4]

Researchers have not been able to identify a single cause of the compression of morbidity in the population. Factors may include progress in preventative measures (such as diet or decreased smoking) and in medical advances in the treatment of conditions such as heart disease, high blood pressure, and diabetes (Fries 2003, 457). In fact, their research indicates the potential value of a more systematic implementation of preventative health strategies in the health-care system. Recognition of the possibility of improving health in old age already exists in our society to some extent, such as the creation of programs that encourage older people to remain fit and active even into their seventies and eighties. For instance, a *New York Times* special supplement on retirement highlighted the increase in the construction of fitness facilities at retirement centers across the country and the creation of fitness classes for retirees (Ellin 2007, 11). Thus, gains

---

4. Baltes does note that the full truth of "compressed morbidity" will be known only when we reach an average life expectancy of eighty-five to ninety.

in health and the postponement of chronic disability indicate that understanding old age today must include recognition of extended vitality and activity.

And yet, as the concept of compressed morbidity also identifies, increased longevity means recognizing that many of us now live to an age in which disability and disease are more prevalent. For although research shows that gains in human longevity have been accompanied by gains in overall health in the United States, the President's Council on Bioethics makes clear that "there remain difficulties, both psychic and physical, that eventually come with growing old" (2005, 2). In a documentary on contemporary aging, Dr. Leon Kass starkly describes our context:

> One of the great achievements over the last half century has been in medicine's ability to do battle with the causes of acute life-threatening illnesses. . . . What this means is that we are now left to suffer from those chronic illnesses that limit our mobility, that make us frail, that in many cases diminish our mental capacities of choice, judgment and self-management, so that more and more people are living long enough to suffer from the as-yet-incurable diseases of body and mind: Parkinson's disease and Alzheimer's disease; major diseases of the nervous system; arthritis; chronic congestive heart failure; chronic pulmonary disease. ("Interviews: Leon Kass, M.D." 2006)

In its report on caregiving for the elderly, the President's Council on Bioethics insightfully captured a paradox of contemporary aging: "The defining characteristic of our time seems to be that we are both younger longer and older longer, we are more vigorous at ages that once seemed very old and we are far more likely to suffer protracted periods of age-related disability and dependence because we live to ages that few people reached in the past" (2005, 7). While medical science has the possibility of improving treatment of age-related chronic conditions in the future, adequately understanding the ethical dimensions of old age today means seeing that, for now, the gift of longer life also entails a significant probability of disability and disease of different degrees. Furthermore, the President's Council notes that in 2000, studies showed that people on average experienced two years of serious disability prior to death due to "prolonged causes of death from age-related degenerative diseases," including Alzheimer's and Parkinson's (2005, 12).[5] Thus one of the ways to describe the ethical challenge of care is figuring out a proper response to this paradox of being both younger longer and older longer.

In any conversation about disease and disability in old age, it must be noted that there is no single common experience of decline and disability: "While aging is a shared biological fact for human beings as a species, the trajectory of biological aging differs dramatically from person to person, due both to one's unique genetic inheritance and to variable environmental influences that shape each person differently throughout life" (President's Council on Bioethics 2005, 24). Some people will suffer physical disability without any decline in mental capacities, and others may suffer mental disabilities while physical ability remains intact. However, within this diversity, there are some general trends. For instance, medical expert Atul Gawande observes that half of those sixty-five and older develop hypertension, and within the same age group, over half report having arthritis (2007b, 50). For those in the fastest growing age group of eighty-five and older, the experience of chronic disease and disability becomes more and more likely.

Baltes states, "For instance, compared to people in the Third Age [ages 60-79] almost five times as many people over 85 suffer from chronic impairments and exhibit low functional scores across a wide range of physical, cognitive, and social indicators" (2006, 36). Similarly, the President's Council reports, "After age 85, only one person in twenty is still fully mobile; and roughly half the people over 85 will suffer major cognitive impairment or dementia as part of their final phase of life" (2005, 8). In addition, while the individual

---

5. It should be noted that there is ongoing, rigorous debate within aging research concerning what should be considered "normal" processes of growing older versus "disease" aspects. For instance, geneticist Linda Partridge's essay explores the main scientific hypotheses concerning "the intrinsic decay in function that sets the ultimate limit to life span" (2006, 40). For further discussion of the scientific debate about the aging process, see Shaw 2005.

risk of developing Alzheimer's disease has not changed since it was first identified in 1907, the number of new cases increases each year because more people are living to the ages for which its prevalence rises sharply (President's Council on Bioethics 2005, 35). Statistics suggest that as many as 40 percent of those age eighty-five and older may be affected, with the expectation of at least a threefold rise in prevalence by 2050 (Alzheimer's Association 2007). In light of such statistics, Baltes realistically concludes, "Although some of the older-old remain very agile and emotionally well-off, their numbers begin to dwindle as they grow older. Physical and mental capacities increasingly diminish the older someone gets, clearly contradicting the belief that today's elderly are necessarily spared the negative aspects of aging" (2006, 35-36).

Furthermore, it is important to understand the *nature* of the diseases and conditions experienced by many older people today. The President's Council states, "Living longer also means suffering numerous chronic but not deadly conditions—such as arthritis, hearing and vision loss, dental decay, bowel problems, and urinary difficulties" (2005, 12). A chronic condition can be defined as "an illness, functional limitation, or cognitive impairment that is expected to last at least 1 year, limits the activities of an individual and requires ongoing care" ("General Aging Facts" 2006). In capturing the reality of chronic illness in the United States, gerontologists Michael Smyer and Sara Qualls write that more than 80 percent of persons sixty-five and older have one or more chronic conditions (1999, 4). And while medical science has made enormous progress in treating acute conditions, there are still limitations to the treatment of chronic conditions that can affect functioning in later years (Deutsch 2007, H10). Fries identifies such conditions as an urgent area of geriatric health care: "The most prevalent conditions of later life, such as osteoarthritis, rheumatoid arthritis, depression, isolation, and Alzheimer's disease, have relatively little effect on mortality yet cause an immense amount of morbidity" (2003, 458). Thus, a major aspect of understanding illness and disability in old age is gaining an appreciation for the way in which they interfere with basic functioning. Data collected for the 2012 report of the Federal Interagency Forum led the authors to conclude: "Problems with physical functioning were more frequent at older ages" ("Older Americans 2012," 33).

The social challenge of long-term care starts to become evident in the fact that the fastest growing age group among the elderly for the next twenty years are those eighty-five and older, for whom there is increased likelihood of chronic disease and disability. Kass states, "So we now will have in this mass geriatric society a very large number of people who are not just old, but who are 'old-old,' not just chronologically, but in body and in mind, and they will need a massive amount of care precisely at a time when there are fewer and fewer people available to look after them" ("Interviews: Leon Kass, M.D." 2006). The long-term care needs of these older persons range from basic tasks called "Activities of Daily Living" (ADL), which include house cleaning, preparing meals, paying bills, bathing, toileting, and dressing, to more complex medical needs such as drug regimens and other medical treatments. Summarizing the challenge our society faces, the President's Council states, "One of the greatest economic and social challenges will be funding long-term care—the provision of daily medical and personal assistance to individuals incapable of looking after themselves, ranging from in-home nurses to adult day-care services to full-time nursing homes" (2005, 10).

To further understand this challenge, it is important to have an empirical sketch of projected long-term care needs. Given the reality of chronic illness in late old age, it is not surprising that 2004 statistics show that about 55 percent of those eighty-five and older require some form of long-term care ("Population Statistics" 2006). In its 2012 report, the Federal Interagency Forum noted that as people age, their use of home health services and skilled nursing facilities increases. For instance, "In 2009, there were 33 skilled nursing facility stays per 1,000 Medicare enrollees age 65–74, compared with about 222 per 1,000 enrollees age 85 or over" ("Older Americans 2012," 51). The same report recorded that the oldest age group had higher use of supported housing options: "among individuals age 85 and over, 8 percent resided in community housing with services, and 14 percent resided in long-term care facilities" (60). When reminded that the eighty-five plus population is expected to double by 2050, the President's Council appears justified in stating, "Looking broadly, we seem to be on the cusp of an historically unprecedented situation, both in the degree of care that elderly individuals will need and in the proportion of society's resources that will have to be devoted to such care" (2005, 46).

While 2013 data shows that only about 1.4 to 1.5 million Americans receive long-term care in a nursing-home setting at any one time, the likelihood of nursing-home placement increases with age (*Nursing Home Data Compendium* 2013, 2). For instance, 2012 data showed that 1 percent of those sixty-five to seventy-four resided in long-term care facilities compared to 14 percent of those seventy-five and older ("A Profile of Older Americans 2013," 5). And of the Americans living in nursing homes, about 45 percent were eighty-five and older ("Population Statistics" 2006). Regarding future projections, an AARP report states, "Current estimates are that 35% of Americans age 65 in 2005 will receive some nursing home care in their lifetime, 18% will live in a nursing home for at least one year, and 5% for at least five years" (Houser 2007).

Another aspect of understanding the ethical challenge of long-term elder care is the financial dimension. Long-term care costs strain the personal budgets of individuals and families, given that, as experts point out, we have yet to adjust to the realities of aging today. Geriatrician Jeffrey Faber spells out the financial implications of increased longevity: "Most people still retire at 65, and they don't live [just] five or 10 years anymore; they live 10, 20, 30 years [more]. And savings that was enough for five or 10 years is simply not enough for 20 to 30" ("Parents & Children" 2006). As Gawande notes, long-term care needs are a major threat to retirement security: "More than half of the elderly who live in long-term-care facilities go through their entire savings and have to go on Medicaid—welfare—in order to afford it" (2007b, 58). Similarly, the President's Council argues that Medicaid has become "in large measure a de facto long-term care program," including many middle-income Americans who spend down their income in order to become eligible for Medicaid (2005, 10). Alternative proposals to shift the cost of long-term care to expanded Medicare benefits would simply move the cost problem to another program that is projecting future solvency challenges. Thus, part of the ethical challenge we face is a matter of financial resources allocated to ensure adequate care is available.

To fully understand the ethical challenge of providing long-term care today, we must also consider the availability and responsibility of caregivers, both professional and family. In recent years some experts have been sounding the alarm concerning the projected shortage of trained geriatric medical professionals relative to the growing elderly population. For instance, according to a 2005 report, if current rates of geriatric certification continue, by 2030 there will only be one-third of the number of geriatric-trained doctors projected to be needed ("Geriatrician Facts" 2006). Gawande provides an insightful observation of the irony we find ourselves in:

> Equally worrying, and far less recognized, medicine has been slow to confront the very changes that it has been responsible for. . . . Despite a rapidly growing elderly population, the number of certified geriatricians fell by a third between 1998 and 2004. Applications to training programs in adult primary-care medicine are plummeting, while fields like plastic surgery and radiology receive applications in record numbers. (2007b, 53)

In light of the projected shortage of geriatricians, Kass, former head of the President's Council on Bioethics, urges, "We need very much to encourage the development of geriatric physicians and nurses who will be there for the longer haul" ("What Needs to Change" 2006). One of the main problems in recruiting geriatricians is that current medical compensation structures provide very low financial compensation to doctors for the kind of care elderly need. For instance, Kass points out that public and private insurance reimbursement schemes are still oriented toward acute-care patient visits rather than toward the long-term management of the chronic conditions prevalent in late old age. Experts further note that the kind of time needed to effectively assess the complex chronic conditions of many older people such as dementia issues or arthritis is not rewarded by our current medical reimbursement system, one that still largely pays out for discrete services performed. In addition, elderly with multiple chronic conditions need care coordination among medical providers, but time spent by doctors in care coordination such as phone calls with other specialists goes largely uncompensated. Factors such as this mean income for geriatricians and primary-care doctors ranks among the lowest specialties in medicine.

In addition to nurses and doctors, there is also increasing need for nonmedically trained care workers. A 2004 report stated that "By 2050, the U.S. will need three times as many paid long-term care workers as are employed now to meet the needs of the aging baby boom generation" ("Caregiving Facts" 2006). Among the several factors leading to a reduction in the number of paid care aides and nurses, the President's Council cites "the strenuousness of the work involved, compensation barely above minimum wage, difficult relationships with patients, language barriers, the lack of health insurance and other benefits, and hindrances to immigration" (2005, 18).

In addition to professional caregivers, it is important to consider the challenges that exist to family caregiving today. Although there exists a popular impression that families no longer live up to their caregiving responsibilities, empirical data continues to show family involvement in the care of elderly relatives. In fact, reports show that elderly spouses and adult children still provide a significant share of long-term elder care in the United States. In 2004 the federal Administration on Aging reported that one in four American households had at least one person providing care for a friend or relative fifty years of age and older ("Caregiving Facts" 2006). Often older people prefer the care of their family to professional caregivers or institutionalized residential care because it is more flexible and personalized.

However, there are several factors conspiring to make unpaid, personal caregiving very difficult. Current challenges to family caregiving include trends such as geographic mobility, the increased number of women in the work force, which has decreased the people available for unpaid caregiving, delayed childbirth, smaller family size, and higher divorce rates. In addition, one report estimates that by 2020 there will be 1.2 million people aged sixty-five and older who do not have a living child, sibling, or spouse (President's Council on Bioethics 2005, 16-17). Gawande articulates the challenge this raises: "More than half of the very old now live without a spouse, and we have fewer children than ever before—yet we give virtually no thought to how we will live out our later years alone" (2007b, 53).

Furthermore, when we consider that many of the family caregivers are spouses or adult children, we confront the fact that the average age of the unpaid family caregiver today is sixty—which means this group includes many people who are beginning to face care needs of their own. The President's Council reports how the general aging of society affects the availability of caregivers: in 1990, there were twenty-one people between the ages of fifty and sixty-four for each person over eighty-five years of age; in 2030, the ratio is expected to decrease to six to one (2005, 17-18). Given the realities both of aging itself and changes in family structure, the President's Council concluded, "Taken together, the need for family caregivers will almost certainly increase while the availability of family caregivers may only decline" (2005, 2). Even in situations where family caregivers are present, additional paid help is often needed. Thus, the need for our public policy system to be adjusted becomes clearer when we consider that it was originally structured with the expectation of uncompensated family care, especially that of women.

In fact, an accurate analysis of the challenge to family involvement in long-term elder care must include special attention to its impact on women. Studies continue to demonstrate that the burden of elder care falls disproportionately on women, and that this carries negative consequences for women in many ways. As the President's Council reports, "Caring for elderly relatives will often come into competition with raising a family of one's own; already women spend as long in caregiving for adult family members as caring for children" (2005, 18). It is estimated that women on average will spend eighteen years caring for an elderly relative in addition to seventeen years on children ("Caregiving Facts" 2006). With delayed childbirth and increased longevity, women often find themselves in a situation of competing care needs from children and elderly parents. As a result of contemporary caregiving demands, women disproportionately suffer the personal consequences of this burden: the emotional stress and fatigue associated with caregiving and negative health consequences (Brewer 2001). There are also financial and career consequences for women due to the inequity of family caregiving. Whether for female spouses of dependent elderly or adult daughters, the demands of caregiving can result in lowered income due to lost and forfeited employment and career advancement opportunities (Yang and Gimm 2013, 501). While the statistics on family caregiving demonstrate that many women continue to take on care duties, the personal and social costs associated with this role must be addressed.

Adequate caregiving is challenged not only by the changing structure of society and family itself, but also by the changes in old age. As previously discussed, today many older persons have multiple illnesses and thus require more complex care. Furthermore, increased longevity has resulted in a lengthening of the time period in which care is needed. The President's Council points out, "It was one thing to say that families should be responsible for the care of their aged relatives in an historical period when life expectancy was 60 or 70 years of age and the period of dependency was limited. But it is quite another when a period of dementia could stretch out ten years, the last five of which require nonstop nursing care" (2005, 46). Furthermore, as our demographics above illustrated, the general aging of society means more of us are living to ages where care is necessary and there are fewer persons in the younger age cohorts. Taken together, the realities of contemporary society and old age today challenge any simplistic notion that present and future caregiving problems would be solved if families would only live up to their filial obligations.

Finally, to understand the ethical challenge of long-term care today is to recognize that it is not merely an economic or personnel issue. From an ethical perspective, we must also consider how the manner in which we provide care impacts the dignity of older persons. Baltes argues, "We are now faced with a new challenge: to conserve human dignity in the later years of life" (2006, 37). Part of the argument of this book is that experience teaches us that adequate care of the elderly and the justice of a society are not secured only by the management of physical and material needs but also by responding to the desire for dignity in late life. Thus, it is important to identify the ways in which our approaches to caregiving can undermine the dignity of older persons. The need for such a critique was made clear by William May's important essay in 1986, "The Virtues and Vices of the Elderly." May describes the structure of relationship in which age-related disability often places the elderly: "Increasingly, the elderly depend upon persons—professional caregivers, planners and designers of facilities for the elderly—who function at some emotional distance from them" (1986, 44).

This aspect of old age contributes to cultural attitudes in which the elderly are cast into the status of the other—they are needy, we are providers; we are growing, they are declining. For instance, May describes the way in which the agency of elderly persons is easily undermined in situations of professional caregiving: "Idealistic professionals tend to define themselves as benefactors, others as relatively passive beneficiaries" (1986, 45). While May acknowledges that professionals certainly vary in their professional habits, he argues that the professional–client relationship always carries a power imbalance that "tempts the insensitive to condescension," a dynamic that may be further exacerbated by the age difference between younger staff and elderly clients (45). Particularly important to the field of ethics, May also argued that professional ethicists can further marginalize older persons with ethical models of caregiving that "can unwittingly exclude old people from the human race by consigning them to a state of passivity, moral and otherwise" (44).

Likewise, aging expert Harry R. Moody, who has been a pioneer in analyzing U.S. public policy regarding aging, particularly in elucidating the ways policies and programs may undermine the capacities and participation of old people, argues in his *Abundance of Life* that an examination of major U.S. aging policies and programs reveals that "The policy goal for the aged was never understood as the development of the capacities of old people" (1988, 110). Moody's purpose is to illustrate that the way policies and programs are shaped affects whether old age is viewed strictly in terms of problematic needs or as containing possibilities and capacities. Unlike some current efforts to shift all the costs of old age to individual and private responsibility, Moody is not arguing for the elimination of public spending for the elderly. Rather, his concern is to adjust policy and spending so that older people are not marginalized and disempowered by the very programs meant to help them.

In another work, *Ethics in an Aging Society*, Moody cites the rise of the nursing-home industry as a clear example of the deficiencies in old age policy. Moody writes, "Nursing home residents are cast in a passive role, often infantilized, with few opportunities to make meaningful decisions about their lives" (1992, 180). Other experts echo Moody's critique of the caregiving structure of nursing homes. For instance, geriatrician David Muller raises the issues of marginalization that occurs with institutionalized caregiving: "[In the nursing home] there's a sense of being marginalized and, as you said, being stored away somewhere, out of everyone's sight, even if it is a relatively nice place" ("Parents & Children" 2006). Likewise, Faber notes that even quality facilities contain inherent limitations as regards the dignity of residents:

> The nursing home where I [started working and training a few years ago] is fantastic. I think it's one of the best ones out there. The staff is great. The physicians are really wonderful and dedicated. But it is an institution, and people do lose their personal identity and give up a lot of their individualism to join the system and get cared for in a group setting, where things happen at certain times, and schedules are adhered to, and you have your room, or you're with your roommate, and you have the nursing station in the middle and the long hall. It feels like a hospital. It is a hospital. ("Parents & Children" 2006)

Nursing homes illustrate the larger point that long-term care today is not merely a financial challenge. For in addition to the financial burden of nursing-home care is the simple fact that no one wants the care provided there because of the way it is delivered.

Related to this problem, gerontologist Larry Polivka has argued for an adjustment in societal attitudes toward the elderly based on learning from the transformation of social attitudes toward disabled adults. Polivka focuses on the frail elderly, particularly those in long-term care institutions. He argues that long-term care policy for the elderly in the United States needs a directional change comparable to that which occurred in the system of care for disabled adults starting in the 1970s. As Polivka explains, the disabled adult community was able to change how we view "disability" so that resources and policies were aimed at making the social and economic environment less disabling, thus allowing for the empowerment of disabled adults' capabilities (1998, 21).

Polivka then contrasts the change of approach in the empowerment of nonelderly adults with the "perception of dependency imposed upon and acquiesced to by many disabled elderly" (1998, 23). Polivka demands recognition of the desire of the elderly, including the frail and disabled, to have their autonomy supported. Autonomy here is understood as "the power of an individual, however dependent, to interact and communicate freely with others, to give and receive affection, and to initiate actions that are consistent with the person's sense of self" (24). Polivka argues that this aspect of human dignity has too often been ignored in long-term care policy for older people: "In my experience, respect for the need and desire of frail elderly people to remain as autonomous as their impairments allow by providing supportive, nurturing environments and services has been, more often than not, compromised by the needs of policy makers and providers to achieve short-term bureaucratic or fiscal goals and the implicit notion that autonomy may well not be an appropriate or achievable goal for the dependent elderly" (24). Like Moody, Polivka's work reveals the way in which our long-term-care structures too often reflect societal interpretations of disability that are disempowering to persons. In an essay on dignity in old age, Moody addresses the issues of disability and societal views of old age: "The 90-year old is no more, and no less, a citizen than a 30-year old. But should old age bring frailty or, in cases of dementia, should age bring with it diminished mental capacity, then a predictable response by others is *Infantilization*: that is, the aged person is no longer treated with the respect of *Adulthood*" (1998, 26). Such analysis calls for a shift from the exclusive category of "need" to inclusion of the category of "capacity."

Jane A. Boyajian, an ombudsman for the elderly in Washington state, uses the parallel language of "self-determination" to suggest the need for a "new agenda" in our approach to the elderly, which respects their desire to make choices and direct their lives according to their value system and life experiences. Boyajian points out the marginalization that can occur when policy is not oriented toward enabling capacity: "We need to see elders not as recipients of our programs, though they are, but rather as members of our community-in-the-present. We need to remember that they are separated from our community partly because of their infirmity or living situation but more because of our attitudes toward them" (1988, 22). In different forms, each of these authors appeals for a change in the vision that guides our social response to long-term-care today and for shaping policy in a way that takes into consideration the moral significance of human dignity as that is related to personal empowerment and social inclusion. Concern with combating disempowering approaches to long-term care of the elderly is thus expressed in various terms by the preceding authors: the elderly as contributing subjects versus passive recipients, as having capacity not merely need, and as desiring self-determination and autonomy. This concern is the basis of a key argument of this book: that just care of the elderly cannot be measured merely in terms of amounts of material and financial resources but whether *the care is provided in such a way as to foster the dignity of older people* as persons who retain agency even in the midst of frailty and disability.

Conclusion

This chapter has sought to address the descriptive task of ethics by outlining the relevant dimensions of our contemporary context that demand thoughtful moral reflection on long-term elder care. I began by identifying two important demographical realities: population aging and increased human longevity. As stated above, neither of these dynamics in and of itself constitutes an emergency social crisis. Furthermore, the stereotype of the older years as nothing but decrepitude and decline is not supported by empirical evidence; Americans have gained not only years, but also healthier years. However, it is also a mistake to ignore the other side of the paradox of contemporary aging: that many more of us do now live to an age in which chronic disease and disability are very common. To ignore this reality with rosy images of the "golden years" means failing to make the adjustments necessary individually and societally that would allow old age to be a blessing. As Gawande argues, there are costs to ignoring the challenges of the new old age: "For one thing, we put off changes that we need to make as a society. For another, we deprive ourselves of opportunities to change the individual experience of aging for the better" (2007b, 52).

The second part of this chapter then sought to identify key ethical challenges arising out of the situation of contemporary aging and long-term care. Again, the need for elder care is not unique to the twenty-first century, but new reflection is required, given the increased number of older people in society, that more elderly are living to ages that involve extended periods of chronic illness, and the stresses on professional and family caregiving structures. Given the financial costs of long-term care and the projected lack of both professional and family caregivers, one major challenge is simply how do we make it possible for the moral responsibility of elder care to be fulfilled? A second major challenge is designing the manner of care so that human dignity in old age is preserved. As Polivka argues, reshaping long-term care for the better will not occur merely by collecting technical and economic facts but "will require a collective change of heart that is fundamentally dependent on the creation of a clear moral vision for long-term care" (1998, 22). Whether the gains in longevity and the aging of populations can be experienced as a social good rather than a crisis and whether older people can maintain dignity in old age depend largely on whether society responds creatively to the ethical challenges of long-term care. Such creative responses are evident in the experiences of the Community of Sant'Egidio and the Green House Project, and thus it is to these two models we now turn.

CHAPTER THREE

Two Models of Long-Term Care: The Community of Sant'Egidio and the Green House Project

In order to shape a contemporary Christian ethic of long-term care, it is important to have concrete models that can invigorate our moral imagination by demonstrating the practical possibility of caring for older people in a way that honors their dignity and promotes their ongoing agency as participating members of society. For there is no doubt that the immensity of the challenges arising from the realities of aging today can dampen our imagination and the willpower needed to make new visions possible. Thus, I have chosen to begin a Christian ethical response to the challenges outlined in Chapter 2 by analyzing two contemporary models of elder care: the Community of Sant'Egidio and the Green House Project. I will show that these two examples provide vital ethical insights that help move us beyond what *is* to what *can be*.

The Community of Sant'Egidio

There are, of course, multiple models of church and faith-based service organizations involved in community service. In a document on the elderly, the Roman Catholic Pontifical Council for the Laity noted the importance of one such possibility—Christian lay associations: "An important role in promoting the active participation of older people in the work of evangelization is now played by the Church-based associations and the ecclesial movements, 'one of the gifts of the Spirit [to the church] of our time'" (Pontifical Council for the Laity 1998). Many of these lay associations or ecclesial movements are marked by a model of intergenerational community. Our first model—the Community of Sant'Egidio—is one such lay association. Furthermore, Sant'Egidio provides a particularly important model because it also seeks to build direct forms of collaboration with government and nonprofit elder care programs.[1] I will first provide general background on the Sant'Egidio organization and then provide specific analysis of its outreach program with older people.

General Background

The Community of Sant'Egidio was founded in 1968 in Rome by Andrea Riccardi. Its name is taken from the church of Sant'Egidio in the Trastevere section of Rome, which has served as the headquarters of this organization since 1973. Like many other lay movements that began at this time, Sant'Egidio's formation was influenced by the event of Vatican II, which, as founder Riccardi explains, "outlined a new path for the Church in the contemporary world" (Riccardi 1998, 157). Part of the new path being outlined during the historic Vatican II council was a reaffirmation of the importance of lay people in the work of the church. Given this atmosphere, Riccardi states, "Sant'Egidio is a reality born after the Council and from the Council" (Riccardi 1999, 29). In 1986, under the auspices of the Pontifical Council for the Laity, Sant'Egidio became an officially recognized lay association within the Roman Catholic Church. Today Sant'Egidio is an organization consisting of approximately sixty thousand members with local chapters established in seventy-three countries worldwide, including in Africa, Asia, Europe, and North, Central, and South America ("The Community"). In the United States, the Community

---

1. Lisa Cahill makes a similar observation about Sant'Egidio's work with the elderly: "Sant'Egidio exemplifies the potential of religious communities to catalyze efforts in public and private spheres, to connect such efforts to personal religious identity and commitment, and to create social practices embodying virtues of solidarity and justice" (2005, 88).

of Sant'Egidio has local chapters in various areas, including Boston, New York, Minneapolis, and Washington, DC.

While officially recognized within the Roman Catholic Church, communities of Sant'Egidio are ecumenical in membership, including Eastern Orthodox, Anglican, and Protestant Christians. In terms of age demographics, Sant'Egidio is intergenerational in its membership, with ages ranging from high school to the elderly. As a public lay association, its members and its leadership are predominantly lay people, although ordained persons and religious may participate and affiliate with Sant'Egidio communities. Furthermore, as author Thomas Cahill describes, Sant'Egidio is a nonresidential form of lay Christian community: "They do not live together; they have normal jobs and normal lives" (1999, 311). Thus, members of Sant'Egidio participate in the organization and activities in a voluntary, unpaid capacity, supporting themselves and their families with regular jobs. Riccardi explains, "All this work [of Sant'Egidio] is done in a completely voluntary way, in addition to each community member's job and ordinary civic commitments. Everyday people with families and jobs, the members of the Community of Sant'Egidio listen to the Gospel and live in concrete solidarity with the poor" (Riccardi 1998, 160). Thus, there is a great deal of flexibility in the membership of this organization with the actual hours spent in activities of the community varying among members depending on their personal and professional situation.

Though nonresidential, the two primary ways in which members of Sant'Egidio share a common life is through gathering for prayer and through various outreach services to the poor. As the Pontifical Council for the Laity describes, "From the outset, specific features of the Community have been service to the very poor and defence of human dignity and human rights, together with prayer and the communication of the Gospel" (Pontifical Council for the Laity, "International Associations"). Framing the organization's mission in light of *Gaudium et spes*, founder Riccardi explains, "Social commitment is very important with us. Trying to respond to the challenges of the world obliges us to move out of ourselves. . . . *Gaudium et Spes* remains the great question, which is: how to live the joys, the hopes, and the agonies of our world?" (1999, 30-31). For example, shortly after its founding, members of the Community of Sant'Egidio began an education program for poor children living in the periphery of Rome. In the 1960s Rome was surrounded by slums with tenements for the working poor, including temporary makeshift houses built to accommodate workers who migrated from southern Italy. From this first initiative, Sant'Egidio has kept service to the poor at the center of its identity, today engaging in a wide variety of initiatives. Reflecting on this history, Riccardi notes, "New kinds of poverty have replaced the old kinds, or have been added on. . . . There's an effort to create a fabric of solidarity with which to engage the poor and marginalized" (1999, 38-39).

Describing the diversity of this fabric of solidarity, Thomas Cahill notes that the social services provided by the Community of Sant'Egidio worldwide include service to the homeless, immigrants, AIDS hospices and treatment programs, abused and abandoned children, and prisoners and death-row inmates (1999, 313-14). Local chapters throughout the world organize and run these various service programs, with the headquarters in Rome coordinating these initiatives and assisting in various funding needs. As an international organization, this structure has allowed Sant'Egidio the flexibility to establish programs that best fit and meet the needs of local areas. For instance, in many European cities, local Sant'Egidio communities provide services to the large number of urban homeless persons ("Friends on the Street"). And in many local communities in Africa, outreach to children through education and recreational programs has been an important initiative ("Africa: The 'Schools of Peace'"). In the United States, local chapters in various cities have focused on outreach to the elderly in nursing homes and at home, after-school programs for children, and prison ministry, including death-row inmates (Gilsinan 2008; Allen 2014).

Before turning to the concrete aspects of Sant'Egidio's care of the elderly, it is also important to outline the organization's concept of friendship, which is the primary metaphor guiding its approach to all service programs and is considered an explicit discipline of its common life. The Pontifical Council for the Laity observes, "Friendship is therefore the distinctive feature of Sant'Egidio, both among themselves, and as an attitude of friendship and interest in the world and other ecclesial experiences" (Pontifical Council for the Laity, "International Associations"). And in his own study of Sant'Egidio, Thomas Cahill writes, "Friendship is a profound experience for these people: they are true friends to one another, and they wish to be friends to the world" (1999, 313). Sant'Egidio thus draws on the mutuality of friendship to guide both its internal life and its outreach to the poor. For Sant'Egidio, the emphasis on friendship has resulted in service programs shaped by a distinct spirit of personalism. In her dissertation on Sant'Egidio's peace work, ethicist Laura Johnston provides helpful observations about Sant'Egidio's practice of friendship:

> Sant'Egidio's use of the terminology of friendship is complex, and is applied to both the internal bonds within the Community as well as relationships of solidarity and dialogue with those outside the Community. . . . One way to describe this conception of friendship would be to explain that Sant'Egidio members engage in dialogue and relationship with the "other" *as whole persons engaging whole persons*. There is an openness to make virtually any contact a personal contact, instead of observing professional boundaries. A member who is involved in a friendship with a needy elderly person does not, then, focus only on analyzing the elderly person's most obvious or tangible needs from the perspective of a social worker, but attempts to build a relationship by celebrating birthdays and other milestones together. (2008, 162-63)

The observations of others are confirmed by the organization's own articulation of its understanding of solidarity with and service to the poor. For instance, the organization Website states, "The third 'work' typical of Sant'Egidio, a fundamental and daily commitment since the very beginning, is the service to poor people, lived as friendship" ("Friendship with the Poor"). Or, as founder Riccardi describes Sant'Egidio's mission, "We consider the poor as friends and relatives of ours. This is the spirit that moves our work and the services provided by the members of the Community of Saint Egidio, whether helping immigrants, the elderly, those with mental or physical handicaps, the homeless, or people with AIDS" (1998, 160).

While Sant'Egidio's use of the terminology of friendship is complex, there are at least two distinguishing aspects of its practice of friendship with the poor that are important to our examination of its work with the elderly. First, as already noted above, Sant'Egidio's outreach initiatives begin with personal engagement provided free of the financial remuneration of human services professionals. Sant' Egidio often uses the term "gratuity" to describe the spirit within which it offers services free of charge, which it believes allows it "to consider needs and desires of the individual not according to an institutionalized approach nor pre-codified or general answers" ("Home Help: What We Do"). Furthermore, as described by Riccardi, friendship is understood as the attempt at being personal, not providing generic services: "The poor, once again, have taught me that they don't exist as 'poor people,' that is, as a homogeneous category, determined by need. . . . As persons they don't just have a need for the most obvious things: the need to eat, to sleep in a warm place, to be taken care of. The poor remind me that each of us needs to be treated as a friend" (1999, 202). Thus, Sant'Egidio outreach work is marked by a spirit of personalism. This personalism is captured in an address by Riccardi: "Always remember that the first thing you do with a friend is not assist her . . . the first thing you do with a friend is talk to her, even discovering in your conversation her thoughts, her desires, and her feelings" (2002).

A second significant aspect of Sant'Egidio's practice of friendship is the recognition of a fundamental equality between people that creates relationships of mutuality. For instance, Riccardi uses the language of solidarity to describe the mutuality and equality of relationships between old and young: "Solidarity is the recognition that the poor and the nonpoor share a common destiny. It is the affirmation of a kinship that our society wants to deny" (Riccardi 1998, 161). One expression of this approach is the way in which Sant' Egidio views those it reaches out to as members, as part of its common, shared life. While recognizing that participation varies among those included in the fellowship of Sant'Egidio, Riccardi states, "But the old or poor person whom we help, with whom we've been friends in Trastevere or Primavalle for fifteen years . . . can't in conscience be excluded from membership in the community. . . . I can't say that there really is a radical difference between the members and the non-members" (1999, 53). As a basis for this approach, Sant'Egidio cites the story of the poor widow whose meager contribution to the Temple was praised by Jesus: "Truly I tell you, this poor widow has put in more than all those who are contributing to the treasury" (Mark 12:43). From this scriptural insight, Sant'Egidio is shaped by a fundamental principle of equality that no person is too poor or too weak to be given the dignity of the opportunity of helping others ("Friendship with the Poor").

Finally, the equality and mutuality of the Community's understanding of friendship are also expressed in the refusal to "romanticize" the poor, as one longtime member of Sant'Egidio stated (Johnston 2008, 152). For Sant'Egidio, genuine friendship means a shared opportunity for growth, challenge, and support. For instance, as we will see below in its work with the elderly, Sant'Egidio believes that part of its solidarity and friendship with the poor entails challenging persons to change and grow. Likewise, Sant'Egidio states explicitly that its friendship with the poor has allowed its own members to be challenged to become more generous and also given its members a deeper understanding of the world and of humanity. Furthermore, Riccardi observes that friendship with the poor and marginalized has, in his perspective, saved the organization from becoming destructively focused on its own internal life and administration, as happens with some religious communities (1999, 30-31). There is, then, for Sant'Egidio, the expectation of a mutual opportunity for growth and development between old and young while recognizing different forms of need and different forms of participation.

Friendship with the Elderly

Having examined general background on Sant'Egidio's history and organization, we turn now to the organization's outreach to older people. From early on in its history, care of the elderly has been a primary and defining aspect of Sant'Egidio's commitment to solidarity with the poor. As Riccardi observes, "The Community has always lived in profound solidarity with the world of the elderly" (1998, 160). The work with elderly persons began in 1972 when members of

Sant'Egidio began encountering elderly persons in the various areas of Rome where they were present. From this beginning, the Website states, "A true 'alliance' of the Community with the elderly grew." In 1980, John Paul II also recognized the connection between young and old in Sant'Egidio in a speech during a visit to the Sant'Egidio church in Rome, "I immediately realized that the community of Sant'Egidio is not 'homogenous' but 'pluralistic,' that is, a diversified community; and I believe that this is wonderful in that you welcome different persons, young and old. I wish to give special stress to this splendid feature: the sharing of your young life with that of old people" (Riccardi 1999, 67). Today this alliance is manifested in various cities throughout the world, including in the United States, and, as we shall examine below, includes various services and outreach to older persons who live at home and in institutions.

Rooted in its general commitment to solidarity, Sant'Egidio's initiative stems from the recognition that the elderly represent a form of poverty in our contemporary world. This form of poverty often goes unrecognized because it is due not merely to physical and material need but also because of social marginalization. Concerning the history of its work with the elderly, Sant'Egidio states the first problem it observed for older people was an isolating solitude and a desire for fellowship. Riccardi observes, "Many old persons nowadays are no different from the lepers that we find in the Gospel. They have the same destiny, living on the margins, the same exhaustion, afraid of what they are and what they represent" (1999, 201). Because social marginalization is a major factor influencing dignity for the elderly, Sant'Egidio argues that society has a tremendous capacity to shape the experience of old age positively or negatively. Riccardi argues, "We have said many times that the blessing of a hundred years becomes a curse. Our society does not know how to take care of or manage a blessing . . . it seems to me that the fundamental problem is understanding and affirming the value of a long life" (2002).

Thus, Sant'Egidio approaches long-term care for the elderly as encompassing the dimensions of participation and fellowship in addition to physical and material needs. For example, Sant'Egidio argues that one of the struggles for dignity in old age involves a sense of exclusion from community participation. Articulating a fundamental need and desire of elderly people, the organization states, "Indeed, the elderly ask a question of integration, of company, that is not only a demand for solidarity and social services. It is a question of full participation in social life" ("The Secret of an Alliance"). Without sensitivity to this dimension of long-term care, societies risk denying and undermining the full dignity of older people. Sant'Egidio states, "The elderly person represents a great contemporary paradox: the gift of a longer life is also held by many to be useless and cumbersome" ("The Meaning of Old Age"). Furthermore, Sant'Egidio suggests that the problem of isolation and marginalization can occur even for elderly persons who are not institutionalized: "Loneliness is a great problem that doesn't just concern elderly living in the institutes but also those who live at home and/or with their family. Loneliness brings discouragement, depression and sadness, states of mind that accelerate psychological and physical decay" ("The Hard Work of Living"). In response to what it sees as the challenges of contemporary aging, Sant'Egidio's outreach has multiple dimensions. In what follows, I shall outline the four main dimensions of Sant'Egidio's approach to elder care: service at home, service in institutions and congregate-care settings, social participation and community, and cooperative alliances.

Service at Home

The first major focus of Sant'Egidio's outreach is to provide care to elderly persons so that they can remain at home. The organization states, "To help the elderly stay in their own home, even when energy declines, is a fundamental objective of the Community" ("Respect for Self-Determination"). This care is provided in two ways: directly by Sant'Egidio members and by setting up and coordinating formal elder-care services. This home-based care can range from assistance with activities of daily living to more specific forms of medical care. Sant'Egidio's provision of personal care in the home includes help getting dressed, cooking, cleaning, accompanying elderly for grocery shopping, and obtaining social and financial services. In addition, home help can involve medical care: Sant'Egidio members are trained to administer basic care such as medicine distribution, blood pressure,

checking for basic hygiene and physical condition, and accompaniment to medical visits. In terms of formal elder-care services, the
coordination of paid care services might include homemaker services,
home health aides, arranging a money manager, and arranging participation in a day program. Sant'Egidio also seeks to help elderly persons who are poor by connecting them to forms of public assistance.
Sant'Egidio has long recognized that many older people end up in
nursing homes simply because they are not capable of accessing and
coordinating home-based and community-based services even when
eligible. Therefore, a key aspect of Sant'Egidio's home service is the
important function of helping to coordinate assistance from various
sectors, what it calls a "synergy" of resources. Without coordination
support, this synergizing task can be difficult for elderly persons who
experience illnesses such as dementia.

The home-based work of Sant'Egidio can be illustrated by the story
of Mary, an eighty-six-year-old unmarried elderly woman living in a
major city in the United States.[2] Mary emigrated to the United States
as a young woman and had no other family in the country. She lived
alone in a one-bedroom apartment in a public housing development.
Mary enjoyed fairly good health, needing only two different prescrip-
tion pills per day for manageable conditions. However, friends found
Mary collapsed on the floor of her apartment with a slight sprain to
her ankle. After evaluation at the hospital, doctors determined that
Mary had collapsed due to nutritional imbalance and dehydration.
After a short stay at the hospital, doctors were planning to place Mary
in a nursing home because they felt it was still unsafe for her to be at
home alone.

However, members of Sant'Egidio were able to work out an alternative plan, having already established a cooperative relationship
with her doctor. The volunteers set up a short-term rotating schedule,
taking turns staying at Mary's apartment overnight, so as to avoid the
need for a stay in a nursing home, and facilitated her recovery to independent living. The volunteers assisted with her medicine regimen,
provided for greater independence by acquiring an automated pill
dispenser, cooked meals, and made sure Mary was drinking enough

---

2. The account of this story first appeared in Cahill and Moses 2008.

fluids. Sant'Egidio members also coordinated local elder services to put together resources that Mary now needed on a permanent basis, such as home health and hygiene assistance and twice-weekly attendance at a senior day center affiliated with a nearby hospital, which included therapeutic exercise and activities. In addition, the group arranged for a money manager to pay bills and keep track of finances. As part of their friendship, Sant'Egidio also continued to involve Mary in various activities of the local Sant'Egidio group in her apartment building, including social gatherings and visiting other elderly at a nearby nursing home.

Explaining its commitment to in-home care, Sant'Egidio notes that this work was born from listening to the desire of elderly friends who expressed their wish to remain in the setting most familiar to them and protective of their dignity. As described on the Sant'Egidio Website, these concrete actions that serve the material and physical needs of the elderly are understood as "gestures of friendship" ("Home Help: The Gestures of Friendship"). Furthermore, the in-home care in situations like Mary's are provided voluntarily by Sant'Egidio members as part of its overall framework of personal friendship. And within the framework of service as friendship, there are no preset limits to the amount of time Sant'Egidio members can spend assisting older people, and thus the frequency of in-home care and visits can be tailored to individual elderly person's needs. In order to coordinate such activities and to attend to the particular needs of each elderly person, local chapters hold regular meetings for members of Sant'Egidio to discuss the situations of various elderly friends and to figure out possible solutions. Thus, while Sant'Egidio's home-based care is rooted in personal friendship, there is a commitment to stability, regularity, and effective organization.

Service in Institutions and Congregate-Care Settings

The second aspect of Sant'Egidio's elder care initiative is focused on improving quality of life for older people in long-term-care institutions and setting up alternative models of congregate residential care. Within existing long-term-care institutions Sant'Egidio seeks to mitigate the negative effects of institutionalization: isolation, marginalization from the wider community, and loss of freedom and agency. For instance, the organization argues, "Institutionalization is often a sentence to isolation that lessens the elderly person's will to live. Some institutes accommodate up to 500 people—it is easy to lose one's own individuality there" ("The Hard Work of Living"). For many elderly, physical disability and nursing-home placement also mean separation from meaningful connection to society. In order to lessen isolation and marginalization, the organization states that its goal is to provide contact with and connection to people and the community outside of the institution. This goal is achieved through frequent (at least weekly) personal visits from members of Sant' Egidio and the nurturing of consistent, long-term friendship. The personal connection of these friendships is also realized through celebration of important life moments such as birthdays and through leisure outings in the community. Particularly for older people who have lost friends in the community and have no ongoing family relationships, the friendship with Sant'Egidio members may be the only contact with the outside world an elderly person has. In addition, Sant'Egidio provides programs within nursing homes, including religious services, social activities, and also involvement in the Community's other outreach programs. For instance, in several nursing homes visited by the Community, elderly residents support Sant' Egidio's AIDS treatment program in Africa or write letters to prisoners ("Friends of Elderly in Institutions").

In addition to working to prevent isolation and marginalization, Sant'Egidio addresses the loss of agency that occurs in institutional settings. As noted in the previous chapter, elderly persons lose personal freedom in institutions because of the demand that they fit generic, fixed schedules of sleeping, eating, and personal hygiene care. Thus, Riccardi has argued that one of the violations of elderly people's dignity is when they have no say in anything in their lives but have everything decided by others (2002). He lists things like when to eat and what to eat, one's daily schedule, and choices made by family and/or professionals that do not include the elderly person's input. In contrast, Sant'Egidio promotes maximizing the self-determination of older people: "Above all, it is important to ascertain whenever possible and to respect the wishes of the elderly" ("Respect for Self-

Determination"). Thus, within institutions Sant'Egidio members often serve as mediators between elderly residents and institutional staff. For instance, when needed, Sant'Egidio members may represent and advocate for resident needs/wishes in care-planning meetings with professional staff members. Furthermore, its consistent presence in facilities helps to assure quality care and prevent abuse of elderly friends.

Beyond working in existing long-term-care institutions, Sant' Egidio has also created two alternative models for congregate living. The first model is based on combining the personal resources of elderly people in order to achieve a form of independent living that would be impossible individually. Sant'Egidio chapters in various cities help to match older people with one another so that they can pool their resources by sharing a communal living arrangement in a particular elderly person's home or apartment. In this way older people who would not be able to afford to live alone in their own homes or apartments and pay for needed services can share the financial burden with others while maintaining independence and community-based living. Sant'Egidio members then assist by setting up social services for the elderly persons living together and by providing direct support through its in-home care program. As in the outreach to older people living in their own homes, Sant'Egidio members may provide assistance ranging from accompaniment for grocery shopping to basic medical needs such as medication ("Friends of Elderly in Institutes").

The second model of congregate living initiated by Sant'Egidio is what are called "family homes," which aim "to provide a closely-knit community, a family and comfortable environment." In this model, a local chapter of Sant'Egidio provides the residence itself, ranging from an apartment to an entire house, and provides a twenty-four-hour presence in the home. Currently Sant'Egidio operates such family houses in these locations: Rome, Genoa, and Naples in Italy, and in Germany and Belgium. These residences seek to maintain a personalized and family-style atmosphere by limiting the number of residents, with current houses ranging from as small as eight persons to a maximum of thirty. The family homes are offered particularly to lower income elderly who are unable to afford paying for their own homes or in-home services and for elderly people with intensive care needs. One of the primary principles shaping this model is to maximize the self-determination and individuality of the elderly. For instance, unlike in large institutions, elderly residents share in meal preparation and housecleaning as they are able and are allowed to personalize their rooms. Furthermore, like a family home, the residential space is open so that the elderly can move freely in and out of various areas such as the kitchen or the living room. In addition, these homes seek to combat marginalization from society through physical location. Unlike many planned institutional residences for the elderly, the family houses are embedded in already-existing neighborhoods and thus help to prevent geographic marginalization. And, as characteristic of all of Sant'Egidio's work with the elderly, local members help connect elderly people with community activities and events ("Friends of Elderly in Institutes").

Another important characteristic of the family houses is a personalized relationship with those who provide care to residents. Sant' Egidio makes use of paid professional services where needed, such as doctors, physical therapists, and house cleaners. However, the majority of care provided in these houses is through the voluntary work of Sant'Egidio members. A consistent group of Sant'Egidio members are assigned to a particular family house and rotate shifts at the house, assisting with meal preparation, personal care needs of residents, and sleeping in the home overnight. For instance, longtime Sant'Egidio member Paolo Mancinelli, who coordinates one of the family homes in Rome, serves weekly on daytime shifts and stays overnight one evening per month. Members of Sant'Egidio receive ongoing training in basic medical and personal care in order to provide proper levels of care for the elderly residents. Thus, the residents have a stable and personal relationship with the people providing their care, which reduces the disempowerment and loss of identity that can often occur in professional caregiving settings. As discussed in Chapter 2, the demographic realities of contemporary aging mean more older people are living to ages where care needs increase dramatically. Thus, Sant'Egidio's model is very relevant to a world in which residential care is a necessity for many elderly. And, while Sant'Egidio remains committed to improving the life of older people in traditional long-term-care institutions, its members also seek to contribute to the reform of residential long-term care by providing their own alternative models of congregate care.

Fostering Social Participation and Community

A third dimension of Sant'Egidio's elder-care initiative is what could be termed the intentional fostering of social participation and community. For within Sant'Egidio's model of service as friendship is a recognition that human dignity is realized partly through a meaningful sense of human solidarity with others. Furthermore, within the mutuality and equality of friendship the elderly are viewed not merely as the object of the care of others but also as subjects with ongoing agency, as part of a community of friendship and not outside of it. A primary way in which Sant'Egidio fosters participation and solidarity is by providing meaningful social interaction with the wider community. For instance, Sant'Egidio invites elderly persons to support and participate in the various initiatives of the organization. Such opportunities have included making sandwiches for homeless people, tutoring children, organizing fund-raisers for the AIDS treatment program in Africa, writing letters to prisoners, and visiting other elderly. In local Sant'Egidio chapters, members work with elderly friends to organize such occasions through which service can be offered to others and elderly people can experience a sense of ongoing social participation. In addition, Sant'Egidio organizes cultural events and summer holidays, which also foster social interaction with the wider community. Sant'Egidio not only organizes such occasions but provides transportation and personal accompaniment. These opportunities for social participation and engagement are offered to elderly at home and in institutions and are open to all elderly persons regardless of whether they are interested in the spiritual dimensions of Sant'Egidio's life.

A second way in which Sant'Egidio seeks to foster participation and community is through an initiative called "Long Live the Elderly," created in anticipation of the 1999 "Year of the Older Person," declared by the United Nations. The purpose of this project is to join the forces of older and younger persons in an effort to channel the capacities of elderly people and maintain their connection to the community. As the organization explains about those who participate in this movement, "They are elderly who serenely live the pride of their age, on the one hand accepting its limits and, on the other hand, being convinced of the resources which old age brings with it" ("The 'Long Live the Elderly' Movement"). This initiative tries to foster a sense of responsibility among the elderly in which they are empowered to contribute to their societies and to receive the dignity of participation, that is, "to live their age as an occasion for a new commitment, firstly overcoming the sense of uselessness and resignation."

The concrete activities of this movement include public-education projects to promote keeping older people out of institutions, increasing community-based living, and creating opportunities for older people to tangibly contribute to the common good of their communities. For example, in July 2009, after an attack on an immigrant in a Roman neighborhood where Sant'Egidio has a family house, the elderly residents of the house and members of Sant'Egidio organized a neighborhood gathering to call for greater tolerance and for peaceful coexistence, inviting immigrants and members of the neighborhood together. In a 2014 conference in Rome that reviewed the "Long Live the Elderly" initiative, government officials and professional experts affirmed its success in promoting intergenerational solidarity and effectively marshaling society's resources for elder care ("Long Live the Elderly").

A third aspect of Sant'Egidio's commitment to fostering participation and solidarity is through dimensions of human experience that do not appear "active" or "useful." In fact, founder Riccardi has been critical of Western society for its privileging of the active life of concrete doing over the spiritual life. Referring to Psalm 71, Riccardi argues that the witness of the elderly person to God and to God's work in his or her life is itself a form of service, of continuing to be called by God though it is a form of "usefulness" that is often denied (2002). The Community of Sant'Egidio thus makes an explicit point of welcoming the prayers and spirituality of older people as a form of participation. This prayer is nurtured and welcomed through personal pastoral care but also by organizing regular prayer services, including within nursing homes, so that even the frail and sick may experience the dignity of caring for others through prayer. For elderly who continue to live at home, Sant'Egidio organizes transportation and personal accompaniment so that they can get to the places where Sant'Egidio communities gather for prayer. In addition, for older people too frail to participate in concrete activities such as fundraising or tutoring children, Sant'Egidio members share news of the organization's various outreach initiatives as an occasion for elderly friends to express genuine concern and care for the larger world. And through the personal friendships with members of Sant'Egidio, older people express a form of participation and solidarity simply through expressions of love and affection for others.

The explicit commitment to fostering participation and solidarity is connected to Sant'Egidio's experience of long-term personal relationships with elderly persons in the community and in institutions. In contrast to social attitudes that view old age as nothing more than illness, dependency, and uselessness, Sant'Egidio states, "Meeting the elderly means discovering in them a great desire to live" ("The Meaning of Old Age"). And founder Riccardi observes, "Old people, terminally ill people, people with AIDS, teach us how much life there is when only a little is left and how worthwhile it is to live it" (1999, 202). Thus, as we have seen, Sant'Egidio's understanding of long-term elder care is the enabling of still-existing capacity in older people, including a commitment to genuine personal relationship in which older people participate in and contribute to human solidarity.

Sant'Egidio refrains from a Pollyannaish view of old age by insisting that wisdom does not come automatically with old age, but requires ongoing change and growth, which we saw is also a part of the biblical vision of old age. Thus, part of the mutuality of friendship is mutual encouragement and challenge, which includes the recognition that old age demands continual spiritual growth. For instance, Sant'Egidio argues that one of the particular temptations of old age today, given its many difficulties, is resignation. As Riccardi states, "The elderly person's sin is not as much omission, not doing, as it is the sin of resignation or desperation . . . in the end, you say, 'my life is terrible and there is nothing I can do; it's only other people who can do anything for me'" (2002). In his reflection, Riccardi argues that the elderly are tempted to conclude that there is nothing they can do for others because they themselves need such extensive care. In response to this, he argues that service to the elderly includes helping them to continue to be of service, "And the idea of helping someone also means bringing them to a point where they can do something for someone else." Thus, to engage the gifts of older people and to ask them to continue to grow and change in old age means approaching them as moral subjects like everyone else. Far from romanticizing old age and the elderly, Riccardi argues, "This means taking the elderly seriously" (2002).

To conclude this section it is important to note that Sant'Egidio's emphasis on participation and solidarity does not ignore the very real challenges and hardships of late old age. In fact, on its Website, the organization includes an entire section on what it refers to as the "hard work" of living as an elderly person. As described in Chapter 2, Riccardi has noted that aging today involves the challenge of both extended years and decline: "there is that undeniable mystery and undeniable reality of growing weaker, the reality of burning out but in the end continuing to live" (2002).

Thus, I would suggest that Sant'Egidio shows the possibility of affirming the ongoing dignity and agency of the elderly within a realistic acknowledgment of the challenges of the Third and Fourth Ages. Trying to capture this paradox, Riccardi has spoken of Sant'Egidio's "contact with the suffering, the prayer, and the dreams of the elderly, without making the elderly into a myth . . . we can't make a myth out of the elderly, because their world is a world of lights . . . but of lights that are going out" (2002). Or, as the organization states, "It's not about idealising an age of human existence that brings many discomforts, forgetting the more problematic aspects of ageing with easy youthfulness. But rather it emphasises that physical decline and growing fragility can be accepted and faced if one is not alone" ("The Secret of an Alliance").

Furthermore, because of the mutuality of its relationship with elderly people, the Community of Sant'Egidio has sought to reflect on how the elderly can turn their hardships and challenges into an opportunity to enrich younger persons and society. Through genuine friendship, older persons are able to communicate basic values about life that can benefit the young: "The elderly can give witness to those who are younger that one can always be happy, in every stage and condition of life and they represent a hope for all" ("The Friendship between Young People and the Elderly"). Riccardi also argues that precisely in their age-related weakness, the elderly offer an important insight to others: "The reintegration of the wound of need is a moment of human growth, because a mature man or woman is a man or woman who recognizes his or her own need and weakness and is not a prisoner of the illusion of omnipotence. . . . This is almost an obligatory point for the elderly, but I would say that it is not optional for anyone" (2002).

However, it would require a fundamental shift in thinking in the church and society for the elderly to be valued even in a condition of frailty. Riccardi states, "When the Church understands weakness as strength, it will reintegrate the elderly, who are the weak par excellence, into its heart." Because of the mutuality of its friendship approach, Sant'Egidio cultivates the relationship with the elderly as a "school of humanity," in which younger persons can learn virtues such as patience and fidelity and the sacred value of human life. In addition, by illustrating forms of service beyond the active stages of life that involve childrearing and professional life, Riccardi argues that older people serve others by reminding them of another dimension of life: the elderly call into question the productivity model of usefulness that has dominated Western cultural ideas (1999, 196). For instance, in the mutuality of friendship, the prayer of the elderly can become a model for others: "The prayer of the elderly person rises from the depths of need, but for me it is the model for the prayer of every man and woman" (Riccardi 2002). As we have seen, Sant'Egidio's focus on participation and community goes well beyond cultural notions of active productivity to guard against exclusion of the frail elderly.

Cooperative Alliances

The fourth dimension of Sant'Egidio's elder care initiative is what they call "the collaboration with all," or what can be described as cooperative alliances with family and the formal elder-care service sector, such as nonprofit and governmental programs. The first dimension of this collaborative approach is Sant'Egidio's relationship to family caregivers. Early on, Sant'Egidio observed that the marginalization and isolation of older people was related to an issue discussed in Chapter 2: shifting patterns in family and work in contemporary society. Due to smaller families, the increase of women in the workplace, and to geographic mobility, the traditional family support network is not present for many elderly today. Furthermore, even in situations where family caregivers are present, Sant'Egidio recognized that the long-term-care needs of today's elderly often prove to be too great a challenge for families to manage on their own. Thus, many families end up feeling overwhelmed by the care needs of an elderly relative, contributing to the sense of old age today as excessively burdensome. As Sant'Egidio argues, "Increasingly we witness the nature of a generational conflict that has, as its product, the frustration and the growing marginalization of many elderly in every part of the planet, who no longer feel part of the community of which they are members" ("The Secret of an Alliance").

In response, Sant'Egidio seeks to strengthen and support family networks as part of just care for the elderly: "It often happens that families, even when they want to help their elderly parents, are not prepared. Here, our support tends to involve, with appropriate incentives, all institutional resources, supporting the wishes of the family and the elderly person" ("The Collaboration with All"). From this perspective, Sant'Egidio has a commitment to strengthening and supporting family caregivers, not replacing them. This commitment involves providing support, counsel, and education for family caregivers and helping them to access formal care services. For elderly who remain at home, Sant'Egidio's home-based service is intended, where possible, to augment and complement the presence of family caregivers, and thus Sant'Egidio members communicate directly with family to coordinate one another's efforts. Helping families to remain part of the care network of an elderly person not only enhances the physical and material support of older people, but often promotes a sense of dignity through ongoing participation in family life. Because many elderly people express a desire to have their families involved in their care, Sant'Egidio also collaborates with family caregivers as a dimension of respecting the self-determination of older people.

In addition to family caregiving sources, Sant'Egidio chapters seek collaboration and association with governmental, nonprofit, and private elder-care programs and agencies. In this sense it is important to note that Sant'Egidio does not consider its elder-care services as sufficient alone but rather as one dimension of the wider society's care of the elderly. Similar to its perspective on the family, Riccardi states, "For us, solidarity does not mean trying to substitute for public institutions" (1998, 160). As already noted in the section on home-based service, Sant'Egidio chapters draw upon and help to coordinate the professional care services available in a local area whenever this is helpful to an elderly friend. Sant'Egidio members not only initially set up these services but develop ongoing relationships with care providers, such as housekeeping and personal-care services. This cooperation not only guards the welfare of older people receiving home-based care, but also helps to facilitate the relationship between formal caregivers and the elderly.

In addition to collaboration with direct-care providers, Sant'Egidio has sought partnership with governmental and civic entities in program development. For example, in some cities such as Rome, Sant'Egidio established a phone hot line, called the "Telephone of Solidarity," that elderly persons and caregivers can use to ask about services. This hot line is also used by staff at hospitals and senior centers to connect older people with elder-care services. In addition, in collaboration with city government and other nonprofit service agencies in different cities, Sant'Egidio has published a guidebook entitled "How to Remain in Your Own Home When You Are Elderly." This easily understood publication coordinates information about health centers and doctors, cultural and activity centers, governmental and nonprofit agencies, and transportation options. Furthermore, as Paola Carcaterra, one of the leaders of the elderly service in Rome, explains, in places like Italy where the Sant'Egidio organization is long established and large, it organizes regular conferences to educate its members, medical personnel, social workers, and family on issues in gerontology and elder care. These conferences include the participation of governmental and academic experts in long-term elder care ("Respect for Self-Determination").

A commitment to collaboration with all also includes political advocacy when circumstances demand it. For instance, in Italy, where foreign immigrants constitute a significant share of elder-care workers, anti-immigrant sentiment potentially threatened the well-being of foreign workers and concomitantly the older people for whom they care. Thus, the Sant'Egidio organization publicly lobbied on behalf of foreign workers' labor rights and also organized the elderly and immigrant care providers to publicly demonstrate together against harmful legislation. Another example of advocacy in the public sector comes from Sant'Egidio's international network. As we saw in Chapter 2, aging and long-term care are no longer a challenge for Europe and North America alone but are becoming a growing issue in developing countries, particularly where poverty limits the government's ability to provide an extensive social-security structure. Given its presence in many of the developing countries of Africa, Sant'Egidio, in collaboration with government agencies, organized its first international conference on aging in June 2010, held in Lilongwe, Malawi. The conference, "Ageing in Africa: Sensitizing the Nations," included governmental and nongovernmental representatives from Malawi, South Africa, Ghana, Uganda, Zambia, Mozambique, Sweden, Italy, and Belgium. One purpose of the conference was to initiate dialogue between Europe and Africa on the challenges of longevity and aging today and to promote policies in African countries that can provide well-being and care for the elderly. Given the demographic and social changes already underway in many African countries, it is important to raise awareness about the transitions in traditional care structures so that public policy can be shaped accordingly ("The Conclusion of the International Conference").

The initiatives of collaboration and advocacy described here demonstrate that Sant'Egidio's impact and network extend beyond its own organization's elder-care services. Furthermore, this approach reflects Sant'Egidio's implicit argument that long-term elder care cannot be secured merely by the isolated efforts of family or faith-based organizations. Instead, Sant'Egidio sees the future answer to the challenge of long-term elder care to be based upon the creation of a rich network of resources and efforts: "Collaboration, co-ordination involving different kinds of assistance, creating a network of solidarity and protective facilities offered by public services, the help of volunteers, the family, the neighbourhood, allows easy solutions" ("Home Help: What We Do").

Conclusion

While Sant'Egidio's origins lie in the lay spiritual renewal of the Catholic Church's Vatican II reforms, I have presented it as a model with far-reaching and broader significance for long-term care of the elderly. Based on its understanding and practice of friendship, Sant'Egidio provides care for the elderly in relationships of genuine mutuality that help to foster the ongoing capacity and participation of older people. Approaching older people through the lens of friendship reveals the ongoing agency and dignity of the elderly, even in the midst of disability and need: "Closeness [to the elderly] reveals the value of their lives: one grasps their strength amid the ocean of their weakness" (Riccardi 1999, 196). The analysis of Sant'Egidio's program has sought to show how recognition of strength and agency of older people shapes all dimensions of its approach to elder care: service at home, service in institutions and congregate-care homes, social participation and community, and cooperative alliances.

However, one could argue that while Sant'Egidio's work with the elderly is a noble image, it is limited because it is based on volunteerism stemming from religious faith, and because friendship cannot be a model for large-scale, long-term-care programs and policy. However, Sant'Egidio's insights and knowledge about the elderly go beyond a particular faith community, and its concrete activities highlight important areas of elder care generally. Furthermore, for Sant'Egidio, personal relationships are part of responding to the real needs of the elderly: "Friendship, direct contact, personal involvement with the elderly, can appear to be inadequate means to confront problems that would seem to require a much more complex and structural response. Nevertheless, in these years, friendship and close relations with the elderly have radically contrasted the spiral of alienation and have broken the isolation of many elderly" ("Assistance at Home"). And while it may be difficult to replicate the volunteer nature of Sant'Egidio's work, this does not preclude the family houses serving as a model for professionally staffed elder- care residences, as we will see in the Green House model in the next section. Likewise, particularly in a country such as the United States, Sant'Egidio provides a compelling model of the potential for voluntary groups such as churches and synagogues to organize care for the elderly in their own communities on whatever scale possible. Based on Sant'Egidio's experience, such programs do not aim at replacing public long-term-care programs and funding but rather aim at collaborative efforts that maximize the effectiveness of elder-care resources. We turn now to a second concrete model of elder care to further shape an ethical response to contemporary aging.

The Green House Project

Though sharing in some of Sant'Egidio's insights and approach, our second model of the U.S.-based Green House Project provides us with another distinctive example to explore.[3] For one, this long-term-care model is not religiously based, as the Community of Sant'Egidio is. Furthermore, the Green House is aimed specifically at frail elderly who cannot live at home or in more independent residential facilities, such as assisted living. Thus, it is an important reform model particularly for long-term care provided in nursing homes or what are called "skilled nursing facilities." We will see that the Green House vision seeks to combat the problems of institutionalized long-term care we began to highlight in Chapter 2 and which Sant'Egidio has also identified through its work in institutions.

General Background

The Green House Project was founded by Dr. Bill Thomas, a well-known geriatrician and activist who became involved in aging issues as medical director for a nursing home in upstate New York (Adler 2008, 24). The Green House initiative has its roots in Thomas's first project aimed at reforming long-term care called the Eden Alternative, which was founded in 1991. The Eden Alternative is a nonprofit organization focused on bringing about a change in the "culture" of long-term-care institutions by combating what Thomas considered to be the three main problems in institutional nursing homes: boredom, helplessness, and loneliness. This organization was founded on "the core belief that aging should be a continued stage of development and growth, rather than a period of decline" ("About the Eden Alternative"). The purpose of the Eden Alternative was to provide training and consultation to

---

3. Some of the analysis and description included in this section are based on observations conducted by the author at the Green House homes located on the Traceway Retirement Community campus in Tupelo, Mississippi, in 2009.

nursing-home administrators and staff and provide official certification for nursing homes that instituted its core reform measures. In this effort, the Eden Alternative promoted ten basic principles to change nursing-home culture, including creating a culture that is "elder-centered," providing easy access to companionship with other people and living things, providing "opportunity to give as well as receive care," and maximizing decision making by elders ("Our 10 Principles"). The specific reform efforts of the Eden Alternative were connected to a more general movement for long-term-care "culture change," which took shape in the 1980s. Legislatively, a serious attempt to bring about institutional change occurred in the federal Nursing Home Reform Act contained in the Omnibus Budget Reconciliation Act of 1987. Meg LaPorte notes that after this time, culture change came to refer to specific aspects of proposed long-term-care reform: person-centered care, individualized treatment plans, and choice and autonomy for residents (2010, 24).

Despite these efforts, subsequent studies have shown that nursing-home institutions have been stubbornly difficult to change (Brown and Pfeiffer 2009, 16; M. LaPorte 2010, 24). In fact, even institutions that attempted reform found it difficult to incorporate the principles of the Eden Alternative. For instance, Kane and her colleagues argue that follow-up studies have suggested that Eden reforms have had "limited effects," indicating that a more radical, systemic level change is required (2007, 832). And Rabig et al. show that the more than three hundred nursing homes that incorporated Eden training and concepts still reported difficulty in making deep-seated, permanent changes (2006, 534). Not surprisingly, as Bob Moos reports, a 2001 Kaiser Family Foundation survey showed that only about one-third of Americans were satisfied with the care a friend or family member had received in a nursing home (2006, 15). Thus Kane and her colleagues concluded, despite a 1986 Institute of Medicine report calling for reform of nursing homes, "The problems of maintaining a sense of well-being in a nursing home are well documented in decades of anthropological, ethnographic, and ethics studies" (2007, 832).

Similar to Sant'Egidio's analysis, Thomas and other culture-change reformers argued that two of the main problems with institutional nursing-home care in the United States were routinization of daily schedules and undermining the capacity of residents. As Angelelli describes, "the way life is organized for elders in far too many long-term-care settings in the US, where care and treatment regiments are determined not by elders or direct-care staff but by the arbitrary dictums of supposed operational efficiencies" (2006, 428). The institutional necessity of ensuring that tasks are completed leads larger facilities to centrally control the times residents wakened, put to bed, fed, and bathed, regardless of personal preference. Gerontologist Brenda Bergman-Evans describes the negative effect of such institutionalization on residents: "The need to control the environment is of fundamental importance to human beings. Yet when one enters a nursing home, choice often becomes a thing of the past. Such basic choices as when to eat, what to wear, or when to go to bed are often in the hands of someone else. The result is often a sense of helplessness" (2004, 29).

In addition, while frailty and disability are usually the reason a person enters a nursing home, gerontological experts also note a process of "learned helplessness," where the traditional model of nursing homes takes all responsibility and initiative from elderly residents so that capacity they still have is submerged under acquiescence to a role of passivity. As Bergman-Evans describes, learned helplessness is "a result of the dependent role that is typically expected and assumed on admission [to a nursing home]" (2004, 29). Rabig et al. also refer to research on "induced disability" in nursing homes, "where residents perceive little control over their lives and environments," which then contributes to decreased functioning and loss of capacity (2006, 534). The undermining of still-existing capacity occurs for elderly in an institutionalized situation where one "consistently receives care without having the opportunity to give care back" (Bergman-Evans 2004, 29). This learned helplessness can contribute to further physical and mental decline for patients.

While Thomas began the Eden Alternative as a nursing-home reformer, the Green House Project grew out of his subsequent conviction that true person-centered care and dignity in late life could not be achieved without creating a whole new model of long-term residential care. As he states, "I believe that America can outgrow the mistake it's been making for the past 40 years, which is institutionalizing older people. But in order to be a real abolitionist, I really had to bring to the table an alternative—something that was not a nursing home—to help people who can't live at home" ("Green House Projects"). Thus, the Green House initiative was launched to provide long-term residential care in small-scale, personalized settings where the autonomy and capacity of older people are nurtured and promoted. Kane et al. state, "The GH [Green House] entails sweeping and comprehensive changes, so much so that some proponents perceive it as the deinstitutionalization of a nursing home" (2007, 838).

Subsequent to the creation of the Green House Project, the first homes were built in Tupelo, Mississippi, under the auspices of the nonprofit Mississippi Methodist Senior Services, which is headquartered in that city. Instead of remodeling its outdated 140-bed nursing-home facility, the administration opted to build four Green House homes on its Tupelo retirement campus in 2003. In June 2003, forty residents from the larger nursing-home building were moved into the new homes, including twenty residents from the locked dementia unit. As a result of the positive outcomes of the first four homes, the organization has converted its entire long-term-care program to Green House homes, using the old building for a rehabilitation unit for short-term residents (Rabig et al. 2006, 533-38). As of 2012, 144 Green House homes have been opened in thirty-two states, with 120 future homes under development in other locations.

The Green House Approach to Elder Care

While particular Green House developments operate independently, they work with the national organization to meet the standards and specifications for using the Green House designation. In articulating its goals, the Green House project states, "We envision homes in every community where elders and others enjoy excellent quality of life and quality of care; where they, their families, and the staff engage in meaningful relationships built on equality, empowerment, and mutual respect; where people want to live and work; and where all are protected, sustained, and nurtured without regard to the ability to pay" (*Guide Book,* 4). Toward this end, Green House homes are constructed and organized in a very intentional manner in order to achieve their ethical vision. In my analysis of this model, I will focus on the two main dimensions that define a Green House home: the physical structure and the human community.

Physical Structure

As noted above, in order to achieve a genuine environment of home instead of institution, the Green House organization specifies certain requirements of physical structure and layout in order to affiliate with its name. These requirements follow from a key Green House insight: there is an inseparable connection between the physical design of long-term-care residences and the way care is provided and experienced. As one article observes, the Green House model "uses architectural design to help it achieve its mission of providing care that offers privacy, dignity, and choices for its elderly residents" (Wallace 2006). The typical Green House home is one-story and averages 6,400-7,000 square feet, and can be a free-standing house or a floor in a multilevel building. Designers have now adapted models for urban, suburban, and rural locations. Thus far, Green House homes have been built in residential neighborhoods and as a part of retirement campuses. However, a key requirement is that each "household" must be free-standing and separated so that "artifacts of institutional life" are not replicated, such as long, connecting hallways (Angelelli 2006, 429). Furthermore, each house is designed for no more than seven to ten elderly residents, though the organization allows an exception of up to twelve residents in situations where an organization faces serious financial constraints. The innovation of this small-scale requirement can be fully appreciated when one considers that the average size for a traditional nursing home in the United States is 120 beds, with larger facilities containing as many as 400 to 500 beds (*Guide Book,* 30).

Within Green House residences, the home environment is further achieved through interior design that includes living rooms, hearth area, open kitchen and dining areas, and free access to outdoor living space. To facilitate open access for elderly with varying levels of functioning, the kitchen is designed with safety locks for drawers and cabinets with sharp objects, and the stove has a safety shield that locks in pots on the stove. Each resident has her own private room and bathroom, and residents are encouraged to furnish their private rooms entirely with personal belongings. This differs from traditional nursing homes, in which residents typically share a room and must bathe in shared, large shower rooms. In addition, the houses are designed so that resident rooms circle around the main hearth area/ living room. Other small but significant requirements further help to avoid an institutional atmosphere: there are no nurses' stations as in typical nursing homes but rather an office/study room where staff can work when necessary; there is no public address system and room call buttons send wireless signals to silent pagers; medicine carts are not allowed, and instead resident medication is kept in each private room in locked medicine cabinets; instead of manual lift devices, each room has a ceiling track to which a lift can be attached to assist in moving residents from their beds to the bathroom. And to enhance the indoor living space, houses are designed with an emphasis on achieving natural light throughout the home (Rabig et al. 2006, 534-36).

For the Green House creators, the physical layout has ethical implications in terms of being able to provide care in a personalized manner that honors the individuality and self-determination of older people. For this reason, the organization argues that the Green House model cannot simply be "overlaid on an existing large facility" (*Guidebook*, 6). As one architectural designer explained, during the design process for a Green House development, the planning team kept asking, "Would you do that in your home?" (Wallace 2006). To help in conceptualizing the Green House layout, see the following sample home design to understand the importance of physical design in the Green House model (see p. 66; Rabig et al. 2006, 537). As is evident in this image, the Green House aims at building real homes, not just "homelike" features in otherwise large, institutional facilities.

The Human Community

Like the intentionality of the physical design, the Green House model insists that the vision of the human community within long-term residences must be transformed in order to provide care that truly fosters the dignity of older people. Key aspects of this radical transformation articulated in the stated philosophy of the Green House initiative include "recognizing and valuing individuality of elders and staff," "honoring autonomy and choice," "supporting elders' dignity," "offering opportunities for reciprocal relationships between elders and staff," "promoting maximal functional independence," and

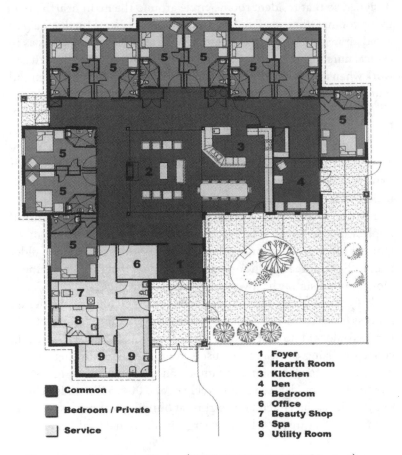

1 Foyer
2 Hearth Room
3 Kitchen
4 Den
5 Bedroom
6 Office
7 Beauty Shop
8 Spa
9 Utility Room

Common

Bedroom / Private

Service

Floor plan of the Green House (THE GREEN HOUSE®Project)

"fostering spiritual well-being" (*Guide Book*, 7). In order to achieve these goals, the Green House model is very intentional in the way that it approaches elderly residents, staff, and the wider community.

Similar to Sant'Egidio, the first key aspect of the Green House's vision of older people is an explicit affirmation of the dignity of the elderly as possessing ongoing potential for growth and participation, not merely as the objects of the medical and personal care of others. As Kane and colleagues describe, the Green House is a model that "emphasized individual growth and development and a good quality of life under normal rather than therapeutic circumstances" (2007, 832). One way in which this affirmation is implemented is by referring to the elderly members of the home as "elders" rather than as patients, residents, or clients. In this way, the Green House vision insists on a holistic view of older people as full persons, refusing to reduce their identity to a medical or social-service status. The agency of elders is further enhanced by organizing the homes in a manner that invites and encourages their contributions and participation. As researchers have described, the Green House emphasizes "competence and participation in daily activities of the household" for elders (Rabig et al. 2006, 534). To facilitate elder participation, the basic design of a Green House home includes a kitchen space that is open to a shared dining area and hearth space. Elders have access to the kitchen at all times, and they are encouraged to assist in meal preparation as they are able and wish to; and, at the least, the open kitchen allows them to be a part of meal preparation if only by watching. Researchers noted that at the first Tupelo Green House homes, the staff and elders were often seen cooking together. Furthermore, as members of a home, elders are welcomed to assist staff in other basic household chores such as setting the table, gardening, caring for household pets, cleaning, and doing laundry. This design differs dramatically from traditional nursing homes, where the kitchen is off-limits to residents and visitors and where all cooking and cleaning tasks are performed by designated staff. Affirming that dignity partly derives from a meaningful sense of responsibility, researchers have observed, "The Green House rejected the idea that the elder's primary purpose is to live out the sick role with exemption from the usual daily expectations and obligations of life and reliance on a health care provider for all assistance" (Rabig et al. 2006, 534-38).

Concomitant to viewing elders as participating members of the household, the Green House does not reduce the elderly to a class of vulnerable persons who must be protected at all costs. As Thomas argues, "And one of the problems we have in nursing homes in America is people try to take all risk away from the elders and to protect them to a degree that in some cases can be smothering" ("Green House Projects"). In other words, proper care of frail elderly should not mean trying to eliminate all the risks of normal human living at the cost of banishing the elderly from meaningful participation and freedom.[4] Thus, in Green House homes, the elderly are allowed to be out of staff vision to move freely in and out of outdoor patio spaces or to be alone in their rooms (Kane et al. 2007, 838). Such allowance for risk is not a matter of neglect but rather the attempt to maintain "normal" life even for frail elderly needing forms of care.

A second major aspect of the Green House vision of older people is respect for self-determination. One long-term-care-facility designer wrote, "The Green House approach empowers frail elders to continue a life of relative autonomy, dignity, privacy and choice" (Volzer 2003, 47). As noted above, one of the major problems with traditional nursing facilities is an undermining of agency and autonomy as a result of the routinization of schedules as determined by the needs of the institution. In contrast, the Green House homes seek to maximize flexibility and personal choice as relates to the daily schedule. Project director Jude Rabig explains the person-centered approach of the Green House: "For decades, we have organized the life of the elder or disabled individual in a skilled nursing facility around the needs of the institution. But in a Green House, clinical care and activities are organized around the needs of the individuals who live there" ("Developing Small Community Homes"). In concrete terms, this means that there is no centralized, fixed schedule in a Green House home and elders are not forced into set schedules for sleeping, getting up, or bathing. And elders and staff design meal times to meet the rhythm of their particular house, with residents able to access food whenever they wish. This flexible household maximizes the exercise of autonomy and self-determination by elderly persons as regards their daily life and personal preferences. As Angelelli writes, the Green House has "the centrality of home as an organizing principle in everyday organizational life, where elders and those who provide the majority of hands-on care are empowered to define for themselves the rhythms and routines of the household, honoring the essential personhood of its inhabitants" (2006, 428).

---

4. In his analysis of Green House homes, physician and author Atul Gawande also argues for the importance of reasonable personal freedom in achieving quality of life for older people in residential settings (2014, 111-47).

Finally, like Sant'Egidio, the Green House movement insists that its vision can be realized by the most frail elderly, including those with severe dementia. Thus, Green House homes aim to serve elderly persons with a full range of care needs, not merely higher functioning people. The organization states, "The Green House model is a de-institutionalization effort designed to restore individuals to a home in the community by combining small homes with the full range of personal care and clinical services expected in high-quality nursing homes" ("Mission and Vision"). Given the infrastructure of clinical and care support, Green House homes can accommodate elderly of wide-ranging care needs, including feeding tubes and end-of-life care. In addition, the Green House model has also been used for Alzheimer's patients and persons with other forms of dementia. Furthermore, one requirement of the Green House model is that elders cannot be asked to leave if care needs increase, including end-of-life care, with exceptions only where clinical needs require hospitalization. This differs from other forms of supported housing such as assisted-living residences, where elderly must move if their care needs increase ("Developing Small Community Homes").

In addition to a transformed vision of the elderly, the Green House approach to community also presents a new way of looking at professional caregivers. As with elderly residents, the Green House project intentionally chose to change the traditional titles of staff in order to reflect the underlying change in role and responsibility. The primary caregivers within each house are persons licensed as Certified Nursing Assistants (CNA), which is also standard in traditional nursing homes. But in order to avoid the negative connotations of the title CNA, the Green House chose the term "shahbaz," which is the Persian word for falcons who serve royalty. In traditional nursing homes, CNA-level staff provide the front-line, hands-on personal care of residents and are supervised by nurses. However, in Green House homes, the shahbaz is considered a "universal" worker whose role is expanded beyond personal care of elders. The shahbaz staff in each home are responsible for cooking, housekeeping, personal laundry, implementation of care plans, scheduling, and also spending time with residents in activities they prefer. Given this expanded role, Green House shahbaz receive 120 hours of Green House training in addition to regular CNA certification

(*Guide Book,* 10). Typically, there are two such staff persons in the homes during day shifts and one per house for the night shifts. An administrative staff person, referred to as a "guide," then oversees one or more Green House homes within a development and is responsible for overall operations and service quality. In line with nursing-home regulations, there is also a professional clinical support team with staff needed to handle technical aspects of medical treatment and physical care, such as doctors, nurses, and physical therapists (Rabig et al. 2006, 535). The clinical team is not situated in individual houses but serves one or more houses with personnel visiting as needed.

Along with expanded responsibility for shahbaz staff is expanded authority and decision making. As the *Guide Book* states, "The elders and Shahbazim are the primary decision-makers for each community" (6). This model maximizes the self-direction and choices of elders by placing decision-making roles closest to them in the form of their direct caregiver. This differs from traditional nursing homes, where decisions such as schedule and meals are determined not by the CNAs but by higher-level administrators and nursing staff who are at a greater remove from the elderly. In reference to the shahbaz, one Green House administrator explained, "We have empowered them to make decisions within their household. And so they take the responsibility of planning their menus, ordering their food, deciding what—what do the elders want" ("Green House Nursing Homes" 2007). As Kane and her colleagues note, this approach reflects a fundamental change in the role of long-term-care staff and challenges the hierarchical nature of the nursing-home-staff structure (2007, 839). Instead, Angelelli suggests that the "true unifying concept" of the Green House is "interdependence" (2006, 428). In this model, the shahbazim staff of each home work in collaboration with and are supported by the administrative "guide" and the clinical support team, which includes nurses, doctors, and physical therapists.

Another significant feature of the shahbaz role is the Green House commitment to "consistent staffing," which means the same shahbazim are assigned to particular houses. This further empowers the caregiving staff by giving them a sense of personal investment in their particular home and the elderly they serve. As Rabig et al. state, "Compared with CNAs, Shahbazim are expected to know their residents better as people, to be more likely to perceive that they have the power to influence resident outcomes positively, and to be more engaged and satisfied with their work" (2006, 535). The emphasis on consistency in relationships then also enhances resident well-being and autonomy. For, as Bergman-Evans reports in her review of nursing-home research, "Another factor that may affect loneliness for individuals is the seemingly never-ending change of nursing home personnel" (2004, 33). Thus, the Green House explicitly affirms the importance of a personal relationship between staff and elders. The ability of staff to share decision making with residents is captured in one Green House worker's observation: "[In the traditional nursing home] I used to feel like my hands were tied. I had to get the elders out of bed at a certain time, even if they didn't want to. Now if someone doesn't want to get out of bed for breakfast one day, I'll bring her a milkshake" (Tarkan, A5). Furthermore, as Angelelli insightfully describes, agency and self-determination are enhanced by the mutuality created in Green House homes: "The preferences of elders and their hands-on care partners are realized *in relationships*, and decision making and self-direction proceed from there" (2006, 428).

In addition to transforming the way elderly and staff are viewed, Green House homes, similar to Sant'Egidio, insist that meaningful participation in humanity be seen as a fundamental dimension of long-term care. Thus, the Green House model actively fosters relationships within the home and connections to the wider community. For instance, rather than the mere provision of nourishment, there is a strong emphasis on food as cultural and community experience. The *Guide Book* states, "The Green House model views food as an essential source of enjoyment, activity, community, and nourishment. The kitchen and the table serve as the centers of pleasure, culture, and community" (28). As noted earlier, meals are prepared in the home by shahbaz staff and elderly who wish to participate rather than arriving prepackaged. Furthermore, the Green House design calls for one large dining table adjacent to the kitchen, which can accommodate all elder residents, staff, and any visitors eating together. Thomas explains, "We've always insisted in the Green House that there be one big table, because that's how—that makes a meal into a community experience, where food and companionship come together" ("'Green

House' Nursing Homes Expand" 2008). This differs markedly from traditional nursing homes with large dining rooms, where residents and staff do not eat together and in which residents are segregated by those who can feed themselves and those who cannot.

Another way Green House homes foster community is by insisting that long-term care for the elderly ought to entail attention to the whole person and not merely technical aspects of care. As former project director Rabig states, "[Green House homes] are places that focus on life, and at their heart is the relationships that flourish there" ("Green House Organizers"). Thus, shahbaz staff are encouraged not only to provide basic care such as maintenance therapy and bathing, but also to spend time doing "noncare" activities with elders. In recognition that meaningful relationships enhance the dignity of the elderly, "Elders and caregiving staff are expected to engage in direct personal relationships. They eat together, talk together, make decisions together, and play together" (Rabig et al. 2006, 534). For instance, in their study of the Tupelo Green Houses, Cutler and Kane reported that bridal and baby showers were organized for staff in the houses and that elders shared in these celebrations (2009, 328). And a study comparing Green House shahbaz staff and traditional nursing-home CNA staff reported that shahbazim spent more time with elders outside of care for activities of daily living (Sharkey et al. 2011, 130). One shahbaz compellingly articulated the importance of personal relationships: "You know, your whole life you eat with family and you converse and some of these people are hard of hearing, and they can't hear. So I thought if I go sit next to her and hold her hand, she'll start eating. And she did. I have been doing this for two-and-a-half years and I love it. I wouldn't trade it for anything in the entire world" ("Green House Nursing Homes" 2007).

Participation and community are also fostered by the Green House approach to relationships among elderly residents. For instance, the Green House approach anticipates that, as in any normal human household, conflicts and tensions will arise in relationships. There is no attempt to eliminate these normal relational dynamics but rather an explicit commitment to constructive conflict resolution and engagement with elders as responsible adults. Thomas provides an insightful explanation of this approach:

We work with the shabazeem, the people working in the house, and the elders and the families around a shared commitment to create a respectful community in the house. You see, I actually think it's the wrong idea to sort of try to move elders around like they were pegs in a box, you know, and say, well, these ones will go together these ones won't . . . one of the problems that we face in traditional institutional long-term care is that everybody wants to make conflict go away. Everybody wants to suppress conflict, whether it's between the staff or with the residents. And in the Green House, we say, oh, we've got conflict? Let's talk about it. We're human beings, we're going to have conflict. So that's the approach we take at the Green House. ("Green House Projects" 2007)

Thus, as we saw with Sant'Egidio, the culture of the Green House home asks for and expects ongoing personal growth from elderly persons in terms of their character and their engagement with others. Relationships within the home are also enhanced in the requirement that, in each house, no more than two elders can be short-term, rehabilitation residents unless the entire house is designated for this purpose. This helps staff and elders relate to one another more personally, rather than being generic, replaceable parts in an institution.

Thus, while the Green House project is a model using paid staff persons, it promotes personal relationships of mutuality as the proper context for long-term care that promotes the dignity of older people. Furthermore, Rabig and her colleagues argue that the Green House model has been able to expand the shape of long-term care without sacrificing clinical well-being. While maintaining the clinical and professional standards required by nursing-home regulations, they suggest that the Green House "gives primacy" to nonclinical measures of quality-of-life, including a sense of security, physical comfort, enjoyment, meaningful activity, relationships, functional competence, dignity, privacy, individuality, autonomy, and spiritual well-being. In this model, "care" is not merely the treatment provided by clinical medical staff, but "helping another person to achieve the highest possibility of quality of life given his or her condition and impairments" (Rabig et al. 2006, 534-36).

Beyond the internal residential community, the Green House model seeks to nurture connections to family, friends, and the wider community. As Lum et al. explain, studies have shown that ongoing family involvement is vital for the well-being of nursing-home residents and provides a major connection to the larger community (2008, 35-36). However, the medicalized and institutionalized environment of the traditional nursing home may discourage or lessen family visits and involvement. In their study, Lum et al. compared the Green House homes in Tupelo to two larger long-term-care facilities. The study showed that family members of elders at the Green House homes were more involved overall with residents' care and scored higher in family satisfaction with care and quality of life (47-48). The researchers observed that the Green House homes allowed for many family members such as spouses to become a daily presence in the home, participating in the meals and activities of the house. A later study of the Tupelo Green House homes also found positive family involvement. Cutler and Kane state, "Family members reported an increase in their visiting patterns because 'it doesn't feel like a nursing home'" (2009, 327). Rabig and colleagues support these studies, arguing that Green House homes enhance family visits and involvement because of better visiting space such as private rooms and involvement with meals (2006, 538). Thus, the Green House model also enhances quality of life for elderly persons by better sustaining meaningful relationships with family and friends. As one Green House resident stated, "When [my family members] come to see me, I'm so proud to show them around. Back at the nursing home, I felt like I was staying at somebody else's place. Here, I know I'm home" (Moos 2006, 16). Finally, in order to promote ongoing connection to the wider community, the Green House model calls for community volunteers who establish special relationships to a particular house. These community persons are referred to as "sages" and provide support and advice to staff and residents. And, like Sant'Egidio homes, Green House homes built in residential neighborhoods allow for easier, more organic connections with surrounding neighbors.

Conclusion

As noted at the outset of this section, the Green House Project goes beyond reform measures for existing nursing homes in the United

States to present an entirely new vision for residential long-term care of frail elderly. However, as a radically new model, the development of Green House projects has not been without scrutiny and questions. One set of questions has to do with regulation and licensing of Green House homes under existing state laws governing long-term-care facilities, which were intended for much larger institutions. However, as Rabig and colleagues explain, because the nursing home "is the only nationwide mechanism to meet the heavy care needs of low-income older people," the Green House was designed to meet the criteria for nursing-home designation and reimbursement (2006, 534). Therefore, the Green House consultative team provides local groups with advice on working with state-level legislative and regulatory bodies. For instance, for the Tupelo Green House project, Mississippi Methodist Senior Services made concerted efforts to educate community, government agencies, and legislators to promote public acceptance. Furthermore, throughout the process, project directors met with relevant state agencies to ensure regulatory compliance and to establish an atmosphere of partnership. Thus, the necessary functions and requirements of a larger nursing home are fulfilled, but with the smaller-scale home at the center: "The key operational unit is the self-contained Green House with its elders and its Shahbazim, although the larger sponsoring entity provides the Green House with various administrative functions of a nursing facility, such as accounting, billing, a medical record system, physical plant maintenance, and supply procurement" (Rabig et al. 2006, 535-536).

Along with regulatory questions, the Green House project has had to confront questions about financial viability. While early Green House projects have been very successful with local nonprofit groups such as Mississippi Methodist Senior Services and St. John's Lutheran Ministries in Montana, one challenge is spreading into the for-profit market in order to have a wider impact on the nation's 16,000-facility nursing-home system. Since the first homes were built in 2003 in Tupelo, reports thus far suggest that, while up-front costs for constructing Green House homes are higher than for a traditional facility, it is possible to operate these homes at the same per-patient cost of a larger nursing home (Kalb and Juarez 2005; Parkin 2000, 28; Schilling 2009, 28-29; Moos 2006, 17). As in traditional nursing homes,

Green House income includes private pay and a state's standard Medicaid reimbursement. While Green House homes may spend more in certain areas, there is an equalizing of cost due to an overall "redistribution of resources" rather than merely adding new costs on top of those in a traditional care center. As Meg LaPorte notes, for-profit entities have had similar findings: higher costs in one area will be offset by lower costs in other areas (2010, 27-28). In addition, project coordinators have reported that the up-front costs for Green House homes can be recouped over the long term. Thus, the financial viability of this model seems promising, with the first for-profit Green House homes built in Arkansas in 2009.

In fact, one area of success that also helps financially is the high level of satisfaction among shahbaz staff. Tupelo Green Houses and other projects have seen lower absenteeism and turnover among staff (Rabig et al. 2006, 538; Moos 2006, 17). And the Tupelo project reported that shahbaz staff turnover was less than 10 percent in Green House homes in the first two years compared with 70 percent in their traditional nursing-home units. Lowering staff turnover not only enhances quality of life for elderly residents, but also makes good business sense: the average cost to nursing homes for each personnel turnover is $2,500 (Angelelli 2006, 429). Higher levels of job satisfaction are attributable partly to the Green House model, which empowers CNA-level staff with greater authority and independence. In addition, the shahbaz staff are paid 10 percent more in Green House homes than CNAs in traditional settings (Tarkan, A5). The Green House projects are able to pay more because of achieving other efficiencies, such as cutting out middle-management positions and lowering staff turnover. As one administrator stated, the Green Houses in his campus were the most "self-sufficient" of the facilities he managed because the shahbaz "step up and solve problems on their own" (Peck 2009, 26).

As to questions about the quality of life for elders living in Green House homes, several studies have tracked outcomes for residents and their families. A 2007 study commissioned by the Commonwealth Fund of New York sought to evaluate the first Green Houses, measuring their impact on quality of life by comparing residents of the smaller homes with two other nursing homes operated by the same system. Quality-of-life questions asked of elders ranged from physical comfort to spiritual well-being, and in the self-reported responses of residents on these questions, the Green House was favored over the other two facilities. Furthermore, on improvement in the functional abilities of residents, the Green House homes exceeded the other facilities. The Green Houses had fewer residents on bed rest, less decline in functioning in activities of daily living, and also lower incidences of depression (Kane et al. 2007, 832-37). Likewise, other researchers have noted that because the Green House home design eliminates long hallways, elders are often able to stop the use of wheelchairs because of the short distances within the house, thus improving basic ambulatory functioning (Rabig et al. 2006, 536). Rabig and her colleagues further back up the initial Green House findings with other studies showing that smaller size has been associated with positive-outcome indicators, including reduced anxiety and depression, increased mobility and self-care functioning, increased social interaction and meaningful relationships, improved staff supervision, and improved eating behavior (534). And other studies have also shown that more direct care time by shahbaz-level staff is given to elders in Green House homes than in traditional facilities (M. LaPorte 2010, 30). In their study, Kane and her colleagues also concluded that the original Green House homes equaled the other two facilities in measures of social activity (2007, 837).[5]

After years of working in traditional nursing homes and in efforts at reform, Bill Thomas concluded, "The old model of nursing homes needs to go away and be replaced with new models" (M. LaPorte 2010, 23).

My purpose has been to present the Green House initiative as one such successful new model for residential, long-term elder care, one centered on promoting the dignity and agency of the elderly. And, as discussed above, Green House developments are thus far proving

---

5. However, in another study, Lum and colleagues have suggested that one area in which the original Green Houses could improve is in providing religious services in the house and facilitating attendance at services in the community (2008, 49). In terms of future improvement, Lum et al. also suggest future Green House homes could enhance access to organized activities inside and outside the homes with attention to developing a new role for the activities director found in traditional skilled-care settings (50).

to be a viable improvement to the existing nursing-home system in the United States. As one nursing administrator observed, "'In general the Green Houses are doing things we have tried to do forever in nursing homes. And residents are living more normal lives because of it'" (Peck 2009, 28). To conclude this chapter we will consider the relevance of the two concrete models presented here to a contemporary Christian ethic of long-term care.

Sant'Egidio, the Green House Project, and the Ethics of Long-Term Care

We began this chapter by acknowledging that the challenges of aging and long-term care today often limit our imagination as to what is possible in elder care and our commitment to bringing about necessary changes in our current system. Medical author Gawande observed, "But it seems we've settled on a belief that a life of worth and engagement is not possible once you lose independence" (2007a). My purpose has been to present two models of elder care that directly dispute that belief and, thus, provide us with new possibilities for the future. Though distinct from each other, the Community of Sant'Egidio and the Green House Project together yield important insights for shaping a Christian ethic of long-term care that honors the dignity of older people and promotes their ongoing agency as participating members of society.

First, as we have seen, both models are shaped by a fundamental understanding of old age as a time of potential growth and development. As one author writes, the term "Green House" was chosen precisely to indicate "a place where elders can thrive and grow" (Adler 2008, 24). As Green House founder Thomas argues, it is imperative to challenge the notion that frailty and disability eliminate ongoing agency: "the first thing is to stop thinking of nursing homes as if they were watered-down hospitals and really to start thinking of them as places where older people can live and grow. And right there, that's a challenge for a lot of people, because if you think about people living in nursing homes, you think about people having strokes and living with dementia. How can they grow?" ("Green House Projects"). The Green House has enabled such visible growth through the small-scale personalism of its home, which welcomes the autonomy and contribution of elders in household activities and relationships. Likewise, as demonstrated, Sant'Egidio nurtures growth in old age through initiatives such as its home-based services and providing opportunities for spiritual growth and personal development. As the organization insists, even amid the frailty and weakness of old age, it discovered in the elderly "a great desire to live" ("The Meaning of Old Age"). For Sant'Egidio this also means affirming that older people are a resource for society not merely a burden or problem. Both organizations show that it is possible to provide care in a way that honors the agency and ongoing potential of the elderly.

Second, because both models are guided by a view of old age as a time of growth and potential, they seek to foster relationships of mutuality in which the elderly can make meaningful contributions to others as well as receiving from others. While realistically acknowledging the limitations that can be experienced in old age, Sant'Egidio still approaches its service from the perspective of friendship, in which old and young mutually enrich each other with their distinct contributions. As the organization explains, "Friendship, expresse[d] as closeness, is the way that allowed us to penetrate deeply into the world of the elderly that we met not as a category of 'assisted people' but as persons. The building up of a mature personal relationship, [a] relationship of mutual fidelity is the essential premise to every action because it allows us to understand individuals not as a member of a category but as persons with their special story" ("Home Help: What We Do"). And, as we saw with the Green House approach, care staff are consistently assigned to homes to promote stable relationships in which staff and elders can come to know one another, to celebrate life events together, and to spend time in activities other than direct care needs.

Thomas argues, "In long-term care, love matters. And the heart of the problem is institutions can't love. . . . In fact, I think it's the signal achievement of the Green House: making a place where love matters" ("'Green House' Nursing Homes Expand"). The mutuality fostered in relationships with older people through Sant'Egidio and the Green House Project also reflects the norm of basic equality in which older people are not treated as a fundamentally different class of persons or merely as passive objects of care. As the Sant'Egidio Website states, "Even if the taste, culture, language was very different, we discovered the possibility of a friendship between different generations, between a youngster and an aged person" ("A Bit of History").

Third, from this vision of growth and mutuality comes the commitment to enabling and encouraging the participation of the elderly as a key expression of human dignity. Sant'Egidio describes the importance of such participation: "Social relations, occupying oneself, culture, work, faith, are fundamental dimensions which are important for everyone, but especially when one is old they can determine the dignity or the lack of dignity of one's existence, the desire to live or to let oneself die" ("Home Help: The Gestures of Friendship"). As described above, Sant'Egidio fosters this participation through involving the elderly in social-outreach initiatives and public advocacy, supporting family relationships, and nurturing nonactive forms of participation such as prayer. Likewise, as one Green House director describes, the project seeks to enable even the seemingly smallest forms of participation: "Letting the frailest gifts be recognized and to soar again, after they've been squelched at the end stage of life" ("Green House Nursing Homes"). The Green House achieves ongoing participation through its commitment to flexibility in which the lives of the elderly are determined not by a rigid institutional schedule but through an open-home design that allows elders to remain a part of the daily rhythm of home life and by creating an environment that encourages stronger ties with family and the larger community.

Fourth, both models are motivated in their efforts by the profound conviction that care of the elderly is a basic measure of a just and healthy society. Given the growing universality of increased longevity, Sant'Egidio founder Andrea Riccardi has argued that excluding the elderly inevitably undermines the well-being of all: "There is an old person inside each of us. The effort to run away from aging is the folly of our society" (1998, 160). From Sant'Egidio's perspective, the health of a society can be measured by its ability to welcome the full range of human life: "The fragility of the elderly asks questions of a society in which weak people are left alone, drawing attention to the social nature of man and to the necessity of reweaving the human cloth which has often disintegrated" ("The Secret of an Alliance").

Thus, Sant'Egidio views the integration of various generations as the sign of a healthy society. The Sant'Egidio organization advocates for just care of the elderly both through its collaboration with public entities and through its educational and awareness efforts. Likewise, as noted above, the Green House project seeks to combat the isolation and marginalization that are features of the current nursing-home system in the United States. As aging expert Bill Keane writes, reformers like Bill Thomas are combating "the debilitating effects of the status quo, with its blind devotion to the institutional medicalization of late life and the dismissal of frail older people from the heart of our society. Overcoming that culture and creating the potential for a society that celebrates the elder as a still complex, growing person with an equal opportunity for dignity in daily life is our generation's greatest challenge" (2004, 44). Beginning with the Eden Alternative and continuing with the Green House project, Thomas and colleagues have sought to reform the long-term-care sector and to transform society's view of the aging experience, particularly in situations of frailty.

Conclusion

This chapter represents one building block in constructing a contemporary Christian ethic of long-term care. One value of concrete models is they allow Christian ethics to speak not only from principles and theological sources but also from the experience of communities of practice. On this point, Lisa Cahill's insight regarding what she calls "participatory discourse" is helpful: "Ethical arguments and their ability to persuade are rooted in and rely on such practices, not just on intellectual cogency and verbal rhetoric" (2005, 27). Ron Thiemann made a similar point in arguing that religious communities contribute to public life and debate not only through traditions of thought but also through embodiment of ethical norms in their practices (1991, 43). My purpose in this chapter has been to identify the ethical norms embodied in the practices of the Community of Sant'Egidio and the Green House Project, norms that are relevant for shaping a Christian ethical response to aging today. In the next two chapters, we turn to biblical and theological sources to augment the insights gained from these two models of care.

CHAPTER FOUR

The Elderly in the Bible

In this chapter we turn to resources particular to the Christian tradition that are relevant to the social issue of aging today and that support the ethical insights arising from the two models presented in the previous chapter. One of the particular resources for constructing a Christian ethic of long-term care is the biblical witness concerning older persons in society. As the Pontifical Council for the Laity (1998) of the Roman Catholic Church has argued, "To grasp the full sense and value of old age we need to open the Bible. Only the light of the Word of God, in fact, enables us to fathom the spiritual, moral and theological dimensions of this stage of life." In drawing upon the biblical witness, I seek to show that the biblical injunctions calling for familial and societal care of older people are set within a theological vision of the elderly as subjects who continue to have purpose before God and within the community of faith, even with the onset of age-related weakness and disability. It is this *combination* of elder care as a requirement of justice and the affirmation of the dignity of older people as called by God that provides an important component for a Christian moral vision of long-term care for the elderly today.

It should be acknowledged at the outset that any attempt to relate biblical material to contemporary aging must take into account different cultural and historical contexts. In his exhaustive study of aging and the Bible, biblical scholar J. Gordon Harris points out there is no simple correspondence between definitions of old age today and old age in the ancient Near East (1987, 11). For instance, partly due to Social Security policy in America today, the age of sixty-five is a generally accepted marker of retirement age, and average longevity in the

United States hovers near eighty. In contrast, Harris points out that, despite claims that figures such as Moses or Joshua are said to have lived past the age of one hundred, average longevity in the ancient period was significantly lower than today. For instance, based on the historical record of the fourteen kings of David's dynasty, the average lifespan of the royal class is estimated at about forty-four years (Knierim 1981, 24; Martin-Achard 1991, 32). Given that kings would have enjoyed superior diet and health, Harris notes that few persons at this time would have reached seventy or eighty years (1987, 12).

As regards notions of retirement and old age, the division between the productivity of adult years and the leisure of old age was not as strict in the ancient period as it became in contemporary Western society. For instance, Harris argues that even for those in physically demanding occupations such as agriculture, transition from such work in later life did not entail retirement from social responsibility: he notes that elder members of the community would have continued to fulfill roles in the family and as advisers or judges for the local clan or the Israelite nation (1987, 13). Furthermore, the biblical material itself reflects a diversity of historical periods and societal attitudes, and thus, we should not operate with the notion of a singular biblical "culture" as regards old age. Similarly, ethicist Stephen Sapp warns against the assumption that there is an identifiable, systematic "theology of aging" in the Bible (1987, 132).

However, keeping in mind such factors, there are general patterns in the experience of aging that provide points of commonality that allow the aging experience in the biblical material to speak to our contemporary context. For instance, the Bible does identify old age in relation to "the seasons of life" and transitions in role: old age is marked by "maturity and leadership" within the society and a transition from the primary years of work, reproduction, and parenting (Harris 1987, 13; Knierim 1981, 30). The Bible also associates certain physical characteristics and changes with old age. The arrival of "white hair" is used to indicate maturity of age and also certain physical losses, such as the infertility associated with menopause and the loss of hearing and sight (Harris 1987, 14; Knierim 1981, 25).

Again, though any use of biblical material to address contemporary aging must appreciate historical and cultural differences, scholars agree that the Bible does recognize a distinct stage of life that at least parallels our experience of old age today. As Harris states, "While the experience of aging in the Bible defies precise definition, the materials mention traits that distinguish that season from other periods of life" (1987, 16). And, commenting specifically on the Hebrew Bible, Rolf Knierim concludes, "The biblical authors have not given us an explicit or systematic anthropological chapter on aging and old age. But they certainly had a concept of old age and aging, and they have given us a variety of perspectives throughout the Old Testament" (1981, 21).

The concept of later life as a distinct life stage is also present in the New Testament, as evidenced by references to the "elders" of the community and in discussions of elderly widows. Furthermore, certain basic moral imperatives concerning the aged do appear throughout the biblical material, which is of particular interest to this project. My own approach shares ethicist James Gustafson's position: "Certain generalizations about God's prevailing aspirations and purposes for human life can be formulated on the basis of the scriptural witness. . . . One need not appeal to strict analogies between events recorded and interpreted in Scripture and events of the present, but rather one can appeal to theological affirmations that are informed and governed by the biblical witness" (1970, 449-50). Thus, while avoiding any simplistic application of biblical material to the contemporary context, we shall seek to draw on the biblical witness concerning old age to inform the church's theological and ethical vision of aging today.

There are, of course, multiple ways in which to "open the Bible" in relation to aging, and it is important to be clear about my own analysis, as there already exist several fine studies of the Bible and old age. One approach is to look for what might be termed the biblical "attitude" toward old age by conducting an analysis of relevant words used in Scripture and to look for direct statements that either affirm or disparage aging.[1] This approach often seeks to draw on biblical attitudes

---

1. For instance, Stephen Sapp's book on the Bible and aging contains sections entitled "Attitudes toward Aging" in which he examines statements from the Hebrew Bible and New Testament (1987, 65-75, 99-111), and Richard B. Hays and Judith C. Hays provide an analysis of terminology related to aging found in the New Testament (2003, 4-5).

toward old age in order to critique attitudes toward aging in contemporary society. A second approach is to examine the biblical text for injunctions or principles that outline moral duties for the treatment of the elderly.[2] Studies such as these are particularly aimed at shaping Christian moral principles that can be applied to family responsibility for elder care. A third approach that is prominent in studies of the Bible and aging is to examine elderly characters in the narratives of the Hebrew Bible and the New Testament.[3] Rather than being limited to direct statements concerning old age, the narrative approach provides a helpful method by which to analyze biblical perspectives on the role and identity of older persons by looking at stories about the elderly.

Given this book's focus on shaping a contemporary Christian ethic of long-term care, we will be examining the biblical material with two primary interests. First, what is the biblical perspective on elder care as an ethical concern? And second, what does the Bible have to say theologically about the identity of older persons in their relationship to God and within the community of faith? Thus, we are interested not only in what the Bible tells us we ought to do *for* old people but also in the identity of older persons *as subjects in their own right.* Having an adequate theological vision of older persons is crucial to understanding how long-term care should be shaped and provided. Towards this end, I draw on biblical scholarship that both presents ethical principles of care and analyzes elderly characters.

---

2. Several studies focus specifically on the precepts of the ancient Israelite legal code, including the Decalogue, which require intergenerational responsibility in both the family and society (Harris 1987, 61-74; Sapp 1987, 81-93, 179-81; Blidstein 1975, 37-39), and Warren Carter demonstrates the continuation of these moral principles in the New Testament (2001, 45).

3. Examples of this approach can be found scattered throughout several studies; for instance, both Harris (1987, 78-80) and Hays and Hays (2003, 6-8) examine elderly characters found in the Lukan material. And though her main focus is on a practical theology for ministry with Alzheimer's patients, Dee Ann Klapp also mentions older characters from the Gospel of Luke (2003, 73-76).

The Ethical Imperative for Care

In addressing the normative task of religious ethics, the first consistent aspect of the biblical witness concerning old age to examine is the moral imperative to provide care for aging members of the family and society. We shall first examine evidence of this imperative in the Hebrew Bible and then turn to an examination of the New Testament. Texts of the Hebrew Bible demonstrate ancient Israelite concern for maintaining just and healthy intergenerational relations in society, including linking respect and care for the elderly with righteousness and faith in God.[4] In his extensive study, Harris argues that one aspect of the moral imperative for respect and care of older members of family and society was the effort to strengthen the structure of society. In this effort, Israelite culture was not unique. As Harris explains, the general perspective of the cultures of the ancient Near East was that "Unhealthy relationships between the generations brought social chaos" (1987, 30). Certainly the fifth commandment of the Decalogue highlights respect for the elderly as a centerpiece of a just society: "Honor your father and your mother, so that your days may be long in the land that the LORD your God is giving you" (Exodus 20:12; cf. Deuteronomy 5:16). The insistence on respect and honor for aged members of family and society can also be found throughout the Wisdom literature, particularly Proverbs. For instance, Proverbs 30:17 declares, "The eye that mocks a father and scorns to obey a mother will be pecked out by the ravens of the valley and eaten by the vultures." As Harris concludes concerning the Wisdom literature, "Individual proverbs rival legal traditions in demanding respect for parents. In this way wisdom teachers reinforce the authority and

---

4. In his study, Harris provides comparison of Israelite attitudes toward old age with ancient Mesopotamian, Egyptian, and Canaanite cultures (1987, 18-29). While highlighting some differences in their perspectives, Harris concludes that it is inaccurate to claim uniqueness for the Hebrew Bible's teachings on aging: "Israel seems to have inherited for its faith and society many ancient oriental themes of respect for the older generation. The Hebrew Scriptures often describe attitudes and practices toward the elderly that reflect principles found in the literature of ancient Mesopotamia, Egypt, and Canaan" (30).

sense of worth of the older generation" (1987, 36). Thus, the Hebrew Bible shares the general perspective of other ancient Near Eastern cultures that the stability of society is enhanced by intergenerational relationships founded on proper respect and obedience from younger persons toward elders.

However, a distinctive aspect of the biblical teachings concerning respect for elders is the insistence on respect for older persons as a sign of righteous faith in God. As Harris explains, ancient Israelite theology "seeks to strengthen social structures by relating respect for the elderly to faith in God" (1987, 30). For instance, Leviticus 19:32 states, "You shall rise before the aged, and defer to the old; and you shall fear your God: I am the LORD." Regarding such passages, Sapp observes, "It would be hard to think of a stronger way for a religion like Judaism to convey the importance of honoring one's parents than to equate such behavior with honoring the one true God" (1987, 85). Thus, the biblical text underlines the importance of respect and obedience toward elderly parents and members of society by suggesting that it is a moral commandment as central as respect and fear of God.

Furthermore, it is important to note the scholarly agreement that, in addition to social and familial honor and deference, the respect and honor enjoined by the Decalogue's moral code were to be expressed in concrete forms of material care. Stressing this often-overlooked aspect of the Hebrew Bible, Knierim explains, "What is less known, however, is that this [fifth] commandment refers primarily to the material support of old parents by their adult children" (1981, 29). Likewise, based on his study of multiple texts from the Hebrew Bible, Robert Martin-Achard argues that respect for the elderly "is a matter of looking after the whole of their lives and assuring them of food, clothing, lodging, and even burial" (1991, 37). Thus, respect for aging parents extended into the period in which they experienced physical dependence and disability. In fact, Knierim suggests the Hebrew legal code provided a "genuine form of social security in which old parents remained part of their families, with dignity and material security" (1981, 29). The expectation of such material support can be seen in the biblical texts that warn against neglect and abuse of aging, vulnerable parents.

Texts that prohibit elder abuse are found throughout the Hebrew legal code, including Exodus, Leviticus, and Deuteronomy. These statutes are connected to the imperative to care for elderly persons because "eliminating abuse of aging parents encourages stability and support for people entering old age" (Harris 1987, 30). Furthermore, the moral imperative of providing material support for aging parents is reinforced by the Hebrew legal code's sanction for neglecting this duty: the death penalty. In fact, Harris suggests that this severe penalty reflects a "passion" for elder welfare in the Hebrew Bible that surpasses other literature of the time (57). Thus, the failure of adult children to materially care for aging relatives was seen as a failure to treat the elderly person with respect and honor as enjoined by the moral code of Jewish law.

In ancient societies, the initial and primary location for the fulfillment of the moral imperative to respect and care for the elderly was the family. However, it is important to be aware that fulfillment of this ethical demand was not *limited to* the family. For instance, Sapp argues that the Hebrew Bible insists on a "general obligation" of respect toward all older members of society, not only one's relatives (1987, 79). The clearest proof of a general social obligation is that the Hebrew Bible's demand for just care of the elderly is set within the larger theological vision of God as the advocate of justice for weak and vulnerable populations, such as the poor, the orphan, and the stranger. For the ancient Israelites, this theological vision is, of course, based on the God of the Exodus story, who acts on behalf of a group of oppressed slaves against the authority of Egypt. The biblical concern for the weak and oppressed thus encompassed older members of society (Harris 1987, 59).

In various stories about elderly characters and through prohibitions of elder abuse, the Hebrew Bible recognized that old age could often bring physical decline, weakness, and economic vulnerability. In such circumstances, elderly persons, like other vulnerable members of society such as orphans and strangers, were to be cared for and protected based on the general biblical norm demanding justice for oppressed members of society. As Harris explains, "In the justice of God, however, the aging also find comfort and hope. . . . Since aging implies eventual weakening of the physical, social, and economic powers of an older person, the elderly may depend increasingly on

God's protection from enemies both within the family and from the outside" (1987, 6).

It is important to note, then, that care and respect for the elderly are not based only on a concern for social stability; rather, when old age brings vulnerability through reduced income or physical disability, the moral imperative to care for the elderly is also reinforced by God's special concern for the poor and weak. Harris concluded, "Protection for the aging in Israel issues out of the center of God's nature as much as out of a desire to support the structures of society.... Divine compassion demands concern for the weak and disenfranchised" (1987, 58).

While the Hebrew Bible emphasizes care and respect for the elderly as an important measure of a just society, evidence of this moral concern in the texts should not be taken as proof that ancient Israelite society was always an exemplar in its treatment of the aged. In other words, the moral norms contained in the Hebrew Bible do not reflect an idealized time period in which the elderly always enjoyed respect and adequate care. The biblical text also reveals, albeit implicitly, periods of social instability and mistreatment of the aged in ancient Israel. Harris writes, "Though the Hebrew Bible does not record a history of treatment for the elderly, it contains indirect evidence that implies that in Israel practices toward the elderly often fell short of its ideals" (1987, 41). For instance, prophetic texts such as Micah identify a breach in just relations between the generations in Israelite society. Thus, even with the strong moral tradition reflected in the biblical texts, ancient Israelite treatment of and attitudes toward the elderly were also vulnerable to wider cultural and political transitions in society. However, despite lapses in actual practice, the ancient Israelite legal and moral traditions preserved a concern for just treatment of aged members of society.

When we turn to the New Testament, scholars generally agree that the early Christian communities reflected the Hebrew Bible's moral insistence on respect and care for older members of the community. Sapp observes, "As did the Old Testament, so also the New Testament expects the basic attitude toward the elderly (especially parents) to be one of respect and consideration" (1987, 117). As seen in the Hebrew

Bible and ancient societies, first-century C.E. Jewish culture continued to view the intergenerational relationships within the family as a
fundamental aspect of "social cohesion." Furthermore, care for aging
parents was also reinforced by cultural norms and laws of first-century
C.E. Greco-Roman society (Harris 1987, 76-80).

However, any discussion of the moral imperative to care for the
elderly in the New Testament must address the fact that the Gospels
and the early Jesus movement often reflect a lack of concern with
issues of social stability given their focus on the new era inaugurated
by the life of Jesus. In this regard, Jesus' life and teachings are often
presented in the Gospels as a challenge to ancient traditions and
authority. For example, the Jesus of the Synoptic Gospels calls followers to renounce normal biological family ties when they obstruct
discipleship: "Whoever comes to me and does not hate father and
mother, wife and children, brothers and sisters, yes, and even life
itself, cannot be my disciple" (Luke 14:26). In addition, the Synoptic
Gospels offer an expanded definition of the term "family," which is
based on the fellowship of those who follow Jesus and not limited to
blood relations. The Gospel of Mark records a well-known example of
this redefinition of family: "And [Jesus] replied, 'Who are my mother
and my brothers?' And looking around at those who sat around him,
he said, 'Here are my mother and my brothers! Whoever does the will
of God is my brother and sister and mother'" (Mark 3:33-34).

However, rather than isolating such texts, they should be seen
within the larger framework in which Jesus challenged ancient norms
that prevented persons from wholehearted devotion to God. Thus, as
Harris explains, it is important to keep in mind the overall framework
of the New Testament texts: "In an era inaugurating the impending
kingdom all believers need the freedom to concentrate on preaching
the gospel. Pressures from defensive and resistant families certainly
would cause great hardship for believers" (1987, 82). Likewise, in his
analysis of the New Testament, Sapp argues that Jesus' point is not
that family ties and obligations are bad per se, but that devotion to
God must take precedence where conflict arises (1987, 126). Given
this, texts such as those cited above are properly considered, when
placed within the overall framework of Jesus' message, not as abso-

lute, abstract condemnations of family ties or as denigrating normal family responsibilities.

In addition, New Testament texts challenging ancient norms regarding family ties and obligation must be considered along with texts in which Jesus can be seen to affirm the value of filial respect for parents and the Hebrew Bible's insistence that care for the vulnerable elderly is part of God's special concern for those who are poor and weak. Sapp argues, "The message of Jesus recorded in the Gospels leaves no room for neglect of the elderly (especially one's own parents) and actually demands an active concern for their well-being, indeed, for the welfare of all who are in any kind of need in one's community" (1987, 129). For instance, in Mark 7:5-13, Jesus criticizes the Pharisees for teaching that a religious commitment to make offerings to God (referred to as the vow of "Corban") absolves one of the responsibility to provide material care for aging parents. Furthermore, in Mark 10:19, when the wealthy man asks what he must do to be righteous, Jesus includes honoring of father and mother in the list of moral commandments he emphasizes.

Moreover, several scholars point to the crucifixion scene in the Gospel of John in which Jesus places his mother under the care of John as an expression of Jesus' own filial duty (John 19:26-27). Far from outright rejection of filial duty, this story, according to Sapp, illustrates that "fulfilling the fifth commandment was an obligation Jesus took very seriously" (1987, 121). Furthermore, in the tradition of the Hebrew prophets' insistence on justice for the poor and oppressed, Jesus exhibits moral concern for vulnerable widows in several instances in his teachings and parables. For instance, in Luke 7:11-17, Jesus has compassion on a widow whose only son, and thus only source of familial support, has died by raising the man back to life.[5] In light of such texts, Harris provides an insightful summary of the Gospel presentation of Jesus' attitude toward care for the elderly: "When normal family relationships were possible, however, Jesus condemned any shirking of duty toward aging parents and demonstrated open compassion toward the 'curse of widowhood'" (1987, 95).

---

5. See also Luke 4:25-26; 21:1-4; Mark 12:41-44.

As regards New Testament epistles, they contain more direct statements affirming ancient Israelite concern for intergenerational relationships within the community. This literature is understood to reflect the historical development of the Christian community in which there is a maturation of the movement and more attention given to social stability and responsibility. For instance, Colossians and Ephesians address intergenerational relations in the "household codes." Ephesians 6:1-3 reiterates the ancient Jewish law promising blessing to those who follow the commandment to honor mother and father: "'Honor your father and mother'—this is the first command-ment with a promise: 'so that it may be well with you and you may live long on the earth.'" And Colossians 3:20 reflects the teaching of the Hebrew Bible that respect for parents is tied to true faith in God: the epistle refers to respect for parents as a child's "duty in the Lord." Furthermore, as we saw with ancient Hebrew texts, honor and respect for parents are understood in the New Testament epistles to include *material* care. For instance, 1 Timothy 5:4 and 8 state that it is an expression of a Christian's religious duty to God to care materially for relatives who are aging widows vulnerable to poverty.

In addition to affirming the filial duty to respect and care for aging relatives, the New Testament epistles also address intergenerational relations as regards aging members of the Christian community, the larger "family" as defined by Jesus.[6] As Harris explains, these texts reflect the aging of the Christian community itself: "The increasing incidence of teachings about widows and older leaders indicates an aging population in the early church. As church leadership ages it needs more support" (1987, 87). In these epistles we see that, as in the Hebrew Bible, the moral injunction to honor elders is not limited to blood relatives; for instance, 1 Timothy 5:1-2 states, "Do not speak harshly to an older man, but speak to him as to a father . . . to older women as mothers."

---

6. While our primary interest here is with the biblical texts, several historical studies show that care for vulnerable elderly persons, particular widows, continued to be a main part of the early church's charitable activity; see J. Laporte 1981; Greer, 2003; Carter 2001.

Furthermore, in line with Jesus' prophetic teachings concerning the oppressed, these epistles extend God's special concern for the poor and weak to widows within the community who lack adequate material support from family. For instance, 1 Timothy 5:9-10 states that such widows should be included on the community's "list" of those who receive support from the church. Based on such texts, Harris concludes that, in the New Testament epistles, "God's concern for justice demands that Christian families *and communities* meet the needs of the most vulnerable of widows" [emphasis mine] (1987, 90-91).

This section has demonstrated that one of the consistent themes in the biblical witness concerning old age is the moral imperative to respect and care for elderly members of society. We have seen that both the Hebrew Bible and the New Testament present care for the aged as one of the measures of a just society, the violation of which is considered to be harmful to social well-being and also to reflect lack of true devotion to God. Furthermore, the Bible's specific concern for just care of the aged is rooted in the general theological affirmation of God's concern for the poor and oppressed of society. The ethical imperative to care arising out of the Bible provides a key norm for a contemporary Christian ethical approach to long-term care for the elderly. In the next section, I will lay out a second key norm: the affirmation of the dignity of the elderly as subjects called by God to purposeful living and participation in old age.

The Biblical Vision of Dignity in Old Age

While the ethical imperative to care for the elderly is a vital aspect of the biblical witness, the relevance of the Bible for shaping an approach to long-term elder care is not limited to statements of duty and obligation toward the elderly, the weak, and the needy. In this section, then, we will examine a second consistent norm in the biblical understanding of old age: the dignity of the elderly as continuing to be addressed by God as subjects who are called to the purpose of serving God's work in the world. In other words, from the perspective of the Bible, the elderly are not merely the objects of the community's care but participating *subjects* within the community, even in the context of disability and weakness. My purpose is to show that this second biblical theme is equally important in shaping a contemporary ethic of long-term care because this vision determines how care ought to be provided.

This section will focus from a theological perspective on narratives about older characters in the Bible, asking what they tell us about older people in relation to God and what this means for shaping an ethic of long-term care. Here my own approach is closely aligned with that of New Testament scholars Richard B. Hays and Judith C. Hays, whose essay "The Christian Practice of Growing Old" focuses on older *characters* in the narratives of the New Testament and their relationship to God (2003, 6). This narrative approach analyzes biblical texts in terms of the beliefs and ethical values the story communicates. In his study, Harris observes that the Bible has various ways to indicate an elderly character, from phrases such as "full of days" to specifying an advanced chronological age (1987, 12-13). And while, as noted at the beginning of this chapter, some of the ages attributed to biblical figures are historically doubtful when compared with evidence of life expectancy in the ancient world, the texts are important for what they have to say about characters designated as elderly. For what is clear is that biblical narratives recognize a distinct life stage at the end of life and thus, through these stories, communicate a vision of old age and the elderly.

The first story to examine is that of Abraham and Sarah in the book of Genesis. Within the Hebrew Bible, the story is a crucial text in the Genesis narrative because it recounts the particular covenant with Abraham and Sarah and the formation of the Israelite people. For our purposes, this is all the more important because the Bible presents the divine call to Abraham and Sarah as occurring when they are old. In Genesis 17, God appears to Abram (hereafter to be called Abraham) to announce his covenant with him. The text states, "When Abram was ninety-nine years old, the LORD appeared to Abram, and said to him, 'I am God Almighty; walk before me, and be blameless. And I will make my covenant between me and you, and will make you exceedingly numerous'" (Genesis 17:1-2). As a part of this covenant, Abram receives a new name, Abraham, and his wife Sarai is now to be called Sarah (Genesis 17:5, 15). The covenant announced to Abraham includes the promises that he will be "the ancestor of a multitude of nations" and possess the land of Canaan (Genesis 17:4, 8). Furthermore, as a sign of this covenant, God introduces a new practice, in which Abraham and all of his male descendants are to be circumcised in the flesh of the foreskin (Genesis 17:9-14). Emphasizing the relationality between God and the elderly couple, Walter Brueggemann's observation is an important one: "In this narrative, there is a striking correspondence between God's call and the response of Abraham and Sarah" (1982, 106).

The surprising part of the announcement in Genesis 17 occurs when God promises, "I will bless [Sarah], and moreover I will give you a son by her" (Genesis 17:16). Within the narrative the announcement is remarkable for two reasons. First, the Genesis text has described Sarah as barren and unable to bear children (Genesis 11.30; 16:1-2). Second, the text depicts Sarah as ninety years old and, thus, portraying her as past the age of childbearing (Genesis 17:17). The surprising nature of God's call and promises in Genesis 17 is revealed in Abraham's response to God, "Then Abraham fell on his face and laughed, and said to himself, 'Can a child be born to a man who is a hundred years old? Can Sarah, who is ninety years old, bear a child?'" (Genesis 17:17). The reaction of Abraham is paralleled by Sarah's reaction in Genesis 18 when the announcement is given to them again by the three strangers who visit Abraham's tent. The text states:

> Then one [of the strangers] said, "I will return to you in due season, and your wife Sarah shall have a son." And Sarah was listening at the tent entrance behind him. Now Abraham and Sarah were old, advanced in age; it had ceased to be with Sarah after the manner of women. So Sarah laughed to herself, saying, "After I have grown old, and my husband is old, shall I have pleasure?" (Genesis 18:10-12)

Despite their initial unbelief, Genesis records that God's promise was fulfilled: "The LORD dealt with Sarah as he had said, and the LORD did for Sarah as he had promised. Sarah conceived and bore Abraham a son in his old age, at the time of which God had spoken to him" (Genesis 21:1-2). And, as God had asked, Abraham named this son

Isaac and had him circumcised according to the new practice instituted in God's covenant with him (Genesis 21:3-4).

What is important for our discussion is that the text portrays
God's saving action in the Abrahamic covenant and the forming
of the people of Israel as carried out through the call Abraham and
Sarah receive in their old age.[7] As Brueggemann notes, the overall
narrative of Abraham and Sarah is the story of "a call embraced" as
God's promise and covenant are established through their going out
from their native land (Genesis 12:1-5) and through the birth of their
son Isaac (Genesis 21:1-7) (1982, 159). In fact, Abraham's response
to God's call in late life receives special recognition by Paul in his
letter to the Romans: "He did not weaken in faith when he considered his own body, which was already as good as dead (for he was
about a hundred years old), or when he considered the barrenness
of Sarah's womb" (Romans 4:19). As Martin-Achard writes, "It is
remarkable that the history of God with his people is inaugurated by
an elderly couple, with no children, who from a human perspective
have no hope of continuing their line through children and grand-
children. . . . Abraham and Sarah are going towards death, but their
itinerary is met with a promise of life . . ." (1991, 38). Though elderly,
the narrative presents Abraham and Sarah as having ongoing purpose within their community.

Another pivotal narrative of the Hebrew Scriptures—the Exodus
from Egypt—provides us with older characters called by God to serve
his saving work in the world. According to the narrative, the entire
story of Moses' prophetic call and activity is the story of an older man.
In his commentary on elderly figures of the Bible, the late Pope John
Paul II observed, "Moses too was an old man when God entrusted
him with the mission of leading the Chosen People out of Egypt. It
was not in his youth but in his old age that, at the Lord's command,
he did mighty deeds on the behalf of Israel" (John Paul II 1999a).

---

7. It is beyond the scope of this chapter to address the implications of
this story for the character of Hagar, the slave girl with whom Abraham has
a son prior to Isaac's birth. For extensive analysis of the stories of Sarah and
Hagar from Jewish, Christian, and Muslim feminist perspectives, see Trible
and Russell 2006.

In the narrative of the book of Exodus, God comes to Moses as he is working for his father-in-law, shepherding his flocks in the land of Midian (Exodus 2:15–3:1). Moses is called by God to announce the liberation of the Israelites from their slavery in Egypt. Exodus records God speaking to Moses: "So come, I will send you to Pharaoh to bring my people, the Israelites, out of Egypt" (Exodus 3:10). Through the designation of a chronological age, the text then explains that Moses and Aaron, who is Moses' spokesman before Pharaoh, were old men when called by God to respond to their prophetic task: "Moses was eighty years old and Aaron eighty-three when they spoke to Pharaoh" (Exodus 7:7).

Following the liberation from Egypt (Exodus 12–14), the narrative records that Moses was called by God to serve as a leader of the Israelites in their formation as a community and in their journey to the land prepared for them by God. In the Deuteronomic text, which continues the story of Moses and the Israelites, we are told that Moses' call to lead the Israelites has lasted forty years, to the age of 120 (Deuteronomy 31:2).[8] During the time of his leadership the biblical narrative introduces another elderly figure who serves as an advisor to Moses in his administration of justice. The elder Jethro, Moses' father-in-law, comes to meet him in the wilderness to encourage him and also offers important counsel to Moses as to how to organize the Israelite administration after the escape from Egypt (Exodus 18:1-27). Jethro serves God's formation of the people Israel through his counsel to Moses: "What you are doing is not good. . . . For the task is too heavy for you; you cannot do it alone. Now listen to me. I will give you counsel, and God be with you!" (Exodus 18:17-19a).

The psalms of the Hebrew Bible further affirm the biblical vision that the elderly continue to live in meaningful responsiveness to God's call. For instance, as evidenced from the text of Psalm 71, the voice of the psalmist is presented as that of an elderly believer. The older person in this psalm continues to respond to God's work in the world through worship and the proclamation of God's deeds to

---

8. Harris argues that passages that glorify certain heroes such as Moses and Caleb by attributing unrealistic chronological ages should be seen within the context of clan memorialization of certain leaders (1987, 43-44).

younger generations: "O God, from my youth you have taught me, and I still proclaim your wondrous deeds. So even to old age and gray hairs, O God, do not forsake me, until I proclaim your might to all the generations to come" (Psalm 71:17-18). Furthermore, Psalm 92 affirms that the elderly are still called to live out their faith in response to God and through their testimony in the community of faith. The psalmist declares, "In old age [the righteous] still produce fruit; they are always green and full of sap, showing that the Lord is upright" (Psalm 92:14-15a). The voices expressed in the psalms indicate that old age is not to be welcomed merely because of what one *has* achieved up to that point, but because of the fruit *one may yet bear* during the added years of life. As Hays and Hays conclude, "older biblical characters signal the possibility of unanticipated fruitfulness in old age" (2003, 10).

The New Testament also provides parallel narratives of persons called by God in old age, particularly in the Gospel of Luke, and references from the Pastoral Epistles. The first Lukan story to consider is that of the elderly couple, Elizabeth and Zechariah, which is a part of Luke's larger infancy narrative concerning Jesus (Luke 1). Luke introduces us to Zechariah as a priest of the Jewish temple and his wife, Elizabeth, who is also the descendant of a priestly family (Luke 1:5). The couple is described as "righteous before God" and "living blamelessly" (Luke 1:6). The text also explicitly indicates their old age in verse 7: "But they had no children, because Elizabeth was barren, and both were getting on in years." Hays and Hays observe, "The parallel to the Abraham–Sarah story is especially strong because of the advanced age of the pair to whom the promise is made" (2003, 6). In his old age, Zechariah continues to serve God through his priestly role in the sanctuary, and it is while serving around the altar that Zechariah receives his new call from God. The angel announces to Zechariah that Elizabeth will conceive and give birth to a son, who will be named John and will be a great prophet (Luke 1:13-17). Zechariah then expresses astonishment that God is inviting them to participate in this event at this stage in their life: "How will I know that this is so? For I am an old man, and my wife Elizabeth is getting on in years" (Luke 1:18).

Despite this initial reaction of unbelief, Luke's narrative presents both Zechariah and Elizabeth as faithful servants of the Lord even in their old age. Hays and Hays observe, "Despite Zechariah's initial doubts, both he and Elizabeth become prophets who discern the new thing that God is doing" (2003, 6). First, Elizabeth declares God's saving activity in the world and her role within it: "This is what the Lord has done for me when he looked favorably on me and took away the disgrace I have endured among my people" (Luke 1:25). Furthermore, following the angel's visit to Mary to announce the conception of Jesus, Elizabeth welcomes her younger cousin and cares for her for three months (Luke 1:56). In fact, it is Elizabeth who is the first to recognize and proclaim the significance of Mary's 'yes' to the angel's announcement: "And Elizabeth was filled with the Holy Spirit and exclaimed with a loud cry, 'Blessed are you among women, and blessed is the fruit of your womb'" (Luke 1:41b-42).

Although Zechariah had lost the ability to speak after his encounter with the angel, the text states that he, too, became filled with the Holy Spirit at John's birth and proclaims prophetic words concerning God's steadfastness to Israel (Luke 1:64-79). According to Luke's Gospel, the two elderly people are depicted as vital servants of God's initiation of a new work of salvation. Hays and Hays comment on the significance of these two elderly characters in the Christian story of salvation: "Thus, in Luke's carefully structured narrative, the older figures Elizabeth and Zechariah become both the instruments of God's purpose and—alongside Mary—the first interpreters of God's saving acts" (2003, 6).

Our second story from Luke's Gospel occurs at the end of the infancy narrative about Jesus and concerns Simeon and Anna. The setting of the story is the temple, where Mary and Joseph have brought Jesus to fulfill a ritual prescribed by the Jewish law concerning firstborn sons. The text describes Simeon as "righteous and devout" and informs us that "the Holy Spirit rested on him" (Luke 2:25). Furthermore, Luke's Gospel explains that Simeon had been piously anticipating and watching for "the consolation of Israel" (the completion of God's redemptive work in the Messiah) and that God's Spirit had assured him that he would see the coming of the Messiah before his death (Luke 2:25-26). Thus, upon Mary and Joseph's arrival at the temple with the infant Jesus, the text states that Simeon was led into the temple by the Holy Spirit (Luke 2:27). When the elderly Simeon meets the family, the Spirit leads him to prophetically announce God's work of salvation and foretell the suffering that will be endured by Jesus and by Mary (Luke 2:28-35).

In this story, the Gospel also introduces the elderly prophet Anna. The text portrays Anna as a pious woman who as a widow had devoted herself to God: "She never left the temple but worshiped there with fasting and prayer night and day" (Luke 2:37). Luke's Gospel also depicts Anna as "of a great age" by claiming she had reached the age of eighty-four (Luke 2:36-37). Like Simeon, in response to meeting Jesus and his parents in the temple, Anna offers praise to God and announces God's work of redemption of the people of Israel (Luke 2:38). Despite being an elderly widow without a husband or family, Anna is shown to have great purpose in responding to and announcing God's redemptive work in the birth of Jesus. Concerning the story of the elderly Simeon and Anna, Hays and Hays state, "These two aged figures also suggest that radical openness to the redeeming power of God may be found among elders—perhaps particularly there" (2003, 7).

Another important story from the New Testament is the story of Nicodemus in John's Gospel. A leader within the Jewish religious establishment, the text presents Nicodemus as an old man. According to the narrative, he seeks out Jesus because he believes Jesus has come from God (John 3:2). When Jesus invites Nicodemus to be born again and welcome the kingdom of God, Nicodemus responds, "How can anyone be born after having grown old?" (John 3:4). Commenting on this text, Harris writes, "Jesus responds by teaching that even one who has aged can begin again by 'being born of water and the spirit.' Age in this Gospel presents no barrier to eternal life or membership in the kingdom" (1987, 91). In their study of New Testament characters, Hays and Hays also suggest that Nicodemus illustrates the message that God's Spirit continues to call persons to new life and new purpose "even in late life" (2003, 7).

As seen in the stories we have examined, the New Testament suggests the transitions of old age from previous social and religious roles do not entail the notion of moving into a period in which one no longer had any purpose or responsibility. Harris comments, "Instead, elderly members remain key to the success of the Christian movement. Old age brings some transitions but decreasing responsibility is not one of them" (1987, 89). This observation is also supported by New Testament examples from the Pastoral Epistles in which older members of the Christian community are addressed as persons who continue to have a call to serve God.

While scattered references in the Pastoral Epistles to older men and women in the community of faith are set within injunctions to respect and possibly provide support for elders, there is also an insistence on the responsibility of older members of the community to continue to respond to God with holy living. For instance, in 1 Timothy, the epistle addresses obligations within the community of faith. As we saw in the previous section, it insists that the community care for widows over sixty who do not have adequate resources (1 Timothy 5:9). However, the epistle also counsels that older widows should continue in prayer, hospitality, service to the sick, and remain committed to "doing good in every way" (1 Timothy 5:10). In relation to such texts, Sapp writes, "Older women thus had important work to do in preparing subsequent generations for their proper place in the Christian family and the church" (1987, 107-108). These older women are thus presented as persons who continue to be called by God to service within the community of faith.

The epistle of Titus echoes this image of older persons within the church. For instance, older men are called to continue living their discipleship through a life that is "temperate, serious, prudent, and sound in faith, in love, and in endurance" (Titus 2:2). Likewise, older women are expected to continue to serve the community of faith through pious living and reverence (Titus 2:3-5). As we saw in the perspective of the Hebrew Bible above, wisdom and holiness are not granted automatically with old age but are seen as fruits of ongoing spiritual dedication. Thus, while these epistles establish the obligation of younger members of the community to care for elderly parents and other members of the church, the letters also address older persons as subjects who continue to have their own call and tasks.

Given the theological vision of older persons as continuing to be called by God, it is not surprising that the biblical witness also consistently presents old age as a sign of divine blessing and a positive affirmation of added years of life. In his examination of the Bible and aging, Harris writes that "advanced years" were viewed as "a sign of divine favor" (1987, 12). John Paul II argued similarly in his 2005 Lenten message: "According to the biblical understanding, reaching old age is a sign of the Most High's gracious benevolence. Longevity appears, therefore, as a special divine gift" (2005). Several passages in Scripture point to God as the source of blessing and old age as a sign of God's beneficence. Deuteronomy 30:20 promises that "loving the Lord . . . means life to you and length of days." And Psalm 91 declares, "Those who love me, I will deliver. . . . With long life I will satisfy them, and show them my salvation." Furthermore, in the Hebrew Bible there exists the concept that righteous living brings with it the promise— the blessing—of old age: "Honor your father and mother, so that your days may be long . . ." (Exodus 20:12).

While the Wisdom literature of the Hebrew Bible also contains vivid descriptions of the difficulties of old age, scholars point out that the texts also approach long life as a gift of God. For instance, Proverbs 10 promises that "The fear of the LORD prolongs life, but the years of the wicked will be short" (10:17). Even physical changes such as the graying of hair are interpreted as a sign of God's blessing to a faithful servant; for example, Proverbs states, "Gray hair is a crown of glory; it is gained in a righteous life" (16:31). As Knierim suggests, in the Hebrew Bible, "if age is granted, it is appreciated as a blessing, as a gift of life reaching its fullness despite the frailties of mortal life's last phase" (1981, 22).

In addition to being a sign of personal blessing, elderly persons in the Hebrew Bible are a social sign of eschatological fulfillment. Given that long life was not the norm in the ancient world, untimely death was perceived to be the greatest enemy (Knierim 1981, 24). Thus, living to old age also becomes associated with the hoped-for eschatological fulfillment of God's reign of justice and peace. For instance, in the book of Isaiah, the prophet speaks of a future time in which "No more shall there be in it an infant that lives but a few days, or an old person who does not live out a lifetime; for one who dies at a hundred years will be considered a youth, and one who falls short of a hundred will be considered accursed" (Isaiah 65:20). And in the prophetic book of Joel, the old are included in God's act of restoration when Yahweh declares, "I will repay you for the years the swarming locust has eaten.... Then afterwards I will pour out my spirit on all flesh... your old men shall dream dreams" (Joel 2:25, 28). From the perspective of the biblical witness, society should therefore welcome the presence of long life and elderly persons as a sign of social well-being.

Given the vision of old age as containing ongoing purpose and as a sign of divine blessing, it is equally significant that the biblical narratives do not romanticize the elderly or ignore the difficulties and physical challenges that many older people face. First, although the Hebrew Bible contains attributions of wisdom to the elderly, texts are also clear that they struggle with vice and temptation and that ongoing holiness and conversion are as necessary in old age as in any age. For instance, Harris points out that the Bible offers numerous "warnings against foolishness and reminds all that aging provides no substitute for wise living" (1987, 66). Wisdom of Solomon 4:8-9 states, "For honorable old age comes not so much by means of length of time, nor is it measured in number of years; But understanding is gray hairs unto people, and an untarnished life is ripe old age."

Deuteronomy 30:20 also describes "length of days" as connected to "Loving the LORD your God, obeying him, and holding fast to him." Knierim concludes, "This is what the biblical tradition means when it speaks of the wisdom of old people. It is the wisdom grounded in the fear, i.e., the reverence, of the Lord" (1981, 34). The temptation to foolishness in old age is recognized, for instance, in Ecclesiastes' declaration: "Better is a poor but wise youth than an old and foolish king, who will no longer take advice" (4:13). The New Testament also contains warnings against vice in old age. For example, Harris points to admonitions that parents, particularly fathers, avoid abusing their children or making "irresponsible, irrational demands" (1987, 86). Passages such as Colossians 3:21 and Ephesians 6:4, which contain such admonitions, imply that elderly persons can be tempted to exploit their children's responsibilities for care and respect and thus create unnecessary tension in the family. Furthermore, the Pastoral Epistles insist that older people who succumb to vice are not fit for leadership responsibilities in the community. For instance, Titus

2:2-3 warns older men against intemperance and imprudence and older women against irreverence, slander, and excessive drinking. As Sapp points out, these texts imply the Bible's realistic perspective that not all older people lived up to the "high expectations and ideals" of a wise old age (1987, 108).

Such warnings to seek wisdom and virtue in old age are consistent with biblical stories of older people who act foolishly and neglect the Lord. For instance, this is evident in the stories we have already examined. Although Abraham and Sarah eventually respond to God's call with faithfulness and trust, their initial response is one of disbelief and scorn toward God's promise of a son (Genesis 17:17; 18:12). And in the New Testament, Zechariah loses his voice temporarily because he shows doubt about God's calling, while Nicodemus initially responds with disbelief to Jesus' teaching that a person can experience rebirth in old age. In addition, Genesis 9 and 19 record stories of the foolish behavior of heroes such as Noah and Lot when they become drunk. The Bible also records that Solomon lost his father's kingdom by drifting away from the wisdom of God (1 Kings 11). Furthermore, the revered prophet Elisha appears to act with intemperance and excessive anger when he curses a group of young boys who tease him for his baldness, which results in their being mauled by bears (2 Kings 2).

Two particular temptations in old age highlighted by Harris are "intransigent conservatism" and a tendency to glorify earlier times (1987, 44-45). For instance, Harris points to the story of an older prophet who causes the death of a younger prophet because he refused to accept the younger man's prophethood (1 Kings 13:1-32). And in Ezra's account of the return from exile and the rebuilding of the temple, some older people within the community disturb the community's celebration by crying loudly over their nostalgia for the first temple, which they consider grander than the one being rebuilt (Ezra 3:10-13). Similarly, the voice of the teacher in Ecclesiastes bemoans the losses of old age as compared to one's youth: "Remember the days of your creator in the days of your youth, before the days of trouble come, and the years draw near when you will say, 'I have no pleasure in them'" (12:1).

In fact, far from presenting a "golden age" image of ancient society or merely a glorified picture of aging biblical heroes, the Hebrew

Bible offers insights into the realities of aging in ancient Israel. For instance, Martin-Achard mentions several stories to illustrate that the "realism" of the Hebrew Bible "does not ignore the infirmities associated with old age" (1991, 32). An example is the patriarch Isaac, who goes blind and struggles with concerns about his encroaching death (Genesis 27:1-4). Likewise, the priest Eli is said to have lost his sight in old age (1 Samuel 4:15). Martin-Achard also cites the "weariness of Moses" reflected in his departing speech to the Israelites: "When Moses had finished speaking all these words to all Israel, he said to them: 'I am now one hundred twenty years old. I am no longer able to get about . . .'" (Deuteronomy 31:1-2).[9] The Psalms also record the voice of an elderly believer struggling with declining health: "Do not cast me off in the time of old age; do not forsake me when my strength is spent" (Psalm 71:9).

In addition, the Scriptures bring to light the disappointment and depression that can afflict the later stages of life as a person reflects on his or her life. For instance, prior to God's intervention, Genesis describes Abraham and Sarah as suffering depression and grief, having passed the normal ages of fertility without being blessed with a son (Genesis 15–18). The disappointment of the dreams and plans of one's life is also preserved in the stories of Eli and Samuel, who experience bitter disappointment upon watching their sons' dishonesty and resulting unfitness to continue their leadership (1 Samuel 2:12-17, 22-25; 8:1-5). Harris observes that even the hero David experiences grief and regret over his actions as a father when his sons rise against him to gain his throne (2 Samuel 11–1 Kings 2:11) (1987, 43).

Furthermore, the Bible records how the weakness of the elderly can render them vulnerable to manipulation. For instance, in his old age and blindness, Isaac is easily manipulated and tricked by Rebekah and Jacob regarding the inheritance of the family (Genesis 27). Similarly,

---

9. Moses' own words regarding his weariness are somewhat contradicted by another text in Deuteronomy "eulogizing" the great prophet: "Moses was one hundred twenty years old when he died; his sight was unimpaired and his vigor had not abated" (Deuteronomy 34:7). This particular passage no doubt reflects another aspect of the Hebrew Bible's view of old age as a sign of divine blessing in acknowledgment of a righteous life (Harris 1987, 37).

Knierim notes that even the great king David, advanced in years and largely confined to his chambers, is drawn into the struggle for the throne by Nathan and Bathsheba, who manipulate David so that Solomon is declared king before his other son can gain the support of the people (1 Kings 1) (1981, 32). And, as we saw in the previous section, the general prophetic condemnation of neglect of the vulnerable includes a concern for the weakness of the elderly. For instance, in Micah's account of an unjust and inhumane society, the prophet mentions neglect of vulnerable parents: "for the son treats the father with contempt, the daughter rises up against her mother, the daughter-in-law against her mother-in-law; your enemies are members of your own household" (7:6).

In the discussion of widows in the New Testament, the Bible also identifies the reality of economic vulnerability faced by many older persons. For instance, there is the well-known story of Naomi, who is left without the support of a husband and sons (Ruth 1:11-12). The New Testament also identifies the economic vulnerability of certain widows who should be included in the list of those supported by the church (1 Timothy 5:9-10). While not all widows mentioned in the Bible are elderly, those who are face an increased vulnerability because they are left to depend on the protection of their adult children or the society (Harris 1987, 15).

Thus, it is fair to conclude that the Bible's witness concerning old age does not ignore the real life experiences of hardship and difficulty faced by older people. Knierim observes, "These [difficult] conditions [of old age] are not enjoyable at all. They are distressing, and the biblical authors express this distress despite their basic claim that aging and old age belong to life" (1981, 27). And yet, within this realism, biblical narratives suggest dignity is not lost in the weakness and difficulties that may accompany old age. For instance, Genesis tells of the old Jacob, who blind and dying in his bed, still summons Joseph to bring his two grandsons before him (Genesis 48). Even though Joseph presents his two sons in the traditional order, with the oldest to Jacob's right and the youngest to Jacob's left, Jacob crosses his arms and lays hands on his two grandsons, thus blessing the youngest with his right hand. When Joseph tries to correct his father (surely assuming his old age and blindness have confused him), Jacob insists on his choice. As Harris states, "[Jacob] is perfectly aware of what he is doing and resists being pampered or forced to change his actions despite his illness and impending death" (1987, 47).

Likewise, in the narrative of David, the elderly prophet Barzillai is called to exercise his prophetic role despite his weakness and limitations (2 Samuel 17:27-29; 19:31-40). In this story, the prophet, said to be eighty years old, provides crucial supplies and counsel to David when he is fleeing Absalom during a period of disputed succession. To reward Barzillai, David offers to bring him to Jerusalem to serve in his court. Again revealing the Bible's realism about old age, Barzallai declines David's offer, acknowledging that age-related illnesses preclude him from such rigors. Harris argues that Barzallai's story, like Jacob's, illustrates that while age-related difficulties may entail real limitations, older persons still possess ongoing purpose before God and in the community (1987, 48).

Our discussion of New Testament figures such as Zechariah, Anna, and Simeon also illustrated that despite advanced age older people still have a place within the community. In the case of Simeon, the author of Luke explicitly notes Simeon's awareness of his encroaching death (Luke 2:29). However, as we have seen, even at the end of life, Simeon is called upon to announce God's saving work in Jesus. Such stories lead Harris to argue: "Aging in the Christian community did not necessarily bring loss of status or responsibility. In some way responsibilities increased as physical stamina decreased" (1987, 95). In fact, the biblical witness suggests that even dying can be an opportunity to exercise purpose and responsibility. Knierim writes, "When people, particularly fathers, were about to die, they assembled their children, gave them final instructions, blessed them, and praised God" (1981, 31). In this sense, death was not something to be denied or feared, but rather lived as a final opportunity to serve God, one's family, and the community. In this way, Simeon is able to depart "in peace," having welcomed Jesus as God's anointed one. Likewise, Genesis depicts Jacob as going peacefully to his death, having instructed his sons for the future: "When Jacob ended his charge to his sons, he drew up his feet into the bed, breathed his last, and was gathered to his people" (Genesis 49:33). These stories are significant because they suggest that faithfulness and service in old age do not require super-human, heroic physical strength or virtue.

Conclusion

In shaping a Christian ethic able to respond to the ethical challenges of long-term elder care, this chapter has demonstrated the importance of the biblical texts as a source of normative ethical insight. We began by acknowledging that the use of the Bible as a normative source must include recognition of the complexity and diversity of the biblical material. For while the Bible does address old age in several texts of the Hebrew Bible and New Testament, one must avoid approaching the Bible looking for a unified, systematic "theology of aging." In addition, the Bible should not be read naively as reflective of the "good old days" in which respect and care for elderly family members were guaranteed. As noted, the prophetic condemnation of neglect of elderly persons reveals that ancient societies, like those of today, were sometimes guilty of injustice toward vulnerable members, which included the aged. With these helpful cautions in mind, this chapter has demonstrated that the biblical witness still yields two relevant norms for shaping a Christian approach to long-term care today: an insistence that care for the elderly is a vital ethical measure of a just society and the theological affirmation of the dignity of older persons as subjects called by God to ongoing purpose.

Analysis of the ethical imperative for care showed that the Hebrew Bible calls for just care of elderly persons, based on a concern for social stability, as an expression of respect and fear of God and as fulfillment of divine justice for the poor and weak. Care and respect for elderly persons included the dimension of material and physical care; and while the family was the primary sphere for such care, there also existed a general moral obligation toward aging members of society. As evidenced by the teachings of Jesus and the charitable practices of the early Christian community, the ethical imperative evident in the Hebrew Bible is also affirmed in the writings of the early church. For although Jesus was critical of traditional norms concerning biological family when these interfered with devotion to God, the New

Testament does not present an absolute denial of family responsibility, including respect and care for older persons. The biblical emphasis on elder care as a normative social responsibility intersects with the basic argument found in the Community of Sant'Egidio's practical work and publications and that of the Green House Project. Both organizations, through a long history of involvement with the elderly, have sought to embody and promote long-term care of the elderly as of fundamental moral importance in contemporary society.

The second consistent theme we examined was the biblical vision of older persons as subjects who continue to be addressed by God as members of the community of faith. In this section, the narratives concerning older characters in the Hebrew Bible and New Testament were particularly important for shaping a theological vision of the identity of the elderly in relation to God and the community. Articulating the implications of this theological vision for the contemporary church, Hays and Hays argue, "In late life, Christians remain subject to the possibility that God will act decisively in history and in their lives in such a way as to turn their lives upside down. They may be called to a new ministry. They may receive new revelation. They may see the fulfillment of a long-awaited hope" (2003, 17).

Furthermore, in affirming that older persons continue to be called by God, the Bible does not deny the possible onset of disability, weakness, and death, but does insist that these difficulties do not exclude the elderly from God's service or from the community. Knierim observes, "The diminishing vitality of individuals did not result in their removal from the society into isolated retirement homes, for example. And it did not result in being removed from societal functions that were proportionate to the potential of an old person" (1981, 28). In the biblical perspective, the dignity of the elderly is based not on being morally or physically perfect but in being persons who continue to be addressed by God and called to service within the community. Thus, there is not only an imperative to care for the elderly but to care in such a way that promotes and protects this dignity.

A contemporary Christian ethic informed by the biblical witness concerning old age must demand an approach to long-term care that reflects the insight that the elderly are not merely the *objects* of the community's care but are participating *subjects* within the community. Again we see an intersection between the biblical witness and the practical work of the Community of Sant'Egidio and the Green House Project. Both organizations, in their own ways, seek to foster and enable the capacities of older people even in the midst of age-related frailty as an explicit commitment of their approach to elder care. Furthermore, both Sant'Egidio and Green House insist that taking the elderly seriously means avoiding a false romanticization of old age. Instead, whether through invitations to serving others or mediating interpersonal conflict in Green House homes, these organizations actively support older people in approaching their old age as time for personal growth. We turn now to the Christian theological concept of discipleship and the vision of the church as a community of mutual love and support as a further resource for a contemporary ethic of long-term care.

CHAPTER FIVE

Discipleship, the Church, and the Elderly

We continue in this chapter the task of identifying resources within the Christian tradition that can help shape an ethical response to the challenge of long-term care. In the previous chapter, we saw that not only does the Bible uphold care for the elderly as a measure of a just society but that the biblical vision of persons called by God to purpose and service, even in the midst of age-related disability and illness, affirms the dignity of the elderly. In Christian theology, discipleship is the concept that captures the biblical vision of persons as subjects called to serve God's purposes in the world. This chapter thus presents another building block for a Christian ethic of long-term care: a theological vision of the church as a community of disciples in which persons live in mutual love and support in order to enable the living out of discipleship. Before turning to recent writings that have begun to explore this vision in relation to aging today, we will examine the general understanding of discipleship and the Christian community as formed by norms of equality and mutual love.

Karl Barth and Discipleship

We begin this chapter with an exploration of Karl Barth's discussion of the vocation of the Christian and the Christian community from *Church Dogmatics*. Barth's discussion asks what it is that Christians share that binds them into one community. For Barth, this is a critical question in light of the enormous diversity within the church. He notes that in the church we find persons characterized by many different types of roles and abilities. He writes, "Those summoned to participate [in the Christian community] . . . are human persons, men and women, old and young, healthy and sick, relatively independent and relatively dependent from a social standpoint, more educated and less, of different outlooks, stronger and weaker even in faith, loyalty, zeal and patience" (1961a, 499). Barth's analysis thus highlights that Christians always exist in relation to one another within a complex web of different conditions and characteristics and, in this sense, the Christian community does not exist in a vacuum sealed off from the multiple roles and identities that distinguish persons in life. Furthermore, Barth recognizes that there are also similarities in roles and characteristics that may create connections between Christians. He states, "There may and will be other relations between [Christians], whether erotic, domestic, friendly, intellectual, economic, social or political. For different reasons they may and will in varying degrees interest, need, suit or like one another" (1961a, 499).

Thus, Barth does not dismiss human connections formed around accidental qualities and preferences as inherently problematic; in fact, Barth acknowledges that such relations have their own strengths. However, given the enormous diversity of such accidental qualities within the church and their temporary nature, none of them can provide sufficient theological answer to explain the basis of a genuine fellowship among Christians. Barth argues, "But for all their strength these [accidental] relations are not absolutely necessary, nor can they be maintained unconditionally. It is not these relations which cement the Christian community together" (1961a, 499). Barth's search for the true bond of Christian fellowship underlying these accidental qualities leads to his discussion of Christian vocation or calling.

To articulate the fundamental basis of the human relation between Christians, Barth turns to their shared relation to the divine. Barth uses spatial language to elucidate this theological reality: "What decisively and consistently binds the people united in [the Christian community] is their common vocation, i.e., the horizontal relation created among them by the fact that in their own place and manner they are all in the same vertical relation" (1961a, 499). The vertical relationship, for Barth, is explained in terms of vocation, the invitation to discipleship in which persons are called by God to the service of the Kingdom of God.

Thus, the fundamental bond that can be seen to draw Christians together is the shared acknowledgment that, in Barth's words, one's life is claimed for "continuation of the divine work . . . in fellowship with the man Jesus Christ, in His discipleship, and therefore in fellowship with God in the service of His kingdom and fatherly providence" (1961a, 482). Thus, from a Christian perspective, Barth's argument is that diverse persons find fellowship with one another in the community of the church based on their fundamental, lasting identity as people called to be disciples of the Kingdom of God. As Barth explains, the mutual recognition entailed in the bond of Christian fellowship is "that a Christian sees in another Christian a [person] who like himself is called to faith, obedience, and service" (1961a, 500).

Barth's discussion of Christian identity as a shared call to God's service is further helpful when it addresses the impediments that often exist to this mutual recognition. Using the familial metaphors of the New Testament, Barth describes the way in which limitations and weakness challenge one's ability to view the other as a fellow disciple called by God:

> For often, and in the strict sense always, it is so difficult to recognize in the other a man who has the same calling and who is therefore a brother. . . . His limitation, frailty and burden are easily seen. But are they really the limitation, frailty and burden of one whom it is worth while to help by granting and securing his freedom and loving him as a brother? *Does he look like someone of whom something important is to be expected*, so that it is essential to help him? [emphasis mine] (1961a, 501)

Barth's acknowledgment is relevant to any discussion of the church's vision of older people, many of whom begin to experience the frailty and limitation he identifies.

However, for Barth, one's identity as a disciple is founded not upon any particular outward activity or stage of life but rather by the reality that wherever God grants life, God calls that life to his service even in forms that may appear "useless" to others. For example, Barth writes,

"A man who is not, or is no longer, capable of work, of earning, of enjoyment and even perhaps of communication, is not for this reason unfit to live. . . . The value of this kind of life is God's secret. . . . Who can really see the true and inward reality of this type of life?" (1961a, 423-24). Barth also argues that service to God may entail such things as simply speaking to a brother or sister or preaching and also the interior work of self-examination and reflection (1961a, 549). Similarly, in another section where Barth discusses human labor as response to God's calling, he argues that there is value both to "the outward work of the young and healthy and the inward work of the sick and aged" (1961a, 549). Thus, although often ignored by modern notions of productivity, Barth insists that "the inward work of reflection" engaged in by the sick and physically disabled is as much a form of response to God's calling as outward forms of "activity." For Barth, then, the church's fellowship witnesses to the full glory of human life: that in every moment of a person's life, including illness and frailty, he or she is called by God to service. This theological identity is lasting and continuous because it is based on one's fundamental, vertical relationship to God and not on changing social roles or physical characteristics.

Barth's discussion of discipleship is also highly relevant to long-term care of the elderly today because it is set within his larger discussion of the value of human life and the ethical demand for its respect and protection. Following sections entitled "Respect for Life" and "Protection for Life," Barth discusses human vocation as the reason *why* life is to be respected and protected.[1] Barth explains this order-

---

1. In Section 55 of Volume III/4, from which the material for this chapter is taken, Barth addresses how the church is to respond to the basic reality that as creator, God has given us the gift of the loan of our lives, or, as he writes, "man's freedom to exist as a living being" (1961a, 324). In the first two subsections, "Respect for Life" and "Protection of Life," Barth argues that the proper response to this gift is first a basic attitude of respect toward the fact that we and others exist and, second, to act in such a way as to preserve this creaturely existence (for instance, in the prohibition against murder). In the third subsection, "The Active Life," Barth argues that our moral responsibility toward the gift of life includes our recognition and living out of the purpose for which our lives are given.

ing: "What is done out of respect for human life and with a view to its protection takes place under the necessity of the question *as to the purpose of this life.* . . . We are commanded to honour and protect life because the active life . . . has need of space and time and opportunity" (1961a, 471). Barth uses the term "active life" to refer to the life to which humans are summoned in which as free and deliberate subjects they are invited to respond to God's action in the world with their own corresponding, creaturely actions. For Barth, God's invitation to us to live includes not only the gift of our existence but also the dignity of existing with real purpose.

As Barth states, in the invitation of God to live, our experience of life is enhanced because we are called from "the isolation and self-sufficiency of a life for life's sake" (1961a, 477). In regards to moral responsibility toward life, Barth insists that theological ethics neglects the full dignity to which persons are called when it is content merely with declarations of respecting and protecting life. He argues that the command of God to live "does not allow one to understand and treat his existence as an end in itself. It does not consist only in the demand that life should be respected and protected" (1961a, 473). As evidenced by his extensive treatment of the first two subsections of respecting and protecting life, it is clear that Barth in no way seeks to undermine the moral importance of valuing and preserving physical existence. Instead, Barth wants to emphasize that God's gift of life to humans "is neither the mere duration of his existence nor a mere vegetative nor animal course of events" (1961a, 470). The gift of life signifies an underlying theological truth that humans are called to purpose and meaning as subjects addressed and called by God to serve his work in the world.

Barth's exploration of the identity of persons within the fellowship of the church provides a helpful parallel to our previous discussion of the biblical witness in which the demand for care of aged members of society is coupled with an affirmation that older people continued to be called by God to his service. Like the biblical vision, Barth's approach insists that respecting the lives of older persons entails not only their physical care and protection but also recognition of their ongoing dignity in the community by virtue of God's call to them. This vision thus demands that the church today not only see increased longevity as a sign of God's blessing of longer life per se, but also recognize that wherever God grants the gift of existence God also grants the dignity of calling that life to his service.

The Church as a Community of Mutuality, Equality, and Friendship

Working from the theological understanding that all Christians have a shared identity as persons called by God to his service, persons at every stage of life thus share a fundamental equality that creates the possibility of mutuality in their relationships. Again, drawing on Barth's theological reflections, the recognition of a shared call to discipleship and service creates a union between Christians that entails a *mutual* moral obligation to one another. Barth argues that the moral responsibility of Christian fellowship is determined by the fundamental calling that binds them together. He writes:

> A Christian sees in another Christian a man who like himself is called to faith, obedience and service, and who is therefore his brother, and that he thus recognizes that he is united with and under an obligation to him as a brother. Under obligation to do what? The only answer worth considering is as follows—to grant to and secure for this other as much of the freedom physically and spiritually necessary for his life in service as a creature, as one man can grant and secure for another, and he specifically to and for this other. (1961a, 500)

In other words, the church exists as a community in which persons practice mutual love, which shows itself in support and care for one another to empower one another for a life of service as disciples. In his discussion of the Christian community, Barth insists on the obligation Christians have to one another in relation to their shared call to discipleship: "But each [Christian] has the task of loosing others [for service], even if these others be only Christians who happen to be in his vicinity" (1961a, 500). For Barth, every Christian is under this moral obligation to fellow Christians, to "help as he can" and "to the very best of his ability."

For Barth, this mutual helping entails spiritual, psychological, and emotional support. But, particularly relevant to the topic of aging, Barth's discussion of the mutual aid of Christian fellowship includes the vital recognition that the freedom to live out one's call as a disciple is connected to the physical reality of human existence. In his discussion of Christian fellowship, Barth makes what appears to be an obvious observation, but one that has significant implications for the mutual moral obligation of care: "The fact that the brother is also a [human being] cannot be overlooked. It has to be acknowledged. But it is precisely as a [human being] that he needs the freedom to be able to be a Christian, and it is to this end that I am summoned *to help him in his humanity*" [emphasis mine] (1961a, 501). Barth's sympathetic stress on the humanity of the fellow Christian leads him to insist that the freedom necessary for a life of discipleship is not merely an internal spiritual condition, but rather includes all aspects of life as a creature: "But for the life of service there is also need of a measure of creaturely freedom, of psycho-physical freedom, of space to breathe and move, of joy, of opportunity for expression and development" (1961a, 500).

To be able to help another in his or her humanity is, for Barth, to become adept at seeing realistically the dynamics that prevent him or her from responding to God's call: "But [the Christian] also perceives the limitation, frailty and burden of [his fellow Christian's] creatureliness. He realizes how restricted he is in his freedom and therefore how threatened in his service" (1961a, 500). Barth's discussion is significant because it argues that attending to the physical and material needs of another is about more than merely protecting physical survival; for Christians, it is a necessary part of freeing one another as creatures to respond to God's call to discipleship.

A recent ethicist who has incorporated Barth's theology into his own exploration of the church as a community of mutual love aimed at enabling one another to live out his or her Christian vocation is Paul Wadell. Wadell's work seeks to deepen understanding of the nature of Christian relationships in the church by drawing on the long tradition of Western thought on friendship. Wadell's research analyzes both the foundational thought of Aristotle and then demonstrates the way in which various Christian thinkers such as Augustine, Thomas Aquinas, and Aelred of Rievaulx adapted Aristotelian insights to explain Christian fellowship.[2] We will examine Wadell's writings here because, using the metaphor of friendship, his work parallels and further expands Barth's insights into Christian identity and fellowship.

One of the consistent themes in Western Christian and non-Christian writings on friendship is that friends are bound together by a shared "good" and that different types of friendship exist based on this good. Wadell argues, "A seventh characteristic of friendship is that friendships are formed around shared goods that help define the purpose and nature of the friendship, as well as the type of friendship" (2002, 61). Paralleling Barth's discussion above, despite the vast diversity within the church, Wadell describes Christians as tied together by a fundamental bond or "shared good," which is the relationship each one shares with God. In fact, Wadell explicitly acknowledges what he sees as the overlap between his discussion of the church and Barth's: "Though Barth never refers to the Christian community as a community of friendship, the relationship he describes between those who confess Jesus is Lord is, in the terms of our discussion, a friendship. Friendships arise between those drawn together in agreement on what they consider their life to be, and their friendship is the activity of pursuing this together" (1989, 116).

Further reflecting on friendship in Christian thought, Wadell explains, "What distinguishes Christian friendships from other friendships is that they are means of growing together in the love of God—that is their purpose and rationale. All friendships are centered in the good that joins the friends together and explains the friendship's life" (1989, 99-100). In his historical survey of Western thought, Wadell shows that previous Christian thinkers have also applied the concept of friendship to the church based upon this insight. For instance, Wadell summarizes Augustine's argument concerning the shared bond of Christian friendship that overcomes differences: "Through the love of friendship, divisions and distances melt away as

---

2. For Wadell's analysis of Aristotle, see Wadell 1989, 27-69; for Augustine, see Wadell 2002, 77-96; for Aquinas, see Wadell 1989, 120-41; for Aelred, see Wadell 2002, 97-118.

the friends, through all that is shared between them, achieve a true and lasting communion of persons" (2002, 87). And he demonstrates the way the medieval monk Aelred understood the bond between Christians through the lens of friendship: "Every friendship is formed around shared goods that identify the friendship and help the friends understand the life and purpose of the friendship. In spiritual friendship the principal good is a mutual love for Christ and a desire to grow together in Christ" (2002, 107).

A second insight from the concept of friendship that Wadell finds helpful for thinking about the church is that the primary activity of friendship is assisting one another in pursuit of the shared good. In other words, friendship is constituted by the shared effort toward fundamental goals agreed upon by persons as good. Thus, applied to the church, the activity of Christian friendship is understood as response to and pursuit of one another's fundamental shared calling before God. Wadell elaborates:

> One of the great gifts of a good friendship is that each friend helps the other grow in freedom by helping them be more fully and authentically who they are called to be . . . not only to call us to our best self but to help us be our best self. . . . Through them we are encouraged to be who God calls us to be. Their friendship gives us the security we need to courageously embrace the vocation entrusted to us regardless of what it might ask of us. (2002, 58)

As we saw in Barth's discussion, the mutual recognition of one's fellow Christian as called by God to service creates a community of care in which persons are obligated to assist one another in responding to this divine vocation. Likewise, Wadell argues that the shared good of Christian friendship means the church is a fellowship of mutual love and care. He explains that "friendships should be freeing relationships" (2002, 58). And highlighting the dynamic of mutuality, Wadell writes, "Friendships are relationships in which each person is committed to the other and each does good things for the other" (2002, 61).

Also similar to Barth, Wadell addresses the reality that in their humanity Christian persons face concrete difficulties and challenges in living out their call to discipleship. The mutual love of Christian friendship is thus practiced by offering concrete aid and care to help one another live out a life of discipleship. Wadell provides a description of the church understood through the mutual care of friendship:

> If the church is truly a community of friends committed to a shared life in Christ, then one of the obligations of discipleship is encouraging one another in living that life and helping each other with the tests and challenges of that life. . . . One sign of the vitality of the church is when in each congregation we find a community skilled in helping one another in what each knows to be the most important commitment of their lives. (2002, 72)

As we also saw in Barth's discussion of Christian fellowship, in Christian friendship persons are able to see beyond exterior limitations and weaknesses to recognize and enable God's calling to their lives.

Wadell's application of the concept of friendship to the fellowship of the church has provided us further elaboration on Barth's claim that the fellowship of Christians rooted in a shared identity before God creates a community shaped by equality and mutual love. Wadell writes, "All of us must be able to learn lessons in caring somewhere, and friendship is a fitting context for doing so. Think of all we can be called to do for our friends, things that call us out of ourselves and challenge us to act on behalf of another" (2002, 68). And, as we saw in Barth, this care is aimed not merely at the preservation of physical existence but also at the enabling of one's vocation as called by God to service. In reference to the concept of discipleship, Wadell writes, "This is why we can say spiritual friendship is a discipleship life, a way in which people who are committed to growing in Christ help one another imitate Christ and grow in gospel virtues" (2002, 108). And, as we saw above, the shared good of discipleship is acknowledged in one's friend even in situations of difficulty and human weakness.

Wadell's use of the language of friendship for the fellowship of the church also serves to complement the approach of the Community of Sant'Egidio, analyzed in Chapter 3. As with Sant'Egidio, theological use of the metaphor of friendship is particularly helpful in relation to care of the elderly because it helps to expand the sense of moral responsibility beyond the family. In fact, while familial metaphors have been significant in Christian thought, friendship also has its own established place within the Christian theological tradition.[3] Patristics scholar Carolinne White notes that parables such as those recorded in Luke 11:5-8 and 15:3-10 reflect the way in which friendship was a part "of the daily life of the society depicted in the New Testament" (1992, 48). The New Testament also records Jesus employing the use of "friend" to describe his relationship with his disciples. For instance, in the Gospel of John, his disciple Lazarus is referred to with this language: "After saying this, [Jesus] told them, 'Our friend Lazarus has fallen asleep, but I am going there to awaken him'" (John 11:11). And Jesus' intense love for this friend is revealed in the text when it is recorded that Jesus wept when he reached Lazarus's tomb (John 11:35-36).

Jesus' dialogue with his disciples in John 15 is another important text in our consideration of friendship in the New Testament. Here Jesus uses the term friendship to describe his love for them and also the love between his disciples: "This is my commandment, that you love one another as I have loved you. No one has greater love than this, to lay down one's life for one's friends. You are my friends if you do what I command you. I do not call you servants any longer, because the servant does not know what the master is doing; but I have called you friends, because I have made known to you everything that I have heard from my Father" (John 15:12-15). On this text, New Testament scholar Luke Timothy Johnson comments, "Here the dominant feature of *philia* is the shared outlook: the disciples do what Jesus commands, but not as servants, because they know what Jesus is about" (2004, 168). Johnson also notes that there is some evidence in the New Testament that early Christians actually used the term "friends" to refer to one another in passages such as Titus 3:15; Acts 27:3; John 15:14; and 3 John 15 (159, 168).

Furthermore, there exist connections between the ancient concept of friendship and New Testament texts even when the language used is not explicit. For instance, Johnson argues that phrases such as "being one spirit" (*hen pneuma*) and "having the same mind" (*hē hautē gnōmē*) reflect connections to the ancient concept of friendship that authors and

---

3. For instance, see Carmichael 2004; Fritz-Cates 1997; McNamara 1964; Wadell 1989; White 1992.

readers of the New Testament letters would automatically draw (L. T. Johnson 2004, 161). Furthermore, a brief survey of key New Testament writings presents an image of the early church as a community in which, because of their shared relation to Christ, members were obligated to support one another spiritually and materially. In the book of Acts we find two significant descriptions of the early community of Jesus' disciples. First, Acts 2:44-45 states, "All who believed were together and had all things in common; they would sell their possessions and goods and distribute the proceeds to all, as any had need." Likewise, Acts 4:32, 34-35 records, "Now the whole group of those who believed were of one heart and soul, and no one claimed private ownership of any possessions, but everything they owned was held in common. . . . There was not a needy person among them, for as many as owned lands or houses sold them and brought the proceeds of what was sold. They laid it at the apostles' feet, and it was distributed to each as any had need." In relation to such passages, Johnson argues, "By saying that the believers were 'one soul,' held 'all things in common,' and called nothing 'their own,' Luke described them as friends" (161).[4]

In letters attributed to Paul, one also finds the concept of friendship in Christ expressed through a reciprocal sharing of material possessions. Paul writes, "You Philippians yourselves know that in the beginning of the gospel, when I left Macedonia, no church entered into partnership with me in giving and receiving except you only" (Philippians 4:15). Furthermore, Johnson highlights that Paul's idea of reciprocity taught that the spiritual goods shared with a community entail a reciprocal obligation to share material goods (2004, 165). For instance, in his letter to the Romans, Paul writes, "At present, however, I am going to Jerusalem in a ministry to the saints; for Macedonia and Achaia have been pleased to share their resources with the

---

4. Johnson recognizes that questions exist as to whether these texts are an idealized description of the early community using the literary theme of classical friendship; however, he points to other texts that substantiate a practice of material sharing in the early communities that confirm the practices presented in Acts. For a discussion of the early Christian community's practices of hospitality and material giving, see Meeks 1993, 104-108.

poor among the saints at Jerusalem. They were pleased to do this, and indeed they owe it to them; for if the Gentiles have come to share in their spiritual blessings, they ought also to be of service to them in material things" (Romans 15:25-29). Thus, Johnson points out that the reciprocity of *koinōnia* in the Christian community is more than an "exchange of affection," but involves concrete "material assistance." This reciprocity of material sharing can be seen, according to Johnson, as "fulfillment" of the Greco-Roman axiom that "friends hold all things in common" (164).

Such material sharing flowed from the concept of the church as a community of persons sharing fellowship based upon the mutual call to be disciples of Christ. As Barth's discussion above reflects, early Christian writings taught an obligation in which Christians were to assist one another as fulfillment of Christ's commandment to love one another. For instance, Galatians 6:2 implores, "Bear one another's burdens, and in this way you will fulfill the law of Christ." And in his letter to the Romans, Paul describes the responsibility Christians have to one another in direct reference to Christ's commandment to love one's neighbor: "We who are strong ought to put up with the failings of the weak, and not to please ourselves. Each of us must please our neighbor for the good purpose of building up the neighbor" (15:1-2). Johnson also notes that the theme of fellowship as "being of one mind" and as the sharing of all things (here including possessions) appears in his letters to the Corinthian community (2004, 166). In regard to such texts, White argues that in the context of the Christian community "mutual love may legitimately be regarded as at least part of the general commandment to love one's neighbor" (1992, 49).

In his analysis of friendship in the New Testament, Johnson observes that Paul's concept of equality in the church does not erase the reality of difference between persons. But rather, mutuality and reciprocity in giving are the basis of Christian equality. Johnson argues, "The real spirit of friendship, therefore, seeks that functional equality that is found in reciprocity, a proportional balance through an exchange of different kinds of goods, or an exchange of the same goods at different times" (2004, 167). For Paul, such equality is exemplified by Jesus' own example: "For you know the grace of our Lord Jesus Christ, that though he was rich, yet for your sake he became poor, so that by his poverty you might become rich" (2 Corinthians 8:9). It is this moral example that then informs Paul's exhortation concerning fellowship in the Christian community: "I do not mean that others should be eased and you burdened, but that as a matter of equality your abundance at the present time should supply their want, so that their abundance may supply your want, that there may be equality" (2 Corinthians 8:14). As applied to care of the elderly, this vision of friendship and equality allows the community to recognize differences of need while still affirming a shared capacity for reciprocity.

In addition to the writings of the New Testament, many early Church Fathers and medieval thinkers used the mutual love of friendship as a way to describe Christian fellowship. For instance, in her exhaustive study of fourth-century patristic writers, White argues that these thinkers "recognized that certain characteristics of the ideal pagan friendship, such as spiritual unity and harmony of interest, reciprocity and sharing, could accord with Christian ideals and even be developed further within a Christian context" (1992, 4). White provides analysis of several patristic writers who employ friendship language, including Basil, Augustine of Hippo, John Chrysostom, Gregory of Nyssa, and Paulinus. And in the medieval period, two important thinkers who draw on the language of friendship to explore the mutuality of Christian love are Thomas Aquinas and Aelred of Rievaulx.[5] Thus the themes of equality and mutuality seen in Barth's and Wadell's approaches to Christian fellowship are well supported by the traditions of Christian thought about friendship found in the New Testament and early Christian thinkers.

The Elderly as Disciples for Life:
Catholic and Protestant Sources

The final section of this chapter will consider the implications of the theological resources examined thus far, in particular the concept of the elderly as disciples called to ongoing participation within the

---

5. For analysis of the thought of Aquinas, see Fritz-Cates 1997, 91-130; and Wadell 1989, 120-41. For discussion of Aelred, see Wadell 1989, 104-10; Hauerwas and Yordy 2003, 174-81.

equality and mutuality of the church's fellowship. First, the theology of discipleship establishes the agency of older people as persons called to ongoing purpose and service. In an essay on revising the church's view of the elderly, Freda Gardner explores the fundamental understanding of persons within the community of faith: "When we are called into relationship with God, we receive a vocation, a purpose, and a way to be. That vocation has been described in various ways, but central to any definition is discipleship" (1994, 184).

Similarly, two documents from the Catholic tradition, written in response to the United Nations' declaration of 1999 as the "International Year of the Older Person," drew on the theme of discipleship and service in connection with old age. In their message "The Dignity of Older People and Their Mission in the Church and in the World," the Pontifical Council wrote that "Christ's call to holiness is addressed to all his disciples, in every phase of human life." Furthermore, the council argued that this entails a revising of the church's understanding of the elderly person's identity: "Far from being the passive recipients of the Church's pastoral care, older people are irreplaceable apostles." And in their own pastoral letter "Blessings of Age," the United States Conference of Catholic Bishops stated that their purpose was "to form a fresh perspective, one that sees older persons as active participants in contributing to the Church's life and mission."

An explicit affirmation of the agency of older people rooted in their ongoing vocation as disciples is crucial for countering attitudes within the church that, because of age or frailty, undermine the full dignity of the elderly. As Gardner explains, "What I am suggesting here is that the church, like the culture, thinks of the elderly as a different species of human being, maybe an obsolete human being" (1994, 184). In his final Lenten message in 2005, John Paul II also insisted that the church needed to give "more specific attention to the world of so-called 'old' age, in order to help its members to live their full potential" (2005). Discipleship thus helps the church to resist wider cultural views of old age as lacking meaningful purpose. For instance, Stephen D. Long writes, "Baptism, like ordination, brings with it lifelong tasks. The goal of the Christian life is not leisure, forced or voluntary, at the end of life, but faithful service" (2003, 149).

The second implication of the theology of discipleship is a fundamental equality of persons expressed through mutuality. This equality then demands an approach to older people as subjects and not merely as objects of the aid of others. For there is a subtle way in which calls for care of the elderly reduce them to a category of need different from everyone else. But within a vision of shared discipleship and the church as a community of mutual support, there are not two classes of persons: those who are dependent and needy and those who are independent and giving. Rather there is an equality in the mutual give and take of Christian fellowship made possible by the shared call to discipleship. As ethicists Hauerwas and Yordy describe, "This christological basis of friendship calls friends to be Christlike to one another in particular ways: to give and receive service from one another, to offer correction when appropriate, to be patient, and so forth" (2003, 178).

Third, viewing older people as disciples who continue to participate in the mutual responsibility of Christian fellowship means that the church has the responsibility to be the kind of community that fosters and enables true forms of contribution and participation by the elderly. One dimension through which the potentials of older people are encouraged is spiritual care. In their document, the Pontifical Council rightly emphasized this moral responsibility: "[The current situation] urges the Church to revise her approach to the pastoral care of older people in the third and fourth ages. New forms and methods, more consonant with the needs and spiritual aspirations of older people, need to be sought . . . helping [the elderly] to derive particular spiritual enrichment from their active participation in the life of the ecclesial community" (1998). Such reform of the spiritual care of older people will take place only with the full recognition of the last stage of life as being as developmentally significant as any other. For instance, Anglican theologian Rowan Williams has argued, "It is not an exaggeration to say that . . . growing old will make the greatest creative demands of your life" (2012, 245).

Spiritual care shaped by a vision of lifelong discipleship and participation within the community must recognize old age as a stage of life that calls for further growth and spiritual and moral development. As the U.S. Catholic bishops argue, "Although many cultures revere older people for their wisdom, wisdom does not come automatically with age. The experiences of a lifetime have sown the seeds, but they must be cultivated by prayer and reflection on those experiences in the light of the Gospel" (1999). Thus, a part of the agency of the elderly affirmed by their identity as disciples is that old age involves ongoing growth, change, and maturing.

Similarly, Rowan Williams warned, "We must not be sentimental. Age doesn't automatically confer wisdom, and the authority of 'elders' of one sort or another can be oppressive, unrealistic, and selfish" (2012, 246). Thus, affirming a vision of older persons as called to ongoing growth is actually a form of honoring their dignity, which counters the infantilization of older people. For a benign form of infantilization of older people occurs when others fail to see them as capable of cultivating moral character because physical or cognitive disability is connected with the absence of moral agency. Hauerwas and Yordy summarize this attitude: "That the elderly are freed from such [moral] obligations in our society correlates with the view that human development ends in early adulthood, or at least in middle age. Many dominant images in American culture portray old people as set in their ways, that is, as not capable of learning anything significant, much less growing in virtue" (2003, 173). As seen in the previous analysis of Christian friendship, mutual encouragement includes a shared commitment to growing in virtue.

Enabling forms of participation from older people must also include transforming the challenges and difficulties of old age into an occasion for contribution and service to others. In this way the church becomes a place where the struggles and difficulties of old age are neither ignored nor used as cause for marginalization, but rather the elderly are supported to creatively respond to these demands as ways to contribute to the moral and spiritual growth of others. As Pinches describes, "the elderly person can be placed in our midst, not merely as a demonstration of our diversity but also as a sign of truths we are at other ages tempted to ignore" (2003, 205). Or as the U.S. Catholic bishops suggest to older people, "All of us need each other, more at some time than at others. . . . Your dependency can be an occasion of grace both for yourself and for others" (1999). Hauerwas and Yordy echo this fundamental insight: "For a few years as young adults we may pretend (egged on by social and cultural forces) that we can live forever as autonomous, self-reliant, self-fulfilling beings. The pretense, however, collapses soon enough. So the presence of the visibly vulnerable elderly is a reminder that we are not our own creators. Consequently, Christians must ask the elderly to be among us so we will not take our lives for granted" (2003, 181).

However, this potential is released only insofar as the church understands itself as a community of mutual support and encouragement. As religious studies scholar Eugene Bianchi notes, "For some people, therefore, the challenges of aging can become opportunities for spiritual and ethical growth, while for others the same experiences foster selfish regression and attitudes of social hostility" (1991, 60). Or, as the Pontifical Council highlights, the transformation of difficulties and limitations "will only be possible in proportion as [elderly] feel loved and esteemed" (1998). Within the mutuality of Christian friendship, the elderly remain subjects of their lives, including the difficult aspects, because they are understood as opportunities to respond to God's call to discipleship. Rather than the challenges and limitations of the elderly being seen merely as problems to be relieved by others, they present possibilities for helping younger generations to grow in their own path of discipleship.

Perhaps one of the most challenging areas in which such contribution can occur is in approaching mortality and death. As the U.S. Catholic bishops describe, "Every other phase of life—childhood, adolescence, and young and middle adulthood—has been lived in expectation of a next phase. The next phase after old age, however long and rich old age might be, is eternal life" (1999). While it is not unusual for the church to offer spiritual care in the context of dying, such care can easily be offered merely in terms of providing comfort. And yet the vision of older people as lifelong disciples urges the church to approach dying as a potential gift to the whole community. For instance, Hauerwas and Yordy suggest, "Perhaps the hardest thing the church must ask of the elderly is to teach us how to die. Such teaching requires a vulnerability none find easy, particularly in a society based on autonomy. Yet none of us knows how to die 'by nature'; we must be taught how to die through friendship" (2003, 183).

In his own writings, the late John Paul II echoed this idea by his suggestion that there was a way in which older Christians could model living well in the face of death when lived within the vision of being called by God. He wrote, "Faith thus illuminates the mystery of death and brings serenity to old age, now no longer considered and lived passively as the expectation of a calamity but rather as a promise-filled approach to the goal of full maturity" (1999a). We saw a similar approach to death in the stories from the Hebrew Bible in which figures such as Moses and Isaac approached their dying as an occasion to perform final actions to serve the community. Furthermore, John Paul II suggests that there is a way in which older persons can approach death with a hopefulness that comes from a holy longing for God. Writing as an old man himself, the pope stated, "At the same time, I find great peace in thinking of the time when the Lord will call me: from life to life! And so I often find myself saying, with no trace of melancholy . . . at the hour of my death, call me and bid me come to you" (1999a). We saw the model of such holy longing in the person of Simeon, who never ceased in prayer and in his service at the temple. Without abandoning the value of his earthly life, Simeon prays these words after holding the infant Jesus at his presentation in the temple, "Lord, now let your servant depart in peace, according to your word; for my eyes have seen your salvation" (Luke 2:29-30).

John Paul II also argued that the honest acknowledgment of the nearness of death can allow an elderly person to uniquely witness to those things that are most important to human life: "Knowledge of the nearness of the final goal leads the elderly person to focus on that which is essential, giving importance to those things that the passing of years do not destroy" (2005). This witness can help younger persons to see that a proper sense of one's mortality means preparing for that eternal passage now, by living well and by ordering one's life around those things that have eternal significance. The possibility of living toward one's death as a morally and spiritually significant moment is prophetic within our current culture that schizophrenically either fears death or advocates for the "right to die" as a way to avoid all suffering and weakness.

In contrast to these cultural attitudes, theologian Joel Shuman writes, "For if we understand that dying well is a morally significant act insofar as it bears evangelical witness to our most profound theological convictions, we also will come to see that there is no more important lesson that the old can teach the young than the lesson of how to receive the gift of such a death" (2003, 164). Within the mutual fellowship of the church where older persons are viewed as called by God to the end, even death can be transformed into an opportunity to contribute to the good of others.

Enabling discipleship and ongoing participation within the church also requires meeting the physical-care needs of older people. As seen in the previous sections, in addition to spiritual care and growth, the church as a community of mutual love includes material sharing and support. While gains in human longevity have been accompanied by gains in overall health, Chapter 2 showed that we now also reach ages in which many more people experience periods of age-related disability and disease. Unless the church understands the mutual care of Christian fellowship to include these physical and material realities, older people will face marginalization when experiencing limitations.

In fact, citing a study of twenty black churches in Philadelphia that reported fairly positive intergenerational congregations, David McCarthy notes the study also revealed that when people start to experience physical limitations churches did not do well in continuing to involve older people (2003, 231). Insofar as the practice of freeing a fellow Christian for service is seen to include attending to physical and material limitations, providing such care is not just a matter of responding to need but of enabling still-existing capabilities. As Hauerwas and Yordy note, "This requires, of course, that old people not merely be 'Sunday acquaintances' but that they be entangled and succored in close friendships" (2003, 180). In addition, such material helping is crucial if a vigorous call to older people to live out discipleship is not to become another experience of marginalization for the frail elderly or those with modest economic means.

One note on material assistance in the church is in order here. Hauerwas and Yordy are right to warn against a mentality in which the church simply thinks of itself as "another social service agency simply to provide the benefits of 'support structures' as do other associations" (2003, 175). This is, of course, a danger when the social service sector or the government see church communities as a less costly way to replace the rightful responsibility of the larger society for organizing and providing certain basic services or when social policy inadvertently undermines care provided by family members. However, from the perspective of Christian friendship, it is equally important for the church not to limit the responsibility for physical care to professional health workers, social workers, or biological family. I would argue this point first from the perspective of theological ethics noted earlier: being made friends in the Christian community expands notions of moral responsibility too often limited to natural social and family ties. For as Hauerwas and Yordy also rightly observe, "By being [a new family through baptism], we also discover the possibility of friendship we had not otherwise imagined. So old people are not stranded in their families; instead, they are members of Christ's body along with all the children and other adults of all backgrounds, talents, sexualities, races, and classes" (180).

Furthermore, as we saw in Chapter 3, the Jewish and Christian understanding of God as concerned for the vulnerable creates an ethical obligation to secure just care for vulnerable members of the community and society, including the elderly. Stephen D. Long, in his essay on the church's responsibility to older people, argues, "The church should never rest content with a care for the elderly situated in the biological family, the market, or the state" (2003, 148). He bases this argument on the idea that "the community of faith has as part of its task the charitable redistribution of its resources to care for those who no longer have them" (ibid.). Thus, it is not alien to the life of the church to be involved in the direct provision of material care.

Finally, understanding the church as a community in which the participation and contribution of older people are welcomed and enabled should not be understood in terms of American cultural notions of "productivity." On this point Barth's warning that too often our world values only "active" forms of service is relevant, as is the experience of Sant'Egidio in calling society and the church to broaden its concept of participation. Likewise, in his 1988 exhortation, "Christifideles laici," John Paul II balanced his call to lifelong service with the recognition that the form of this service will change over the course of life: "[The elderly] must always have a clear knowledge that one's role in the Church and society does not stop at a certain age at all, but at such times knows only new ways of application" (1988). Thus, the call to discipleship in old age does not represent a call to try to be "forever young" but rather a call to remain open to serving God's work in the world within the concrete realities of this stage of life. Commenting on the value of nonactive forms of service, John Paul II wrote, "The Spirit acts as and where he wills, and quite frequently he employs human means which seem of little account in the eyes of the world. How many people find understanding and comfort from elderly people who may be lonely or ill and yet are able to instill courage by their loving advice, their silent prayers, or their witness of suffering borne with patient endurance" (1999a).

Similarly, in trying to counter a common attitude toward older people in the church, the U.S. Catholic bishops wrote, "Even those who obviously need pastoral care—the homebound, the disabled, the seriously ill—are also able to give pastoral care, for example, by praying for their families, caregivers, and others, by sharing their own faith lives, or even through the simple yet powerful ministry of presence" (1999). The church then has a responsibility to affirm and nurture such forms of service and participation that do not fit culturally dominant definitions of productivity or usefulness.

Conclusion

This chapter has sought to draw on the theological vision of elderly persons as disciples within a community dedicated to empowering members to respond to the call of discipleship. This analysis has highlighted the norms of equality and mutual love within the theological resources of the Christian tradition. The norm of equality arises from a shared dignity as disciples who, in Barth's words, are characterized by the same vertical relationship to God. And yet this equality does not ignore differences rooted in the person's concrete humanity, including differences in levels of physical, emotional, and material need. Instead, the mutual love of Christian friendship obligates members of the church to empower one another for discipleship precisely by attending to the *particularities* of each person. Furthermore, viewing the elderly as subjects broadens our understanding of responsibility to them as serving their agency, not just ameliorating their need, with this agency understood theologically, not merely in terms of societal notions of productivity. Often unwittingly, the physical limitation and disability that accompany old age are interpreted as the absence of an ongoing call and moral responsibility in the community of faith.

But as we saw in this chapter, there is a profound moral connection between welcoming the gift of the lives of older persons and our recognition and response to the purpose for which their lives exist. Theological ethics must insist on this more comprehensive vision of moral responsibility if life in old age is truly to be lived and not merely endured. In the final chapter, I turn to a discussion of the way the ethical insights presented in Chapters 3, 4, and 5 can be applied practically to the church's own internal ministry with older people and its engagement with the wider society.

CHAPTER SIX

Responding to a Dramatic Feature: Witness, Dialogue, and Cooperation

In a study of the challenges to elder caregiving facing the United States, the President's Council stated, "We will need greater ethical reflection on what the young owe the old, what the old owe the young, and what we all owe one another" (2005, 3). This chapter will outline potential contributions of the church to this public reflection in terms of both action and dialogue. For at the outset of this book I suggested the joys and hopes, the grief and anguish of contemporary aging are not merely the private concern of individual elderly persons or of families but a common human question for our time. The structure of the chapter is based on the ethical vision presented in the previous chapters, which drew on the concrete experiences of two models of elder care and the particular resources of the Christian tradition. The first section focuses on the norm of elder care as a measure of a just society. The second section focuses on norms for the way we care—mutuality, equality, dignity, and participation. In each section I will provide practical application of these norms in terms of both the church's internal life and ministry and its external engagement with the larger society.

Of course, the questions and challenges presented by contemporary aging are varied and numerous, but our focus is on the church's role and responsibility for long-term care and the related public policies and programs to which it ought to engage critically and cooperatively. Even within this focus, it is impossible to touch on every aspect of public policy and programs related to long-term care of the elderly. What I seek to provide is a beginning by highlighting a few key areas to which the ethical vision presented here points and outline what it would look like for the church to respond. Furthermore, while the primary context for this book is the United States, the relevance of these practical applications is not limited to one country. For one, the model of Sant'Egidio is international, and the experience of its elderly outreach program spans multiple continents. Two, as noted at the outset, the demographic realities outlined in Chapter 2 are increasingly a global reality and are projected to be permanent trends. Thus, the challenges arising from contemporary aging will have to be dealt with by most, if not all, societies. In fact, in recognition of its international reach, the United Nations has identified aging as one of the main "global issues" today ("Global Issues—Ageing"). Therefore the ethical vision and practical measures proposed here can serve as contributions not only to a national conversation but also to a global one as to the responsibility we all have for securing just and dignified long-term care for the elderly.

The Responsibility to Care: Elder Care as a Social Responsibility

The work of the Community of Sant'Egidio and the Green House Project reflects the position that long-term care for the elderly is a fundamental measure of a just society and a social responsibility. Chapter 4 established that the biblical witness considers care of the elderly as fundamental to healthy intergenerational relations within a society and as fulfillment of God's special concern for the poor and weak. Chapter 5 drew on a theology of discipleship and the church to argue that the love of Christian fellowship includes material assistance to others, what Barth called helping another in his or her "humanity." In addition, both the biblical witness and the theological vision of Christian fellowship support the argument that care for the elderly is the common duty of all, inclusive of but not restricted to family duty. Following from this vision, the church should prioritize care of the elderly as an indispensable *social* ethical imperative in its own internal life and in its dialogue with the wider society. Three practical ways to do this involve educational awareness initiatives, providing care both directly and indirectly, and advocacy on the allocation of public resources.

Educational Awareness Initiatives

First, in relation to education awareness, the church should contribute to informed understanding of the challenging realities of the aging process. While it is true that gains in health have accompanied gains in longevity, it remains the case that chronic illness, frailty, and disability still affect a significant number of people in late old age, and impact their ability to care for themselves and live independently. As the President's Council on Bioethics (2005) argued, it is this paradox of being both "younger longer and older longer" that presents the specific challenge for us today. Thus, to adequately respond to the ethical imperative to care, the church must cultivate an accurate understanding of the illnesses and disabilities of late old age and provide education about these realities. For example, as explored in Chapter 4, a study of the way aging biblical characters faced the various physical and emotional difficulties of aging could provide the framework for a parish-level adult education series that also included gerontological and medical resources about old age today. In addition, the training seminars and educational sessions sponsored by the Community of Sant'Egidio provide a model for congregational education and public awareness programs. Likewise, a diocese of the Episcopal Church in Texas began sponsoring annual conferences on aging in 2004. These conferences were aimed primarily at older persons from the church and other institutions and provided educational seminars presented by geriatricians and aging experts from across the country. Such educational initiatives can provide vital resources for persons within the church and the wider community and serve to make long-term care a more widespread, shared concern ("Congregational Best Practices").

Direct and Indirect Provision of Care

Second, in its own response to existing care needs, the church should seek ways to both provide direct services and to facilitate connections with public resources. Here the model of the Community of

Sant'Egidio is vital in illustrating ways in which religious communities can organize care for older people and overcome limitations that may marginalize them from the community. Recognition that the mutual support of Christian fellowship entails physical and material helping is particularly important in thinking about providing needed care and enabling older persons to respond to God's ongoing call in their lives. Based on Sant'Egidio's experience, support could include a church creating a consistent, organized system of transportation so that older persons can get to doctor's appointments and the grocery store or come and help with a weekly soup kitchen; getting stamps and bringing them to an older person who writes to church members in the hospital or to someone in prison; creating stable, reliable relationships in which an older person can be helped in getting dressed or remembering to wear a protective undergarment so he or she can still participate in community events; or making sure an elderly friend's medicine dispenser is filled accurately so that she can manage her high blood pressure and dementia. As the Pontifical Council for the Laity (1998) urged, "Steps should also be taken to ensure that [older people's] involvement in [church] events be not hindered by physical or architectural barriers, or by the lack of specialized personnel to accompany and assist them." Such mundane tasks take on great significance when the church recognizes, like Barth, that helping another person in his or her humanity is to help a Christian to realize her dignity as a servant of the kingdom of God.

While the Community of Sant'Egidio is an established lay organization with a particular commitment to outreach programs, its activities could also conceivably be undertaken on a smaller scale by parish groups. One example is the "Life Care Ministry" of St. John's Lutheran Church in Stamford, Connecticut. In the 1980s, this church used a sizable financial gift to establish a ministry program specifically for seniors, including the hiring of a full-time program director. As a part of this ministry, volunteers were recruited and trained to provide help with basic care, such as household chores, transportation needs, and financial planning. Similar to the home assistance we discussed in the Sant'Egidio model, the Life Care Ministry program provided regular weekly visits, including for elderly persons who needed assistance and companionship following hospitalization. The program also organized the youth of the church for service days in which they helped with seasonal chores such as leaf raking. As the program director stated, its ministry initiative was born from recognizing the significant proportion of its membership sixty-five and older. By establishing a paid staff position dedicated to elder care, this church tangibly expressed a commitment to long-term elder care (Thompson 1986, 66-74). As we saw in the discussion of New Testament writings in Chapter 4, such material assistance has long been understood as an expression of Christian love and a duty of the ecclesial community.

Another example of concrete care assistance is the development of adult day programs or centers. As defined by the National Adult Day Services Association, adult day centers provide a "community-based care option for people with disabilities within the larger constellation of long-term care services." In the United States, adult day centers are designed to provide daytime care settings for elderly persons still living in the community, either in their own homes or with families, but who have some form of disability, ranging from mild limitations to Alzheimer's disease. These community-based centers provide care ranging from social activities to meals to specialized therapeutic services and are operated both by nonprofit entities and for-profit companies ("About Adult Day Services"). Such day programs are particularly crucial in providing respite care during the day to relieve family caregivers.

With the urgent long-term-care needs facing us today and in the near future, more churches must consider participating in such care programs, either through providing physical space in collaboration with a senior care agency or for actually operating an adult day program within the outreach ministries of a parish. For instance, Edenton United Methodist Church in Raleigh, North Carolina, has operated the Ruth Sheets Adult Care Center since 1991 as a ministry of its parish. As a part of its program, the center recruits church volunteers to facilitate recreational activities, to foster one-on-one companionship for elderly participants, and to lead religious services. The center also partners with local elementary schools to facilitate intergenerational visits and activities. A nonprofit center such as the Edenton UM Church program operates both on fees paid by participants and on church fundraising ("Ruth Sheets Adult Care Center"). Expanded involvement of local churches in this area of elder care would represent a significant contribution to long-term care, particularly if coupled with a commitment to making such centers affordable for low-income elderly who would have difficulty securing home services privately.

The church can also contribute indirectly to care of the elderly through provision of spiritual and emotional support for caregivers, particularly with the aim of fostering mutually enriching fellowship. As Drew Christiansen notes, not only can family caregivers provide physical care, but they can also help provide the companionship older people need in order to meet the challenges of increasing frailty and illness, what he calls "spiritual friendship." And yet, Christiansen observes that the possibility of such fellowship is often limited by "the temporal, psychic and physical demands of caregiving, by the varieties of roles discharged by the primary caregiver, and by the difficulties both generations experience in role reversal" (1991, 119-21). Furthermore, caregivers are often simply ill-equipped to share and discuss the personal and spiritual challenges elderly people face, such as mortality. In their pastoral letter, the U.S. Catholic bishops rightly emphasize the church's responsibility in this regard: "The parish has a responsibility to provide spiritual and other support for caregivers, for example, by helping to form support groups . . . or periodically recognizing and blessing caregivers" (1999). Given the role of personal caregivers in providing fellowship for frail elderly and assisting in medical and care decisions, the church must actively support caregivers to sustain their commitment in a manner that enhances the dignity of older people.

As illustrated by the Sant'Egidio example, in its engagement with the public sphere the church can also make a significant contribution to long-term care by collaborating with nonprofit and public service agencies and assisting elderly and families in accessing public services. In her analysis of congregational care provided to seniors in black churches, Anne Wimberly describes such efforts as "mediating actions" (2003, 111). Wimberly notes that black churches in the United States have a long history of providing this mediating role, both educating members about and connecting them to available resources. As Sant'Egidio discovered, one of the main reasons elderly persons and their families fail to secure services that would allow the elderly to remain in their homes is lack of information about available services. Thus, mediating actions are a crucial aspect of the church's responsibility in fostering a commitment to long-term care. These actions can include hosting information sessions at a local church about community senior-care services and guiding an elderly person and her family through the process of applying for and managing those services. An example of a church-sponsored program that seeks to counsel family caregivers about available elder services is the Caregiver Coaching Program begun in 2009 at St. Simon the Cyrenian Episcopal Church in New Rochelle, New York, in collaboration with Fordham University. The program recruits volunteers from the congregation to serve as "coaches" and provides training from social workers and other aging experts based on a curriculum developed at Fordham. Coaches are then matched with family caregivers and serve as a resource in care decision making, particularly connecting elderly and family members with resources that enable older people to remain at home ("Congregational Best Practices" 6-7, 42).

In addition to mediation, churches should seek out forms of appropriate collaboration with other nonprofit and public programs. As the U.S. Catholic bishops urged, "One parish cannot meet all these needs of the older person; however, the parish must recognize these needs and be able to direct older persons, their family members, and caregivers to appropriate resources. We encourage parishes to join with local providers of aging services that respond to the needs of older people" (1999). For instance, we saw how the Sant'Egidio Community publishes a resource guide for community-dwelling elderly persons with funding from local government sources. Another example is a church-affiliated community outreach project launched in Texas. This project was launched in an underserved, primarily African American neighborhood in order to increase senior access to health services provided in the local senior center, which was run by the city government. The clinic staff launched an outreach effort to local black churches in order to recruit community volunteers who could do the work of visiting seniors in the area to educate them about available health services. Participating churches promoted the initiative to members and allowed church facilities to be used for training volunteers. In the Texas model, the church did not try to replicate already-existing health services but rather became the needed link in enabling more elderly residents to connect to those resources (Madison and McGadney 2000, 32). Such collaborative efforts illustrate the way in which churches can make significant contributions to long-term care without needing to replace public entities or to provide all services directly.

Just Allocation of Public Resources

A third application of the shared responsibility to secure just and adequate care for the elderly in our society involves public advocacy for adequate allocation of resources for elder care. In their pastoral letter, the U.S. Catholic bishops state, "Moreover, within the larger community the Church should strive to be an advocate with and for older persons" (1999). While acknowledging the differences between ancient and contemporary societies, there is enduring moral relevance to the biblical vision of intergenerational solidarity, with a strong insistence on adequate provision of material resources for the elderly, particularly the most vulnerable among them. Such sharing between the generations is urged as necessary for the health of society. Further, as seen in New Testament texts concerning the early church, Christian fellowship entailed the expectation of a generous sharing of resources, whether spiritual or material. Thus, the church must critique social attitudes and public rhetoric that suggest older people are less deserving of societal resources or that providing social and material security for the elderly is unfair to younger and future generations. As the U.S. Catholic bishops write, "As bishops, we warn against a society and a Church that, however unintentionally, pits young against old. We do not believe that resources are so limited that the gains of one group come only through the losses of another group" (1999).

While programs such as Medicare or Social Security are often thought immune from legislative budget cutting, several scholars have documented a reoccurring temptation to engage in a rhetoric of generational competition. As Williamson and Watts-Roy describe, a major argument often advanced in the "generational equity" debate is that "the elderly are getting more than their fair share of societal resources, particularly federal government resources" (1999, 4).[1] An example of the continuation of this debate is a 2005 article entitled "The Greediest Generation," in which prominent opinion writer Nicholas Kristoff wrote, "But I fear that [the Boomer generation] will be remembered mostly for grabbing resources for ourselves, in such a way that the big losers will be America's children." Kristoff goes on to catalogue gains that have been made in reducing elderly poverty since the enactment of programs such as Social Security and Medicare in the twentieth century and contrasting this with the stubbornly resistant statistics on childhood poverty in America. From the perspective of our ethical vision of care for the elderly, the problem here is not that Kristoff calls for more resource allocation to improve childhood health, education, and material security; the problem is his suggestion that resource allocation for the old is the *direct* cause of a resource deficit for the young. In such instances, Christians are called to repudiate such false choices and work to push our society to act on its financial capacity to care for *all* generations. Or, as Lisa Cahill and I have argued, "Childhood and old age should be provided for in tandem, expressing the commitment and investment of the whole society" (Cahill and Moses 2008, 227).

One concrete area in which the church could advocate for adequate and more effective resource allocation is medical research. For instance, a 2010 *New York Times* article reported that the budget of the National Institutes of Health (NIH), which is the main medical research center of the United States, still does not reflect the reality of aging demographics and the illnesses that threaten late old age. The article reports that growth in spending at the various institutes of the NIH is slowest at the National Institute on Aging, the NIH arm devoted to research related specifically to the elderly. In the article, the director of the NIH argues that spending on areas such as heart disease and diabetes are related to aging and thus indirectly benefit elder health care (Freudenheim 2010). Experts consistently note, however, that persons sixty-five and older continue to be underrep-

---

1. In their article, Williamson and Watts-Roy provide a helpful historical overview of the generational equity debate in the United States, from the creation of Social Security in 1935 up through the 1990s (1999, 7-19).

resented in clinical trials and public health research, which limits understanding of the health of older people, such as the impact of certain medications and surgical interventions (Krisberg 2005, 20). Furthermore, it is also important to distinguish between medical spending that primarily extends lifespan but does not necessarily improve quality of life. As seen in Chapter 2, a primary factor affecting quality of life in old age is chronic illness such as dementia and arthritis. Thus, advocacy on medical research should insist on adequate funding of research aimed specifically at these illnesses. As Lisa Cahill and I have suggested, justice demands that priorities for medical research need to be focused more on alleviating the present threats to elder well-being such as arthritis and dementia than on exotic genetic technologies aimed at further extending longevity (Cahill and Moses 208, 219-22). Now that advances in medical science and public health have created the widespread reality of the Third and Fourth Ages, resources should be committed to enhance dignity and well-being in this life stage.

A second area for the church to focus its advocacy is the availability of professional elder-care providers. For instance, in 2010, the American Geriatrics Society (AGS) reported that it would take around 16,000 geriatricians to adequately care for the *current* population of those sixty-five and older; and yet, as of 2010 there were only 7, 029 certified geriatricians in the United States, which is less than 1 percent of physicians nationally ("Current Geriatrician Shortfall" 2010). This problem applies not only to doctors: the AGS reports that as of 2010 less than 1 percent of RNs, pharmacists, and physician assistants were certified in geriatrics. Not only is there an existing problem with a shortage of trained geriatricians, but continuing low applications to geriatric and adult primary-care medicine programs predict shortages for the future as well. For instance, the AGS noted that in 2008 only 110 graduates of American medical schools entered geriatric residency. In contrast, based on the projected population of those sixty-five and older for 2030, the AGS argued that a conservative estimate indicates the need for training 1,200 geriatricians per year for the next twenty years ("Projected Future Need for Geriatricians").

The shortage of health-care professionals trained in geriatrics is a serious problem, given the impact on quality of life and health in old age. As Gawande argues, "Good medical care can influence which

direction a person's old age will take" (2007b, 55). The ethical responsibility to care must therefore include advocacy for a change in our
priorities: changing policies and resource allocation to increase the
number of geriatric health-care professionals and to educate professionals and communities about the importance of elder health. In this
regard, there already exist some promising proposals and initial steps
toward improvement, and the church should push for such efforts
to be supported and expanded. One line of effort is to encourage
more medical students to pursue geriatrics and also to better train
already practicing primary-care physicians. For instance, the Health
Resources and Services Administration of the U.S. Department of
Health has created programs to channel funding to health professions
schools that provide geriatric training to medical students, faculty,
and practitioners ("Geriatrics Health Care Training Programs").

In addition, under the Obama administration's health-care reform
measures, funding has been directed toward enhancing geriatrics
curricula and developing geriatrics teaching faculty ("Ensuring Older
Americans"). The Institute of Medicine has also argued that licensure
and certification processes for health-care workers should be revised
to include demonstrated competence in older-adult care, which, they
argue, would further encourage curricular and training reform. However, given the dire shortage of geriatric health-care workers, the special committee of the Institute of Medicine has urged the creation of a
"National Geriatric Service Corps" focused specifically on elder care
(Committee on the Future Health Care Workforce, 7-11).

Other efforts at reform are focused on financial barriers to increasing the number of geriatricians. The AGS reports that of six major
specialties, including radiology, dermatology, neurology, internal
medicine, and family medicine, geriatrics ranks last in physician salary ("Loan Debt and Salary Statistics"). This can pose a significant
barrier to entering geriatrics, given the enormous increase in medical
school debt graduates are carrying. As the Institute of Medicine points
out, income disparity for geriatric specialists is directly related to the
traditional medical reimbursement schemes. For instance, typically a
larger portion of a primary-care provider's income derives from Medicare and Medicaid, which have traditionally offered low reimbursement for primary care. Related to this is the fact that primary care of

older adults, many of whom have complex needs, often requires more time during office visits; thus, primary-care physicians serving older adults are not able to schedule a high volume of patient encounters, which results in lower billing (Freudenheim 2010b). Thus, there is a need for a medical reimbursement system that actually rewards the kind of care older adults need, care management that in the long run lowers medical costs such as hospital readmission.

As regards these financial disincentives, the AGS has noted some important first steps begun under the Obama administration. In terms of medical reimbursement disparity, the Patient Protection and Affordable Care Act of 2010 (ACA) offers a 10-percent Medicare bonus payment to geriatricians and primary-care providers for certain primary-care services that fall under "evaluation and management" services ("President Signs Final Health Reform Legislation"). The legislation also provides for scheduled reviews to identify valuable services that are undervalued in terms of reimbursement. Related to older-adult care models, the ACA encourages the creation and evaluation of new models of elder care that better address complex chronic health conditions and more effectively coordinate care provision ("Ensuring Older Americans"). Another significant reform measure increases funding for the scholarship and loan repayment program of the National Health Service Corps, which includes financial assistance for health-care professionals providing care for the elderly (Freudenheim 2010b). Based on the ethical imperative of care, the church should affirm such policy steps and continue to advocate for even further reform in the future.

Another example of reform efforts includes projects aimed at recruiting and training nurses for community outreach programs that focus on elders and the coordination of needed care. For instance, Gawande cites a program of Johns Hopkins School of Public Health that provides a three-week course in geriatric care to local nurses and then places them in primary-care clinics to work with elderly patients. As the organization website describes, "A Guided Care Nurse, based in a primary care office, works with patients and their families to improve their quality of life and make more efficient use of health services. The nurse assesses patient needs, monitors conditions, educates and empowers the patient, and works with community agencies to ensure that the patient's healthcare goals are met" ("Care for the Whole Person"). This approach is reasonably affordable for insurers, and initial studies have shown positive effects in quality of care for elderly patients and in reducing health care costs (Gawande 2007b, 59; "Guided Care").[2] Freudenheim also reports research showing that hospital readmission costs can be reduced 20 percent or more when frail elderly patients "are managed by teams of nurses, social workers, physicians and therapists, together with their own family members" (2010b). The church can provide one voice within society supporting such creative new models of elder care and calling for their expansion.

Finally, a crucial area for advocacy on resource allocation is the recruitment of and improvement in working conditions of lower-level care providers. For there is also a predicted shortage of long-term-care workers such as certified nursing assistants and home health aides. Here the example of the Green House model is instructive in demonstrating the link between dignified elder care and job satisfaction for certified nursing assistants. The Green House homes improve working conditions for CNA-level shahbaz staff by empowering them with greater responsibility and authority, by fostering meaningful care relationships through consistent staffing, and by higher pay achieved through savings from restructuring administrative organization. Higher levels of job satisfaction in Green House homes are evidenced by a lower staff turnover rate, which in turn saves more money. The Green House Project insists that providing just care of the elderly is inseparable from redirecting resources for CNA-level workers. Given the enormous amount of state and federal funding that goes into home-based and institutional care, the church should advocate for new polices that require such care providers to more widely adopt the Green House staffing model and higher wages for CNA staff.[3]

---

2.   For a fuller explanation of this type of "coordinated care" approach to geriatrics, see the AGS's fact sheet, "The Principles of Geriatric Care." The special committee of the Institute of Medicine also provides extensive treatment of new models of older-adult care in their report (Committee on the Future Health Care Workforce, 75-122).

3.   For one study on the possibilities of implementing the Green House care staff model in traditional institutions, see Bowers and Nolet 2014. For

Let me conclude this section by noting the benefit to families of the church's participation in and advocacy for a shared moral commitment to elder care. As discussed in Chapter 2, informal caregiving by family members continues to constitute a significant portion of the personal and household care for elderly in America today. And older people often express a desire for family members to be involved in their care. However, as we also saw, several contemporary realities are creating serious strains on family caregiving, including the sheer length of chronic illness in old age today, geographic mobility, and workforce trends for women. In this context, the President's Council observes: "Guilt and stress afflict even the most devoted, strong, and resourceful families, who today frequently find themselves in a bind, especially when adult women try to care for their enfeebled parents or in-laws while holding down jobs and caring for their own small children" (2005, 45). As highlighted in Chapter 2, in fact, the unequal distribution of care responsibility within families disproportionately impacts women's health, professional advancement, and income.[4]

While this book has focused on the responsibility for elder care of church and society rather than on family per se, there are nonetheless practical implications for helping to address the challenges families face.[5] Following from the example of Sant'Egidio, I suggested the church can provide and advocate for forms of direct care without aiming to *replace* family but rather to complement and collaborate. And as experts such as Moody have observed, access to home-based care services actually enhances and encourages continued family involvement in care rather than supplanting it (1988, 152-54).

---

further discussion of factors influencing recruitment of and job satisfaction of CNAs, see Probst et al. 2010.

4. Both the U.S. Catholic bishops and ethicist Drew Christiansen explore the relevance of justice to family caregiving in terms of creating an equitable sharing of responsibility between family members with particularly sensitivity given to the historically high burden women have assumed for elder care (U.S. Conference of Catholic Bishops 1999; Christiansen 1994, 253).

5. For studies that focus specifically on Christian ethics and family caregiving, see Sapp 1987; and Christiansen 1991, 1994, 1995, and 2005.

Programs such as "Cash and Counseling" can also help to alleviate the financial impact of family involvement in caregiving. Because Medicaid benefits are distributed in the form of a "cash benefit," elderly persons can choose who provides their personal care, including paying relatives or friends who help them (Squillace et al. 2002, 225-26). Such financial remuneration for family members can serve to promote family involvement in societies that are heavily dependent on dual-income households. As the Pontifical Council argued, "The need for the family to be able to benefit from adequate means of material support should also be emphasized: economic assistance, welfare and health services, and appropriate housing, pension and social security policies should be available to the needs of the family" (1998). Thus, more than ever, it is vital for the church to insist on a *social* responsibility for elder care, which also strengthens and encourages family efforts.

Responsibility for the Way We Care: Dignity, Equality, Mutuality, and Participation

A second insight drawn from the Community of Sant'Egidio and Green House models, and from biblical and theological resources, is the responsibility to provide care for the elderly in a manner that promotes dignity, equality, mutuality, and enables meaningful participation in the community. The experiences of the Community of Sant'Egidio and the Green House Project illustrate the possibility and importance of such care. And this experience is supported by stories of elderly characters in the Bible that present an understanding of older persons as subjects who continue to be called by God even amid age-related disability and frailty. Chapter 5 further considered the elderly in light of the theological understanding of lifelong discipleship and the church's fellowship as characterized by mutual love, equality, and participation.

Following from this vision, I have sought to go beyond ethical models of care that primarily view the elderly in roles of need and dependence and instead approach the question of moral responsibility in our aging society from the starting point of the elderly themselves *as moral subjects* with aspirations and responsibilities. Thus, in addition to insisting on a responsibility *to care*, the ethic presented here urges the church to embody and advocate for *models of care* that respect old age as a time of ongoing growth and calling and elderly persons as participating members of the community, not merely the passive objects of the care of others. As in the previous section, I will first address practical applications of this vision in the church's internal practices and then its engagement with the wider society.

Opportunities to Serve

First, in relation to the church's own internal ministries, there must be renewed awareness of the elderly as lifelong disciples who are called by God to the end of life and the provision of opportunities to live out that calling. While the church must avoid a false glorification of old age, it should also avoid the opposite extreme of viewing the elderly *only* through the lens of need, decline, and frailty. As the U.S. Catholic bishops urge, "Former responses that saw older people solely as the recipients of care are not adequate" (1999). The church must insist that, while the *form* of service may change over the lifespan, older people are invited by God to serve even amid weakness and frailty. Similarly, in the biblical and theological vision, old age is a stage of life that involves purpose and responsibility and is not merely a time of leisure and entertainment. In their essay on elderly in the New Testament, Hays and Hays write, "This christological pattern [of service to others] for the years of late life challenges and subverts many of the conventional models for aging that we see around us: old people as helpless, useless burdens on society, or old age as a time to sit back and reap the rewards we have earned through a lifetime of work" (2003, 13).

For the church to truly care for the elderly—that is, to help one another in moral and spiritual growth—thus requires more than a monthly visit from the priest or Eucharistic minister or worse, church programs that mimic wider cultural attitudes by providing nothing more than entertainment and leisure activities. Our discussion of Sant'Egidio provides a concrete model for ways this can be done. As we saw, Sant'Egidio seeks not only to provide older people with basic physical and material care but also to facilitate ongoing service to others, such as providing transportation and accompaniment to religious services and involving elderly friends in service activities such as letter writing to prisoners. For the most weak and frail elderly friends living in residential facilities, Sant'Egidio members offer prayer services and consistent friendship in which elderly persons are able to nurture meaningful social bonds with others. In their own reflection on prayer as service, the Pontifical Council (1998) affirms that even the most frail elderly can be encouraged to experience an ongoing sense of purpose and responsibility:

> Prayer is a service. It is a ministry that older people may perform for the good of the whole Church and the world. Even the most infirm and handicapped of them can pray. Prayer is their strength, it is their life. Through prayer they can break down the walls of isolation, emerge from their condition of helplessness, and share in the joys and sorrows of others. . . . An older person, confined to bed and reduced to the end of his or her physical strength, can, by praying, become like a monk, a hermit. And through prayer he or she can embrace the whole world.

The church's responsibility is to nurture and make visible such forms of service.

Two other examples that parallel Sant'Egidio's approach are Shepherd's Centers and the Gray Panthers movement. Elbert Cole started the Shepherd's Center movement in 1971 in Kansas City, Missouri. As the national organization states, Cole "recognized the need to redefine and restructure the way Americans approach aging" ("A New Image of Aging"). Today, Shepherd's Centers of America is a network of interfaith congregation-based centers with "a commonly understood mission to empower older adults to use their wisdom and skills for the good of their communities" and thus, to "provide meaning and purpose for adults throughout their mature years." In an article on volunteer ministries with older adults, James Seeber describes Shepherd's Centers as ministries aimed at "transitional elderly" to enable them to "maintain a life that has meaning and to receive support services they need to avoid premature institutionalization" (2003, 172). Indeed, as Elbert Cole himself describes, the Shepherd's Centers have always sought to include programs "designed to deal with the question '*Why* survive?'" by providing elderly with the opportunity for lifelong learning and service to others. Thus, a major component of these centers has been to encourage older persons to help other elderly to stay at home longer through volunteering in programs such as Meals on Wheels.

A second example is that of the Gray Panthers, founded in 1970 by Maggie Kuhn, who was forced into retirement at age sixty-five from a job in the national organization of the Presbyterian Church USA. Kuhn convened a network of friends who, like her, were retiring from careers in national religious and social work organizations. Their purpose was to address some of the problems faced by retired persons, "loss of income, loss of contact with associates and loss of one of our society's most distinguishing social roles, one's job" ("Gray Panthers' Founding"). From its beginnings, the organization was founded on the view of old age as more than a time of entitlement and rather as a time in which the task is to use one's time and freedom in retirement to contribute to the betterment of society.

From Kuhn's speech at the 1972 General Convention of the Presbyterian Church, the Gray Panthers became a national organization of affiliated local networks with the purpose of promoting old age as a time of service to and advocacy on major social problems, such as the Vietnam War, racism, and a national health-care system for all. Today the organization continues to organize older persons in advocacy campaigns on a range of public policy issues, from the Iraq War to Social Security to environmental responsibility ("Gray Panthers—Issue Resolutions Summary"). Furthermore, committed to being more than a special interest group for issues exclusive to old age, the Gray Panthers have sought to promote old age as a time of intergenerational solidarity with young people for the purpose of improving society for all ages. Therefore, the Gray Panthers have an explicit commitment to being an "intergenerational, multi-issue organization."

The models of Sant'Egidio, Shepherd's Center, and the Gray Panthers provide important examples of ways in which the church, in its own internal ministries, can promote and empower the agency of the elderly expressed as service. Shortly before his death, an elderly John

Paul II focused his Lenten message on precisely this theme. He called on the church to reflect more deeply on the reality of human longevity today, "in order to deepen the awareness of the role that the elderly are called to play in society and in the Church, and thus to prepare your hearts for the loving welcome that should always be reserved for them" (1999a). The pope's invitation was an important one because within it the connection is made between the moral imperative to preserve dignity in the lives of older people and the ability to see the elderly as persons whose lives still possess purpose and meaning.

In their own letter, the U.S. Catholic bishops argued that the church's specific response to older people is a measure of the well-being of the entire church: "How the faith community relates to its older members—recognizing their presence, encouraging their contributions, responding to their needs, and providing appropriate opportunities for spiritual growth—is a sign of the community's spiritual health and maturity" (1999). And similar to the insights of Elbert Cole, the Pontifical Council (1998) urged: "The ecclesial community, for its part, is called to respond to the greater participation which older people would like to have in the Church. . . . It must therefore re-examine its apostolate on behalf of older people, and open it up to their participation and collaboration."

This vision of older persons is prophetic in a culture that, on the opposite end of productivity, presents old age as a time one has earned for self-indulgent leisure. By revising its own internal ministry to older people, the church counters current social attitudes that approach the elderly as a retired, passive class of people who are "past their prime" or "out to pasture." Such a view was evident in the Allstate ad in Chapter 2 (p. 17) in which the older man has nothing to do but constantly check his watch, in contrast to the active, purposeful work of the earlier versions of himself. Previous transitions in life entail social recognition of needed preparation for the next, more responsible stage of life: childhood to school age; adolescence to young adulthood and greater independence; university years to professional work; adult transitions in work and family life, which imply even more significant responsibility. However, passing into retirement is largely seen as an opting out *from* responsibility and the absence of a transition *to* something. The experience of old age as a period of role attrition is more acutely problematic in our context today given the enormous gains in longevity and health we now enjoy well after the traditional retirement age of sixty-five.

When society lacks a meaningful way to affirm genuine purpose and obligation in this stage of life, it consigns the elderly to a position of passivity in our society, increasing their vulnerability, because they are seen as a burdensome, unproductive class of persons. Thus, responding to the reality of aging and long-term care today is not just a matter of whether we can continue to enhance physical and economic quality of life, but also whether this life can be welcomed as having positive value and purpose.

Ensuring Participation and Overcoming Marginalization in Long-Term Care

Guided by its theological vision of the equality and mutuality of Christian friendship, the church should engage the wider society in creating models of elder care that ensure participation for the elderly. Catholic social thought, in fact, offers a long tradition of reflection on justice as participation within the larger understanding of social justice. Participation is a moral concept that arises out of the Catholic tradition's emphasis on human beings as social creatures and thus, as persons whose dignity is inseparable from their relationship with and to the larger community. Because of the mutual interdependence of persons and community, social justice stresses the principle of participation, which is both a duty of persons and a responsibility of society. The U.S. Catholic bishops provide a succinct articulation of this dimension of justice: "Social justice implies that persons have an obligation to be active and productive participants in the life of society *and* that society has a duty to enable them to participate in this way" (1998, 595). In fact, social justice is sometimes referred to as "contributive" justice because it entails the duty and desire of persons to contribute to the common good without which society cannot provide for the well-being of all members. In other words, justice as participation is a rich moral concept that addresses the many ways in which persons contribute to and take responsibility for the shared social life of the community as an expression of their human dignity and personality.

Two significant Catholic documents published on the occasion of the United Nations' designation of 1999 as the "International Year of the Older Person" draw upon justice-as-participation in their engagement with civil society and governments. In their message "The Dignity of Older People and Their Mission in the Church and in the World," the Pontifical Council (1998) stated that a society which is truly just for all ages is one "committed to creating the conditions of life able to fulfill the great potential that older people still have." From the perspective of social justice, this is a moral right; as the council argues, "older people have a right to a place in society." Furthermore, they recognized the connection between human dignity and community: "Of the various problems that commonly afflict older people today, one—perhaps more than any other— injures the dignity of the person: *marginalization*." Thus, the council insists that reintegrating the elderly is a social responsibility: "Society and its institutions are called to give older people scope for personal development and participation, and provide them with forms of social assistance and health care consonant with their needs and responding to the need of the human person to live with dignity, in justice and freedom."

This responsibility includes empowering older people to "participate in the decision-making processes that concern them both as persons and as citizens." In their own 1999 pastoral message, "Blessings of Age," the U.S. Catholic bishops also drew upon a social-justice approach in the call for "new initiatives that encourage the participation of older persons in society and in the Church." The bishops promote "the principle of participation" as the moral vision that allows older people to be cared for in a manner that respects them as partners in decision making and planning rather than the mere objects of the decisions of others.

The language of participation is also valuable because it connects the church's moral-vision traditions in the wider culture that shares this vision of justice, particularly the contemporary human rights tradition. For instance, the view of justice as a social responsibility to enable participation is also reflected in United Nations' documents concerning the elderly. In its contribution to the 1999 International Year of Older Persons, the United Nations advocated for "a society for all ages" in which "every individual, each with rights and responsibilities, has an active role to play" ("Towards a Society for All Ages").

Toward this end, the United Nations produced a document entitled "United Nations Principles for Older Persons," which offered principles that governments were encouraged to implement through public policies and programs. The document identified "participation" as one of five principles needed to create a just society for the elderly. The United Nations' definition of participation recognizes the mutual responsibility between the person and society: "Older persons should remain integrated in society, participate actively in the formulation and implementation of policies that directly affect their well-being and share their knowledge and skills with younger generations. . . . Older persons should be able to seek and develop opportunities for service to the community and to serve as volunteers in positions appropriate to their interests and capabilities."

As we saw in the Catholic social tradition, the principle of participation means that people have a responsibility to contribute to their society while society has a duty to foster and enable that participation. For instance, recognizing that independence and connection to one's community are vital to participation, the "United Nations Principles" states, "Older persons should be able to reside at home for as long as possible." And, in order to maximize still-existing capacity, the document also insists that "Older persons should be able to pursue opportunities for the full development of their potential. Older persons should have access to the educational, cultural, spiritual and recreational resources of society." Thus, a clear recognition exists that the ongoing participation of older people will be significantly affected by our political and social response. As the NGO forum of the UN assembly stated, "The ageing of the population implied by the enormous progress in the development of peoples all over the world represents an important challenge for public policies and social welfare systems in order to allow the elderly to continue to participate for as long as possible in society and to have available services that are affordable, appropriate and adapted to their requirements" ("Final Declaration and Recommendations").[6]

Because a social-justice vision recognizes participation as fundamental to the protection of human dignity, it calls society to avoid the concomitant violation that is marginalization in the way we provide long-term care. And yet, despite a recognition by some of the importance of participation of securing dignity for the elderly, many experts point out that too much of our long-term-care system still undermines participation and agency and results in marginalization and disempowerment. In his own critique of the current system, aging expert Larry Polivka argues that we still fail to nurture the capacities and agency of the elderly because the provision of "supportive, nurturing environments and services has been, more often than not, compromised by the needs of policy makers and providers to achieve short-term bureaucratic or fiscal goals" (1998, 24). Instead, elder-care expert Jane Boyajian argues that participation ought to guide our agenda in long-term care: "Every person seeks to participate in creation. Our specific charge is to promote the environment in which all can continue to do this and experience well-being to the fullest degree possible, despite age, circumstance, or disability" (1988, 29-30). There are several practical reforms within our long-term-care system that would better ensure participation and minimize marginalization.

One very direct application of the norm of participation is changing the way public funding for long-term care has been structured toward institutionalization of the elderly. Although in recent years

---

6. The capabilities approach to human rights of philosopher Martha Nussbaum makes similar arguments concerning how one measures the justice of society. In her work, Nussbaum articulates a list of basic human capabilities whose realization is fundamental to human dignity. Societies are then evaluated based on an assessment of whether persons have sufficient means—educational, economical, political, etc.—to actualize the core capabilities. What is particularly relevant to aging is Nussbaum's acknowledgment that, because of illness, disability, or age, persons differ in their ability to express the basic capabilities but nonetheless all have the right to resources and care that enable existing capabilities. For Nussbaum's discussion of the capabilities approach that specifically addresses disability and aging, see Nussbaum 2006.

several states have moved toward increasing home- and community-based services, policy expert Stephen Moses notes that, because of government funding of nursing-home care through Medicaid and Medicare starting in 1965, "institutionalization predominated, and home and community-based care languished for decades" (Stephen Moses 2007, 562). Citing multiple studies of quality of care in these institutions, Moses draws a grim assessment of the ability of this system to enhance the overall well-being of frail elderly. He describes the long-term care system in the United States as marked by "access and quality problems," "discrimination against public benefits recipients," "loss of independence," and "welfare stigma" (561). And, as the Pontifical Council (1998) notes, part of the problem with our institutionally biased long-term-care system is marginalization: "The confinement of older people in such institutional structures may translate itself into a kind of segregation from society." Given these persistent problems, it is vital for the church to engage the wider society and advocate for reform of the manner in which long-term residential care is provided in the United States.

Because we know that remaining at home can greatly enhance self-direction and freedom and help maintain social ties, the church should first advocate for continued support for and refinement of home- and community-based long-term-care services. In fact, in its 1999 *Olmstead* decision, the Supreme Court established that unnecessary segregation into an institution could constitute discrimination based on disability and that the frail and disabled had a right to receive care in a community setting where "feasible and reasonable." And, in the last couple of decades significant momentum developed to direct public funds toward home- and community-based care.[7] Not only do people prefer to receive care in their homes, but these models also consistently prove to cost states less than institutional care (Span 2010b).

---

7. Such services can include personal care, housekeeping assistance, meal programs, and day respite centers. For a discussion of recent legislation promoting a shift toward home- and community-based care, including the 2010 Affordable Care Act, see Harrington et al. 2012.

Despite this trend, which was applauded by seniors, gerontologists, and state officials, data suggest that these gains are threatened by short-term budget concerns related to the Great Recession that began in 2007-2008. Reporter John Leland (2010) writes that at least twenty-five states cut programs providing home- and community-based services following the recession, which affected programs such as Meals on Wheels and Alzheimer's day centers. The research organization Center on Budget and Policy Priorities, which focuses on the effects of budgetary policy on low- and moderate-income populations, points out that cuts in care services came at a time in which low- and moderate-income clients and families are least able to absorb the costs for such services (Johnson et al. 2010). On the individual level, as the stories in Leland's article illustrate, these cuts result in an insecure, confusing system for the elderly and disabled persons who depend on them; as one elderly client in Oregon expressed, "They yanked the rug out from underneath us. . . . I'm scared. I'm petrified."

The experience of the Great Recession reveals the need to advocate for permanent change in federal and state funding mechanisms that would better protect home services from short-term fiscal crises. Despite the fact that the 2010 Affordable Care Act contains provisions intended to promote home- and community-based long-term care, Harrington et al. note that such incentives and standards are voluntary, as opposed to mandatory, legislation governing institutional long-term care (2012, 185).[8] And, as Leland reports, existing federal Medicaid regulations make it easier for states to cut from home-based services than from nursing-home funding. This results in a system that, as Span describes, is a "patched-together, undependable jumble that hardly deserves to be called a system. It's not nearly that rational" (2010b).[9] Harrington et al. also report that despite gains in home- and community-based spending, long waiting lists to qualify for special programs in several states reveal that existing need is not fully

---

8. For a thorough discussion of the implications of the Affordable Care Act for home- and community-based services, see Miller 2012.

9. For an extensive, state-by-state report on Medicaid spending for home- and community-based services versus nursing homes, see Kassner et al. 2008.

addressed (2012, 171). A vision of justice as participation demands that home- and community-based services remain a priority in our public debate concerning resource allocation directed toward the elderly.[10] This is especially true concerning the medical and nonmedical services currently available that can help to maintain participation and independence even within the limitations of late life disease and disability.

Going forward, it is also crucial to support measures that increase the ability of middle-income seniors and families who do not qualify for public funding to afford the long-term care of their choice, including both home- and community-based services and residential care. One important option in that regard is purchasing long-term-care insurance. Health policy expert Mark Meiners notes that long-term-care insurance policies have been available in the private market since the 1980s, and have evolved from nursing-home care only policies to today covering a wide array of long-term-care options (2012, 155). While long-term-care policies differ, their basic purpose is to provide benefits in situations of disability that can be used to pay for care such as home-based care, adult day programs, assisted-living facilities, or nursing homes. For persons who would not qualify for long-term care through Medicaid benefits, the purchase of long-term-care insurance can be a vital aspect of planning for future care needs which would maximize independence and living at home.[11] As Paula Span reports, while long-term-care insurance can be highly beneficial, until now only about 10 percent of America's seniors have purchased a policy, and the vast majority of these policy holders are elderly with higher incomes and assets (2010a). Thus, even when older people are willing to pay for policies, the expense can prove more than they can afford.

---

10. See also Moses 2007, 355-56; Cahill and Moses 2008, 223-26.

11. Joshua Wiener reports that the average cost of private-pay nursing-home care in 2010 was $67,525 and home-based care provided by an agency aide averaged nineteen dollars per hour (2012, 121). Wiener concludes, "These expenses are beyond the financial reach of most Americans." In addition, adequate long-term-care insurance has the potential to decrease the number of middle-income persons forced to "spend down" assets in order to qualify for Medicaid (Wiener 2010, 128S-129S).

In terms of increasing the affordability of long-term-care insurance, multiple options exist, including expanding the private market, fostering public/private partnerships, and the creation of a public option. For the private market, one important policy option is to maintain, revise, and perhaps even increase current tax breaks for purchasing such policies. Public policy expert William Weissert explains that the federal government and some states currently offer a tax deduction in which the premium can count toward medical expenses that constitute a deduction when reaching a certain level of personal income (2012, 144). Any future tax policy overhaul at the national level must take long-term-care financing into consideration in order to maximize older people's ability to contribute to and direct the cost of care. In addition, private market policies could be made more affordable by providing subsidies for lower-income elderly and increasing employer-based group policies (Weissert 2012, 144).

Another option for expanding participation in long-term-care insurance is the public–private partnership model already begun in some states. Meiners reports that in the 1990s some states began using special Medicaid provisions to provide greater asset protection for middle-income elderly who purchased private long-term-care policies (2012, 161). These provisions created incentive for this income group because Medicaid could be tapped to cover care expenses that exceeded one's policy provisions; this allows persons to maintain a higher level of personal assets even while qualifying for Medicaid benefits. As with tax breaks, such partnerships can be used to expand the private long-term-care insurance market to more seniors.

A third option for increasing financial preparedness for long-term-care costs includes the creation of a public long-term-care insurance program. Because insurance premiums remain unaffordable for lower- and some middle-income persons and because private insurers can disqualify applicants, the public option is seen by some experts as a vital part of increasing Americans' readiness for long-term-care needs in old age.[12] Such was the reasoning behind the inclusion of the "CLASS Act" in the 2010 health care overhaul bill, which created a

---

12. Here it is important to note that while the overall economic and educational status of older Americans has steadily improved, a 2012 report

"publically sponsored, voluntary long-term-care insurance (LTCI) option for all working adults" (Meiners 2012, 152).[13] While long-term-care reform advocates long advocated a public option, experts note the CLASS Act faced many hurdles, which ultimately led to the announcement by DHHS Secretary Sebelius in October 2011 that the program could not be implemented as stipulated in the law.

Despite postponement of its implementation, policy deliberation and passage of the CLASS Act provide important lessons for future discussion of long-term-care financing. As in the larger health-care reform bill, society must find a way to ensure that all older people have the chance to prepare for long-term-care expenses in a way that maximizes their participation and dignity. The Affordable Care Act shows that this can be achieved in the private insurance market by eliminating exclusion based on preexisting conditions or it can be achieved through the creation of a public option, as in the CLASS Act. As noted in our discussion of the Green House model and Sant'Egidio elderly residences, many older people will always need some form of residential care at some point; therefore it is vital to ensure that long-term-care insurance positions them to secure the highest quality care rather than being left at the mercy of poor quality, Medicaid-dependent facilities. Whether for a public insurance program or for greater participation in the private market, our society must do a better job educating persons about the realities of aging and long-term care and the options that would maximize their ability to receive care in the least restrictive environment possible.

In addition to policy related to the funding of long-term care, the church needs to advocate for adequate regulation of and improvement to home- and community-based service providers. In many states,

---

shows that socio-economic disparity along racial lines is still evident among older Americans (Federal Interagency Forum, "Older Americans 2012," 24).

13.   Wiener notes that the design of the CLASS Act was based on publicly sponsored long-term-care insurance programs already established in Germany and Japan (2012, 119). For a more detailed description of the CLASS Act, see the nonpartisan "HealthReform GPS," sponsored by George Washington University and the Robert Wood Johnson Foundation ("Reform Overview").

home- and community-based service providers have thus far not been subjected to the same regulatory scrutiny as nursing homes. Regulation is particularly needed in relation to the sector of the home-care service industry geared toward moderate-income seniors and families who must pay privately for such services. Because of the enormous expense of these services, many turn to providers who are not certified by long-term-care regulatory protections. In addition, while remaining at home can enhance personal freedom, it can also leave elderly who lack strong social and family networks vulnerable and isolated. Experts argue that it is important to have national standards for the private home-care sector in order to avoid the kinds of abuses and scandals that once occurred in unregulated nursing homes (Gross 2007a).[14]

Guided by an ethic of long-term care that fosters the ongoing participation of the elderly, the church must also join with others in promoting necessary reforms of residential, institutional care settings. Despite the likelihood that many of us will spend some time in a nursing home during our old age, satisfaction with the quality and nature of care in nursing homes remains low. Rabig and her colleagues observe: "Despite intense regulation and substantial expense, adequate quality of care and quality of life are not consistently provided to the more than 2 million individuals who receive care in nursing facilities each year" (2006, 534).

Based on the two concrete models of Sant'Egidio and the Green House Project, I would argue that it is both possible and imperative for the church to engage the wider society in demanding serious reform of the institutional long-term-care system. As Green House founder Bill Thomas forcefully articulates, "First, we must make it our goal to abolish the institutional long-term care facility. They are a very recent creation (in historical terms) and they have served us poorly indeed. The idea of placing millions of elders in these settings is simply not conceivable anymore. The system is broken and must

---

14. Harrington et al. discuss elements of the Affordable Care Act intended to enhance monitoring of Medicaid-funded home- and community-based long-term care services in states who opt to participate in the legislation's pilot programs (2012, 174, 177).

be replaced" (Keane 2004, 45). Thus, for the sake of those elderly for whom residential care is more appropriate, the church could join with civic partners in replacing the old system of institutionalized care.

First, states should be urged to take measures that encourage the long-term-care industry to move toward smaller models such as the Green House in a deep and permanent way. As discussed in Chapter 3, Green House projects have been proven both to enhance the well-being of elders in terms of physical health and psychological health and to be economically feasible at Medicaid reimbursement rates. There are several ways that states could encourage more providers to shift away from large, inflexible institutions to this smaller, more elder-centered model. For instance, developers of the Green House project in Montana noted that one factor increasing up-front costs was having to meet expensive requirements designed for larger institutions, such as the size of kitchen range hoods ("Green House Nursing Homes").

To avoid hurdles such as this, Arkansas revised its long-term-care legislation to make sure existing nursing-home regulations would not prevent development of Green Houses in that state (M. LaPorte 2010, 31). Legislative measures such as this are crucial for encouraging for-profit companies to take up the Green House model and for enabling nonprofit and religious groups to be able to afford start-up costs. Along with advocacy, religious groups should strive to be leaders in promoting permanent change by incorporating the Green House model into their own long-term-care facilities, such as the Methodist-affiliated Green House development in Tupelo, Mississippi, which was the first in the country. [15]

Another area in which state-level regulation can be changed to encourage development of the Green House model regards "Certificate of Need" (CON) licenses through which the state regulates the number of nursing-home "beds" to avoid excess capacity. As the Green House *Guide Book* reports, in states that are trying to reduce

---

15. For example, see reports of new projects being developed by Catholic-based organizations around the country, Adler 2008; Minda 2010. For other models of church-sponsored housing in the United States, see Netting 1995.

the number of current nursing-home beds, it can create hurdles for Green House developers to attain a CON license for new houses or even to transfer an existing CON license to new beds created in a Green House project (42). In such cases, it is necessary to advocate for legislative action that would allow granting new CONs specifically for Green House projects. For instance, the *Guide Book* reports that such legislative advocacy was successful for proposed Green House developments in Massachusetts and Wyoming (42).

Another way that some states have created incentives to develop Green House models is to make public funds available for start-up capital. As one industry article noted, "It will take some creativity and capital to transform [decaying nursing facilities] into home-like environments at a cost-effective way" ("Changing the Nursing Home Culture," 4). In her article on taking the Green House model mainstream, Meg LaPorte describes several ways in which states have provided funds for start-up costs. For instance, some states, such as North Carolina and Arkansas, have begun to use civil money in penalty funds received from nursing homes that were not in compliance with regulations to fund grants to support reform initiatives and pilot projects. Such state penalty funds can be offered in the form of incentive grants to providers willing to convert existing facilities or to create new developments. Furthermore, to offset any additional costs in shifting to the Green House model, Arkansas sought approval from the federal Medicare and Medicaid agency (CMS) to be able to pay an additional four dollars per day to Green House providers for Medicaid residents (M. LaPorte 2010, 31-33).

Second, as both the Sant'Egidio residential houses and the Green Houses illustrated, it is vital to provide meaningful opportunities for growth and learning in residential settings as part of just care for the elderly. As the United Nations Programme on Ageing states, respect for the capacity of older people means fostering continued personal development: "Environments for growth, learning and moving toward creative fulfillment should be within the reach of all. What we are learning today about the extraordinary range of abilities and interests of older persons can help us in the task of creating such environments and remove obstacles for new generations" ("Implications of an Ageing Society"). In this regard, regulatory agencies should be measuring not only *whether* activities are being offered to long-term-care residents but what *kind* of activities are offered.

An early example of a program that viewed old age as a time of growth is the Elderhostel movement, launched in New Hampshire in 1975. Elderhostel was designed to provide people over sixty with a short-term residential college experience in which they could take noncredit courses in a variety of subjects. The original vision of Elderhostel was to use older-adult educational opportunities as a way in which to reverse the alienation felt by many elderly and also to provide them with new "modes of participation" (Mills 1993, 35). As one author explains, Elderhostel offered a different vision of old age in a society that "tied education to youth" and thus "continually underestimated older people's potential and need for learning" (Mills 1993, 171). Admittedly, Elderhostel does not provide a model that suits every older person; and in fact, it continues to draw primarily from healthy, well-educated, economically advantaged seniors. However, serious effort could be made to adapt education models such as Elderhostel to long-term-care facilities. For instance, the church could play an important role in connecting long-term-care residents to educational opportunities in the community, such as bringing in local university faculty for educational sessions or creating partnerships with nonprofit agencies.

Third, the model of mutuality in Christian friendship urges the church to advocate for and cooperate to create structures within which older people can cultivate real friendship and possibilities for intergenerational relationships as a fundamental component of promoting overall well-being and health. As the President's Council warns, "There is sometimes a powerful temptation to believe that elderly persons' lives are so limited that fellowship is insignificant, a temptation to regard being with them as little more than sitting awkwardly in a small room in a smelly nursing home. If, because they remind us of our inevitable decline, we shun their company, we isolate them even more" (2005, 25-26). Furthermore, Seeber argues that elderly people need more than family relationships to experience well-being: "A decade of research on the value of informal social support ties (friendships, 'neighboring,' volunteers, etc.) has established that while immediate family may provide 'instrumental support' (financial and other material help), close friends, neighbors, and church networks provide 'emotional support.' Such ties promote psychological and emotional well-being and freedom from loneliness" (2003, 177).

Despite the importance of meaningful friendship and intergenerational connections, much in the experience of older people conspires to cut them off from such relationships. For instance, because of increasing frailty, older people often move to a retirement center in a city where an adult child lives, but the negative side effect of this is removal from longstanding friendships combined with increased difficulty in creating new, substantive social relationships. Furthermore, friends of the same age also begin to experience decreasing mobility and thus become limited in their ability to make visits and maintain relational ties, such as the impact of no longer being able to drive.[16] Finally, elderly people more than others today face the stark fact that those who survive into advanced old age lose friends, family, and spouses to death. Therese Lysaught writes, "[Elderly people's] communities unravel in a particularly poignant way, as they find themselves facing again and again the deaths of those with whom they have lived for decades, with whom their entire lives have been intertwined: parents, siblings, spouses, children, mentors, friends" (2003, 272). Thus, for those elderly persons living well into their seventies and eighties, loss of personal relationships is a common experience.

Given these challenges, the church must insist that overcoming marginalization and fostering mutual, participatory relationships is imperative to providing just care for the elderly. To foster meaningful friendships and nurture connections to the wider community, long-term-care facilities should consider the extent to which the location and design of buildings either facilitate visits from outside contacts or

---

16. In her poignant memoir of life in a nursing home, Florida Scott-Maxwell describes this reality: "We live in a limbo of our own. Our world narrows, its steady narrowing is a constant pain. Friends die, others move away, some become too frail to receive us, and I become too frail to travel to them. Talk exhausts us, the expense of telephone reduces us to a breathless rush of words. . . . Letters can be scarce so we tend to live in a world of our own making, citizens of Age, but otherwise stateless" (1968, 137).

impede such ongoing connection.[17] Furthermore, through creative partnerships with schools or child daycare centers, opportunities for sustained intergenerational relationships could be promoted. In her essay on the issue of isolation and the elderly, Elizabeth MacKinlay argues that attention to substantive relationship is vital to adequate elder care: "The need of residents of nursing homes to have someone to share with them is very apparent. Good physical care and activity programs are important, but not enough. There is need for holistic care that involves forming trusting, intimate and respectful relationships" (2001, 97). As we saw in Chapter 3, Sant'Egidio and Green House homes provide a compelling model of an approach to care that includes intentional commitment to this important relational dimension.

Conclusion

This chapter has provided an initial vision of what it would look like for the church to respond practically to the challenge of long-term care, guided by a Christian ethic rooted in elder care as a social responsibility and in the norms of mutuality, equality, dignity, and participation. The shared responsibility to care demands efforts at educational awareness, providing care both directly and indirectly, and advocacy for just allocation of public resources. The norms of mutuality, equality, and dignity point to the importance of maximizing participation through which older people are enabled to remain within meaningful, reciprocal human relationships and contribute to others as they are able. Practically speaking, this leads to a revision of the church's approach to ministry to the elderly in which opportunities for service in the broadest sense are provided. And in the public realm, efforts are made to reform the delivery of long-term-care policy to increase

---

17. This is not merely the problem of larger institutions but can also be a challenge for smaller models such as the Green House. During my visit to the Tupelo Green Houses, the staff guide identified isolation from and involvement of the wider community as a major challenge they also face. Evaluation of Green House homes embedded in residential neighborhoods might provide helpful insight as to the relationship between location and ongoing community connection.

access to forms of care that promote participation such as home- and community-based options and small-scale homes like the Green House.

Both in terms of the responsibility to provide care and to do so in a more just manner, I have argued that the church can contribute to the wider society by providing a witness through its own internal ministries and by dialoguing and cooperating with governmental and civic entities. Though this chapter in no way exhausts the possible forms of the church's response, I have provided concrete priorities and programs to which the church could direct its energy and advocacy. The suggestions offered illustrate that the question of whether the new old age will be experienced as a blessing or a burden will be answered largely by *our response*. As the President's Council writes, "Free societies are also creative societies, with a capacity to adapt to, as well as overcome, hard and novel circumstances" (2005, 19). This chapter has shown that the church has a contribution to make to the deliberation and action of free societies as regards long-term elder care that truly promotes the dignity and well-being of older people.

CHAPTER SEVEN

Meeting the Challenge of Long-Term Care: A Question for Us All

Is the new abundance of life now produced by gains in longevity to be seen as a problem or an opportunity? Are younger and older generations simply interest groups, or are all generations bound in obligations toward a common good? To insist that the future remains open is to insist that human beings have in their power the capacity to act, on whatever scale, and to move toward an abundance of life shared by all generations.

Harry Moody (1988, 265)

To bring this book to its conclusion, I return to where I began: the voice of Sant'Egidio's elderly friend Kate, who in her late seventies said, "I can do a lot if I have others to help me." This work has been an attempt to make Kate's desire—the desire of elderly people for respect as subjects who desire ongoing participation—a prominent and lasting part of our society's approach to long-term care. All societies must respond to social challenges such as aging within the limitations of their history, resources, and political and cultural institutions. But defaulting to the family or to existing policy and institutions will not suffice in providing long-term care that enables and protects the dignity of the elderly today and tomorrow. Instead, the question we must ask ourselves *corporately* is whether or not we are willing to marshal the energy, creativity, and resources to make old age a blessing and not a curse.

Our response to this question will largely depend, quite frankly, on whether our societies believe older people possess ongoing value and dignity as equal members of our communities or whether they are merely needy dependents who drain resources. Despite the glossy brochures of senior residential developments and the promising claims of retirement investment portfolios, too often cultural attitudes and existing long-term-care policy and programs relegate the elderly to the margins of society and exclude them from participation in our common life. This is particularly true for the frail elderly, those in the fastest growing cohort of the oldest old, who start to experience disability and illness requiring the care of others. For these elderly it is increasingly difficult to experience their lives as having ongoing purpose and meaning and to be accorded equal dignity within the human community.

That the experience of dignity in old age is profoundly affected either positively or negatively by the attitudes and treatment of the larger community—and not some inevitable aspect of getting old—was powerfully articulated by the late Jewish theologian Abraham Heschel at the first White House Conference on Aging, in 1961. In the speech, entitled "To Grow in Wisdom," Heschel exposed the denigration of older people that follows from a fundamental, often implicit, assumption that the elderly no longer possess capacity and a desire for purpose. Because of this, Heschel argued that too much of what our society offers the elderly is merely entertainment, diversion, and distraction, what he called the "trivialization of existence." For Heschel, this trivialization was incompatible with the full dignity of the elderly: "After all, *to be retired does not mean to be retarded*" (1972, 74).

Heschel's statement is all the more powerful for its use of a term that is no longer considered acceptable; for it identifies a connection between the way older people are viewed and past attitudes toward persons with intellectual disabilities. In both cases there is a cultural failure to see a class of persons as possessing the capacity for personal growth and meaningful participation in society. Heschel movingly described the impact this has upon the aged, particularly the frail:

"The aged may be described as a person *who does not dream anymore,* devoid of ambition, and living in fear of losing his status. Regarding himself as a person who has outlived his usefulness, he feels as if he had to apologize for being alive" (1972, 73). In response, Heschel summoned society to a new vision of the elderly rooted in what he called the "grandeur of being human" that derives from a sense of responsibility and significance to others.

That half a century later there still exists an ethical challenge to affirm and enable the grandeur of older people became evident to me through practical experience. Like almost any middle-aged adult in America today, I began to see the problems in our long-term-care system because of aging family members. The experiences of my extended family were then amplified by my exposure to the work of Sant'Egidio with older people in the United States, Italy, and Africa. As the opening story of Kate illustrates, what I saw in public housing developments and nursing homes were older people still desiring engagement in their community and meaningful participation in human fellowship. But what I also saw was a system that, intentionally or not, failed to recognize this desire and capacity and more often than not pushed older people to the margins where their potential and dignity were hidden and untapped. At the same time, I met family caregivers struggling to meet the care needs of frail elderly and feeling unsupported by society. Time and again, I also saw paid caregivers undervalued by organizational structure and low pay. At the same time, the models of Sant'Egidio and the Green House Project convinced me that it was both possible and morally incumbent on societies to provide long-term elder care in a manner that fosters the values of equality, mutuality, and dignity and enables ongoing participation for older people, though the forms of that participation may change over the lifespan.

Thus, this book has unfolded much as my own thinking about the ethical challenges of aging developed. Because of the practical experiences above, my approach insists that the starting point for ethical responsibility in our aging society is the elderly themselves as moral subjects with agency and dignity. It also argues that aging must be seen as a primary social-ethical issue of our time, and not merely a bioethical dilemma related to death or a matter of familial duty. As the Pontifical Council (1998) argued, "To accompany older people, to approach them and enter into relation with them, is the duty of us all. The time has come to begin working towards an effective change in attitude towards older people and to restore to them their rightful place in the human community." Also, it is through the experiences of new models of elder care such as Sant'Egidio and Green House that Christian ethics is able to return to resources such as the Bible and the theological tradition to gather stories and insights that can help the church to respond to contemporary challenges. For in our society's discussion of long-term care and the elderly, I have argued that the church has a contribution to make. And I have sought to demonstrate the relevant ethical norms from experience and the Christian tradition's resources that should inform the church's own internal practices and its wider engagement.

In Chapter 2, I presented an analysis of the dramatic feature of aging today that helps us to understand the pressing challenge of long-term care. Aging experts have identified a paradox of contemporary aging: while more of us are living longer and healthier, more of us are also living to ages at which chronic disease and disability are common. At the same time that care needs are growing in our society, there exist strains on our capacity to provide this care: experts warn of the current and projected shortage of paid, professional caregivers, including trained geriatricians, and identify features of contemporary life that frustrate the desire of families to provide care for aging relatives. In addition, I have provided evidence of the inadequacy of and dissatisfaction with our current long-term-care system, not only in terms of financial unsustainability but also in terms of its failure to promote the dignity, agency, and participation of older Americans.

The descriptive analysis of Chapter 2 was then followed by two concrete models of long-term elder care that provide alternatives to our current situation and stimulate our moral imagination. These models can motivate social commitment to change by demonstrating the practical possibility that long-term care can be different. As gerontologist Larry Polivka argues, meaningful reform of our long-term-care system will come not merely as a result of intellectual understanding, but only with "a collective change of heart" (1998, 22). Another value of such models is that they allow the church to speak not only from its principles and values but from its experience as a community of practice. Thus, two models of long-term care were presented that illustrate an approach to caring for older people that honors their agency and fosters their ongoing dignity as participating members of society.

The Community of Sant'Egidio, a religiously based, largely volunteer organization, provides different forms of elder care as an expression of its Christian commitment to friendship with the poor. The Green House model grew out of geriatrician Bill Thomas's long efforts at nursing-home reform and his conclusion that the U.S. system of institutional long-term care must be replaced by smaller, family-style homes. These two examples—Sant'Egidio in its understanding of friendship and the Green House in its innovative model of small homes and staff–elder relationship—prove that long-term care can be provided in a way that views old age as a time of potential growth and development, makes possible the contribution of the elderly to others within mutual relationships, and maximizes the agency of the elderly to shape and direct their lives.

Following from these examples, Chapters 4 and 5 turned to the particular resources of the Christian tradition for supporting ethical and theological insight. One of these sources is the biblical witness, which I suggested provides two key affirmations. First, the Hebrew Bible and the New Testament writings insist that care for the elderly is one ethical measure of a just society. In the biblical texts, this position is advocated in terms of a concern for a healthy society, as an expression of respect for God, and as indicated by God's special concern for the poor and weak. We also saw that the ethical imperative for care is presented as a responsibility both toward one's own family members and to aging members of the community and society. Second, particularly in relation to stories of older people in the Bible, the biblical witness is adamant that older persons continue to be called by God to service and purpose, even in the context of age-related weakness and disability. In line with this, the Bible presents a realistic picture of older people: the ability to respond to God's calling does not come automatically with old age; the elderly, like everyone else, must cultivate wisdom and remain open to growth and change in order to live faithful lives. Furthermore, the Bible presents this service as changing over the course of a lifetime, taking into account real limitations such as physical deterioration. Nonetheless, the Scriptures insist that limitations and the need for others' care do not exclude older people from being participating members of the community.

A second key resource was a theological vision of discipleship and the church as a community of mutual love and material support. Here Karl Barth's understanding of the fundamental equality of Christian identity and the relation between Christians as defined by the reality of God's calling to discipleship to Jesus Christ are important. Following from this, the fellowship of the church is understood as a mutual helping aimed at empowering one another to live out his or her discipleship. The work of Paul Wadell supplements Barth's thought by drawing from Christian reflection on friendship to express the equality and mutuality of Christian fellowship. The importance of these theological reflections is in establishing the dignity and agency of older persons as lifelong disciples who remain participants in the mutual love, support, and challenge of Christian community. Drawing on several contemporary Catholic and Protestant reflections on old age, the chapter then explored what the theology of discipleship means for the church's understanding of and ministry with the elderly. What is needed is clear recognition of the elderly as participating subjects in the life and ministry of the church, rather than viewing them merely as the passive objects of its care. The vision of the church as a universal fellowship and community of friendship also furthers the argument for elder care as a shared moral responsibility that, while encompassing and supporting family caregiving, extends beyond biological family.

Finally, Chapter 6 sought practical application of the ethic of long-term care developed here for the church's internal practices and for its engagement with the wider society. While the discussion was not exhaustive, it did identify priority areas where the church actually has something helpful to say and do. As exemplified by Sant'Egidio and supported by biblical and theological sources, I presented specific ways for the church to be a community of material aid and spiritual support oriented to the capacities of the elderly: provide direct care services such as adult day centers; facilitate access to public resources by the elderly and their families; offer spiritual care and education to caregivers; collaborate with nonprofit and public programs such as community-based health services; provide and facilitate opportunities for the elderly to minister to others; and create forums in which older people are challenged and supported in ongoing personal and spiritual development.

Inspired by the framework of *Gaudium et spes,* which calls the church to engage the wider society in dialogue, freedom, and mutual respect, Chapter 6 also highlighted key areas that demand the church's public advocacy based on its ethical vision, particularly as this vision overlaps with secular concepts of justice as participation: to critique attitudes and rhetoric that suggest the elderly are less deserving of resources than younger generations; to promote just resource allocation in health-care spending, such as increasing the availability of quality geriatric care and recruiting more front-line caregivers through improvement of working conditions; to redirect public long-term-care dollars toward more home- and community-based sources; to increase access to adequate long-term-care insurance for lower- and middle-income Americans; and to demand deep, lasting reform of the U.S. residential long-term-care system, including incentives for shifting to the small, family-style models represented by Sant'Egidio's elderly homes and the Green House Project.

Whether longer life is experienced as a blessing or a burden individually and societally, here in the United States and globally, depends largely on adopting such practical measures in response to the challenge of long-term care. This perspective is effectively captured in a statement by the United Nations Programme on Ageing: "The present imperative is that societies must respond to the extraordinary potential and range of variability in individual ageing, and seize the opportunity to rethink our notion of limits and recognize the far-reaching benefits societies stand to gain from the continuing contributions of their older citizens" ("Toward a Society for All Ages"). And yet that argument has not been posited in a way that denies the very real challenges and difficulties currently experienced in late old age. There is no doubt that illnesses such as Alzheimer's and Parkinson's question our concepts of human dignity and agency and what constitutes morally obligatory or proportionate care.

For instance, in a poignant *New York Times* opinion piece, author Susan Jacoby (2010) wrote about her older female relatives who lived long enough to suffer debilitating chronic pain, dementia, and physical disability. Her point was that "age-defying" declarations that "90 is the new 50" harmfully ignore our natural concerns and wish to avoid the conditions we see many of our elderly loved ones experiencing and the painful conflicts family and friends experience in trying to provide care. Nor are many of our cultural attitudes toward weakness and limitations helpful in coping with these existential realities. As theologian Walter Burghardt observes, "The only ideal of old age we accept in the States is an aging without change or limits or loss" (1991, 66).

Precisely because these difficulties cannot be completely eliminated, Chapter 5 highlighted the importance of the Christian community's responsibility in helping older persons to live these challenges in the context of friendship. In the mutuality of friendship, even the painful realities of late old age can become occasions for the elderly to contribute to others by reminding us of neglected aspects of human experience and the importance of loving relationships. As the Pontifical Council (1998) wrote, "Older people, in their search for companionship, challenge a society in which the weaker are often abandoned; they draw attention to the social nature of man and to the need to repair the fabric of interpersonal and social relationships." In turn, this mutuality allows others to cultivate capacities of faithfulness and compassion through supporting and assisting the elderly.

Even in relation to constructively embracing the existential difficulties of old age the church can find places of cooperation and dialogue with the wider society. For instance, the hospice movement has made great strides in shifting cultural attitudes about the dying process from viewing it as a failure of modern medicine to seeing within it a normal life experience that contains possibilities for spiritual growth and meaningful human connection. Likewise, Dr. Ira Byock, a palliative-care physician, draws on the human rights tradition's affirmation of the "inherent dignity" of all human beings to insist that the lives of chronically ill and dependent persons still possess meaning and purpose. Furthermore, he suggests that caregiving represents a vital aspect of a humane society because "the impulse to honor and care for our most vulnerable members—infants, elderly, injured, and ill—is part of our humanity" (2010, 1). To illustrate his point, he tells the story of his own grandmother, who was cared for at home by Byock's family; in the loving interdependence of his father's relationship with his grandmother, Byock explains that he learned that human dignity still remains in the context of frailty and dependence.

Similarly, Arthur Kleinman, anthropologist and psychiatrist, who cared for his wife of forty-five years who had Alzheimer's disease, concluded that "caregiving is also a defining moral experience. It is a practice of empathic imagination, responsibility, witnessing, and solidarity with those in great need. It is a moral practice that makes caregivers, and at time even the carereceivers, more present and thereby more fully human" (2010, 29). Echoing the argument that the value of caregiving rests in our response, Byock likewise observes: "Our society is aging, and soaring numbers of chronically ill people live among us. . . . They do not have to be social problems. . . . We have the collective responsibility to care for them with tenderness and love. Most of us will be physically dependent and intimately cared for by others before we die. This does not destine us to become undignified. It simply confirms that we are human" (2010, 1). What the church and the society can do, then, is to provide the support and conditions that maximize the possibility for aging and caregiving to be experienced as something that enriches our humanity.

Unlike many dramatic features of our time, the challenges of contemporary aging potentially confront every person. The truth is, given the growing universality of increased longevity, people ignore these challenges, literally at their own personal peril. As Andrea Riccardi, founder of Sant'Egidio, observes, "The condition of the old person raises disquieting issues for everyone. Nobody is excluded from this, not even the richest" (1999, 196). And these disquieting issues can either result in collective fear and crisis or become a source of profound solidarity and creativity. As Green House founder Bill Thomas asks, "Can we imagine a society that *welcomes* aging and makes good use of all that it has to offer us?" (Keane 2004, 46). This book has sought to provide one ethical vision to move toward such a society—a society in which the help we provide older people like Kate recognizes and fosters her ongoing participation and dignity, and thus preserves her valued place within the human community.

Bibliography

Aaron, Henry J. 2006. "Longer Life Spans: Boon or Burden?" *Daedalus* 135.1: 9-19.

"About Adult Day Services." National Adult Day Services Association. http://www.nadsa.org.

"About the Eden Alternative." The Eden Alternative. http://www.eden alt.org.

Adams, Rebecca, and Jean Brittain. 1987. "Functional Status and Church Participation of the Elderly: Theoretical and Practical Implications." *Journal of Religion & Aging* 3.3/4: 35-48.

Adler, Jane. 2008. "A Home, Not a Hospital: Small-Scale Nursing Homes Provide Opportunities and Challenges for Communities." *Planning* 74.6: 24ff. *General OneFile*. Available online.

"Africa: The 'Schools of Peace.'" The School of Peace, The Community of Sant'Egidio. http://www.santegidio.org.

"The Aged." Friendship with the Poor, The Community of Sant' Egidio.http://www.santegidio.org.

Allen, John. 2014. "Francis Visit Cements Sant'Egidio as Winner." *Boston Globe*, June 16, 2014.

Alzheimer's Association. 2007. "Statistics about Alzheimer's Disease." http://www.alz.org.

Angelelli, Joe. 2006. "Promising Models for Transforming Long-Term Care." *The Gerontologist* 46.4: 428-30.

"Assessing Housing Options." 2007. AARP. http://www.aarp.org.

"Assistance at Home." Friendship with the Poor, The Community of Sant'Egidio. http://www.santegidio.org.

Baer, David, and Ellen O'Brien. 2010. *Federal and State Income Tax Incentives for Private Long Term Care Insurance*. AARP Public Policy Institute. http://www.aarp.org.

Baltes, Paul B. 2006. "Facing Our Limits: Human Dignity in the Very Old." *Daedalus* 135.1: 32-39.

Baltes, Paul B., and Jacqui Smith. 2003. "New Frontiers in the Future of Aging: From Successful Aging of the Young Old to the Dilemmas of the Fourth Age." *Gerontology* 49.2: 123-35.

Barth, Karl. 1961a. *Church Dogmatics*, Volume III, Part 4. Edinburgh: T & T Clark.

———. 1961b. *Church Dogmatics*, Volume IV, Part 2. Edinburgh: T & T Clark.

Bartoli, Andrea. 2001. "Forgiveness and Reconciliation in the Mozambique Peace Process." In *Forgiveness and Reconciliation: Religion, Public Policy, and Conflict Resolution*, edited by Raymond Helmick and Rodney Petersen, 361-81. Radnor, PA: Templeton Foundation Press.

Bergman-Evans, Brenda. 2004. "Beyond the Basics: Effect of the Eden Alternative Model on Quality of Life Issues." *Journal of Gerontological Nursing* 30.6: 27ff. *General OneFile*. Available online.

Berkman, Lisa F., and M. Maria Glymour. 2006. "How Society Shapes Aging: The Centrality of Variability." *Daedalus* 135.1: 105-14.

Berndtson, Chad. 2007. "Is It Easy Being Green? Tracking the Latest Developments in Green House Senior Living: Its State-of-the-Art, Homelike Residences Have Only Been Around a Few Years, but in That Time, the Green House Project Has Become One of the Long-Term Care Industry's Most Compelling Design Developments." *Contemporary Long Term Care* 30.1: 22ff. *General OneFile*. Available online.

Bianchi, Eugene C. 1991. "A Spirituality of Aging." *Concilium* 3: 58-64.

"A Bit of History." The Aged, The Community of Sant'Egidio. http://www.santegidio.org.

Blasberg-Kuhnke, Martina. 1991. "Old People in the Church: The Subject Option in Old Age." *Concilium* 3: 72-80.

Blidstein, Gerald. 1975. *Honor Thy Father and Mother: Filial Responsibility in Jewish Law and Ethics*. New York: Ktav.

Bowers, Barbara, and Kimberly Nolet. 2014. "Developing the Green House Nursing Care Team: Variations on Development and Implementation." *The Gerontologist*. 54.S1: S53-S64.

Boyajian, Jane A. 1988. "On Reaching a New Agenda: Self-Determination and Aging." In *Ethics and Aging: The Right to Live, the Right to Die*, edited by James E. Thornton and Earl R. Winkler, 17-30. Vancouver: University of British Columbia Press.

Brewer, Loretta. 2001. "Gender Socialization and the Cultural Construction of Elder Caregivers." *Journal of Aging Studies* 15.3: 217-36.

Brown, Dave. 1998. "Senior Power." *Social Policy* 28.3: 43-45. *Academic Search Premier*. EBSCO. Available online.

Brown, Kaye, and Nadine Pfeiffer. 2009. "Tracking Environmental Enhancements: A North Carolina Study Investigates, 'How Much Change in Culture Change?'" *Long-Term Living* (May 2009): 16ff. *General OneFile*. Available online.

Brueggemann, Walter. 1982. *Genesis: Interpretation, A Bible Commentary for Teaching and Preaching*. Atlanta: John Knox Press.

Bureau of the Census, U.S. Department of Commerce. 1999. *Aging in the Americas into the XXI Century*. http://www.census.gov.

Burghardt, Walter J. 1991, "Aging, Suffering and Dying: A Christian Perspective." *Concilium* 3: 65-71.

Byock, Ira. 2010. "Dying with Dignity." *Hastings Center Report* (April 2010): 1.

Cahill, Lisa Sowle. 1996. "The Bible and Christian Moral Practices." In *Christian Ethics: Problems and Prospects*, edited by Lisa Sowle Cahill and James F. Childress, 3-17. Cleveland, OH: Pilgrim Press.

———. 2005. *Theological Bioethics: Participation, Justice, and Change*. Washington, DC: Georgetown University Press.

———. 2006. "Justice for Women: Martha Nussbaum and Catholic Social Teaching." In *Transforming Unjust Structures: The Capability Approach*, edited by Severine Deneulin, Mathias Nebel, and Nicholas Sagovsky, 83-104. Dordrecht: Springer.

Cahill, Lisa Sowle, and Sarah Moses. 2008. "Aging, Genetics, and Social Justice." In *Aging, Biotechnology, and the Future*, edited by Catherine Read, Robert Green, and Michael Smyer, 216-31. Baltimore: Johns Hopkins University Press.

Cahill, Thomas. 1999. *Desire of the Everlasting Hills: The World before and after Jesus*. New York: Doubleday.

Callahan, Daniel. 1987. *Setting Limits: Medical Goals in an Aging Society*. New York: Simon & Schuster.

Carcaterra, Paola. 2010. Personal interview. November 7, 2010.

"Care for the Whole Person, For Those Who Need it Most." Guided Care. http://www.guidedcare.org.

"Caregiving Facts." 2006. *Frontline: Living Old*. PBS online. http://www.pbs.org.

Carmichael, Liz. 2004. *Friendship, Interpreting Christian Love*. New York: T & T Clark.

Carter, Warren. 2001. "Adult Children and Elderly Parents: The Worlds of the New Testament." *Journal of Religious Gerontology* 12.2: 45-59.

Cassel, Christine K. 2009. "Policy for an Aging Society, A Review of Systems." *Journal of the American Medical Association* 302.4: 2701-2702.

"Changing the Nursing Home Culture." 2008. Alliance for Health Reform Issue Brief, March 2008. http://www.allhealth.org.

Christiansen, Andrew. 1982. "Autonomy and Dependence in Old Age: An Ethical Analysis." PhD diss., Yale University.

Christiansen, Drew. 1974. "Dignity in Aging." *Hastings Center Report* 4.1: 6-8.

———. 1991. "Creative Social Responses to Aging: Public Policy Options for Family Caregiving." *Concilium* 3: 115-22.

———. 1994. "Intergenerational Relations." In *Duties to Others*, edited by C. S. Campbell and B. A. Lustig, 247-57. Dordrecht, Netherlands: Kluwer Academic Publishers.

———. 1995. "A Catholic Perspective." In *Aging Spirituality, and Religion: A Handbook, Volume 1*, edited by Melvin Kimble, Susan H. McFadden, James W. Ellor, and James J. Seeber, 403-16. Minneapolis: Fortress Press.

———. 2005. "Of Many Things (Old Age)." *America* 193.9: 1.

Clements, William. 1981. "Introduction: The New Context for Ministry with the Aging." In *Ministry with the Aging*, edited by William M. Clements, 1-17. San Francisco: Harper & Row Publishers.

Clements, William M., ed. 1981. *Ministry with the Aging*. San Francisco: Harper & Row Publishers, 1981.

Cole, C. S. 2006. "Grant Results Topic Summary: Long-Term-Care Housing and Supportive Services." The Robert Wood Johnson Foundation, December 22, 2006. http://www.rwjf.org.

Cole, Elbert. 1981. "Lay Ministries with Older Adults." *Ministry with the Aging*, edited by William M. Clements, 250-65. San Francisco: Harper & Row Publishers.

Cole, Thomas R., and Sally A. Gadow, eds. 1986. *What Does It Mean to Grow Old?, Reflections from the Humanities*. Durham, NC: Duke University Press.

Cole, Thomas R., W. A. Achenbaum, and P. Jakobi, eds. 1993. *Voices and Visions of Aging: Toward a Critical Gerontology*. New York: Springer Publishing Company.

"The Collaboration with All: A Widespread Culture of Solidarity." Friendship with the Poor, The Community of Sant'Egidio. http://www.santegidio.org.

Collis, Ronald L. 2010. "Green House Homes Grow Up." *Provider, Extra News Online*, May 2010. http://www.ahcancal.org.

Come rimanere a casa propria da anziani. 2004. Rome: Community of Sant'Egidio.

Committee on the Future Health Care Workforce for Older Americans, Institute of Medicine of the National Academies. 2008. *Retooling for an Aging America: Building the Health Care Workforce.* Washington, DC: National Academies Press.

"The Community." The Community of Sant'Egidio. http://www.sant egidio.org.

"The Conclusion of the International Conference on Old People in Africa: The Debate and the Proposals." The Community of Sant' Egidio. http://www.santegidio.org.

"Congregational Best Practices." *The Episcopal Church Older Adult Ministries.* The Episcopal Church, n.d. http://www.episcopal church. org.

"Cost of Care." 2006. *Frontline: Living Old.* PBS online. http://www.pbs. org.

Culpepper, R. Alan. 1995. "The Gospel of Luke: Introduction, Commentary, and Reflections." *The New Interpreter's Bible: A Commentary in Twelve Volumes.* Nashville: Abingdon Press.

"Current Geriatrician Shortfall." 2010. The American Geriatrics Society. http://www.americangeriatrics.org.

Cutler, Lois J., and Rosalie A. Kane. 2009. "Post-Occupancy Evaluation of a Transformed Nursing Home: The First Four Green House Settings." *Journal of Housing for the Elderly* 23.4: 304-34.

Daniels, Norman. 1985. "Family Responsibility Initiatives and Justice between Age Groups." *Law, Medicine, & Health Care* 13.4: 153-59.

———. 1988. *Am I My Parents' Keeper? An Essay on Justice between the Young and the Old.* New York: Oxford University Press.

"The Demand for Geriatric Care and the Evident Shortage of Geriatrics Healthcare Providers: Fact Sheet." The American Geriatrics Society. http://www.americangeriatrics.org.

Dembner, Alice. 2006. "'Green Houses' for the Golden Years." *Boston Globe*, September 30, 2006. http://www.boston.com.

Deutsch, Claudia H. 2007, "Training to Be Old." *New York Times,* April 10, 2007. http://www.nytimes.com.

"Developing Small Community Homes as Alternatives to Nursing Homes; 'Green House' Model a New Approach to Long-Term Care." 2005. *AScribe Health News Service,* November 7, 2005. *General One-File.* Available online.

Devor, Nancy Gieseler, and K. Pargament. 2003. "Understanding Religious Coping with Late-Life Crises." In *Aging, Spirituality, and Religion: A Handbook, Volume 2,* edited by Melvin A. Kimble and Susan H. McFadden, 195-205. Minneapolis: Fortress Press.

Dickerson, Ben, and Derrel Watkins. 2003. "The Caleb Affect: The Oldest-Old in Church and Society." *Journal of Religious Gerontology* 15.1/2: 201-13.

Duhigg, Charles. 2007. "Congress Putting Long-Term Care under Scrutiny." *New York Times,* May 25, 2007. http://www.nytimes.com.

Dunn, James J. 2000. "The First and Second Letters to Timothy and the Letter to Titus: Introduction, Commentary, and Reflections." *The New Interpreter's Bible: A Commentary in Twelve Volumes.* Nashville: Abingdon Press.

Ellin, Abby. 2007. "Shuffleboard Gets Pushed to the Closet." *New York Times,* April 10, 2007: Section H.

"Ensuring Older Americans Access to Healthcare." The American Geriatrics Society. http://www.americangeriatrics.org.

"Evaluating the Green House Model." The Green House Project. http://thegreenhouseproject.org.

"Fact Sheet." 2008. Institute of Medicine of the National Academies. http://www.iom.edu.

Fahey, Charles J., and Martha Holstein. 1993, "Toward a Philosophy of the Third Age." In *Voices and Visions of Aging: Toward a Critical Gerontology,* edited by T. Cole et al., 241-56. New York: Springer Publishing Company.

Federal Interagency Forum on Aging-Related Statistics. 2011. "Older Americans 2010: Key Indicators of Well-Being." Administration on Aging, Department of Health and Human Services. January 14, 2011. http://www.agingstats.gov.

———. "Older Americans 2012: Key Indicators of Well-Being." Administration on Aging, Department of Health and Human Services. http://www.agingstats.gov.

————. "A Profile of Older Americans 2013." Administration on Aging, Department of Health and Human Services. http://www.aoa.gov.

"Final Declaration and Recommendations of the World NGO Forum on Ageing." 2002. Global Action on Aging, April 2002. http://www.globalaging.org.

"Find a Home." 2011. *The Green House Project.* http://thegreenhouse project.org.

Flynn, Meghan. 2008. "Model for the Future: A Large-Scale Renovation Signifies Big Cultural Changes for This Long-Term Care Facility, Which Already Uses Innovative Methods to Foster a Culture of Home-like Living." *Inside Healthcare*: 92ff. *General OneFile.* Available online.

Fretheim, Terence E. 1994. "The Book of Genesis: Introduction, Commentary, and Reflections." *The New Interpreter's Bible: A Commentary in Twelve Volumes.* Nashville: Abingdon Press, 1994.

Freudenheim, Milt. 2010a. "Despite Aging Baby Boomers, N.I.H. Devotes Only 11 Percent to Elderly Studies." *New York Times,* June 29, 2010. http://www.nytimes.com.

————. 2010b. "The New Landscape: Preparing More Care of Elderly." *New York Times,* June 29, 2010. http://www.nytimes.com.

"Friends of Elderly in Institutes." Friendship with the Poor, The Community of Sant'Egidio. http://www.santegidio.org.

"Friends on the Street." The Community of Sant'Egidio. http://www.santegidio.org.

"The Friendship between Young People and the Elderly." Friendship with the Poor, The Community of Sant'Egidio. http://www.sant egidio.org.

"Friendship with the Poor." The Community of Sant'Egidio. http://www.santegidio.org.

Fries, James. 1980. "Aging, Natural Death, and the Compression of Morbidity." *New England Journal of Medicine* 303.3: 130-35.

————. 2003. "Measuring and Monitoring Success in Compressing Morbidity." *Annals of Internal Medicine* 139.5/2: 455-59.

Fritz Cates, Diana. 1997. *Choosing to Feel: Virtue, Friendship, and Compassion for Friends.* Notre Dame, IN: University of Notre Dame Press.

Gardner, Freda. 1994. "Another Look at the Elderly." In *The Treasure of Earthen Vessels: Explorations in Theological Anthropology in Honor of*

James N. Lapsley, edited by Brian H. Childs and David W. Waanders, 174-93. Louisville, KY: Westminster/John Knox Press.

"*Gaudium et spes, Pastoral Constitution on the Church in the Modern World.*" 1996. In *Vatican Council II: Constitutions, Decrees, Declarations,* edited by Austin Flannery, 162-282. Northport, NY: Costello Publishing Company.

Gawande, Atul. 2007a. "Rethinking Old Age." *New York Times,* May 24, 2007. http://www.nytimes.com.

———. 2007b. "The Way We Age Now." *The New Yorker,* April 30, 2007: 50-59.

———. 2014. *Being Mortal: Medicine and What Matters in the End.* New York: Metropolitan Books.

"General Aging Facts." 2006. *Frontline: Living Old.* PBS online. http://www.pbs.org.

"Geriatrics." Health Resources and Services Administration, U.S. Department of Health and Human Services. http://bhpr.hrsa.gov.

"Geriatrics Health Care Training Programs under Title VII and VIII of PHSA, Fact Sheet." The American Geriatrics Society. http://www.americangeriatrics.org.

"Geriatrician Facts." 2006. *Frontline: Living Old,* PBS online. http://www.pbs.org.

Gillette, Becky. 2006. "'Meaningful' Environment Underpins 'Green House' Care." *Mississippi Business Journal* 28.50: A1-2.

Gilsinan, Kathy. 2008. "Sant'Egidio at 40: Sant'Egidio, Linking Friendship and Service in World-Changing Ways." *National Catholic Reporter,* May 16, 2008. http://ncronline.org.

"Global Issues—Ageing." The United Nations. http://www.un.org.

"Gray Panthers' Founding." Gray Panthers, Age and Youth in Action. http://graypanthers.org.

"Gray Panthers—Issue Resolutions Summary." Gray Panthers, Age and Youth in Action. http://graypanthers.org.

"Green House Nursing Homes." 2007. *Religion and Ethics Newsweekly,* PBS online. http://www.pbs.org.

"'Green House' Nursing Homes Expand as Communities Reinvent Elder Care." 2008. *PBS Newshour.* http://www.pbs.org.

"Green House Organizers Say Survey Shows Success of New Approach." 2004. *Older Americans Report* 28.44: 351. *General OneFile.* Available online.

"Green House Projects Let Elders Age in Homes." 2009. *Talk of the Nation*. NPR. *General OneFile*. Available online.

Greer, Rowan. 2003. "Special Gift and Special Burden: Views of Old Age in the Early Church." In *Growing Old in Christ*, edited by Stanley Hauerwas et al., 19-37. Grand Rapids, MI: William B. Eerdmans Publishing Company.

Gross, Jane. 2007a. "New Options (and Risks) in Home for Elderly." *New York Times*, March 1, 2007. http://www.nytimes.com.

————. 2007b. "Prevalence of Alzheimer's Rises 10% in 5 Years." *New York Times*, March 21, 2007. http://www.nytimes.com.

Guide Book for Transforming Long-Term Care. 2010. Arlington, VA: Green House Project.

"Guided Care: Better Care for Older People with Chronic Conditions." 2010. Guided Care. http://www.guidedcare.org.

Gustafson, James M. 1970. "The Place of Scripture in Christian Ethics: A Methodological Study." *Interpretation* 24: 430-55.

————. 1988. *Varieties of Moral Discourse: Prophetic, Narrative, Ethical, and Policy*. Grand Rapids, MI: Calvin College and Seminary.

Haddorff, David. 2010. *Christian Ethics as Witness: Barth's Ethics for a World at Risk*. Eugene, OR: Cascade Books.

Haight, Roger. 1990. *Dynamics of Theology*. Maryknoll, NY: Orbis Books.

Hamilton, William. 2005. "The New Nursing Home, Emphasis on Home." *New York Times*, April 23, 2005. http://www.nytimes.com.

"The Hard Work of Living." Friendship with the Poor, The Community of Sant'Egidio. http://www.santegidio.org.

Harper, Sarah. 2006. "Mature Societies: Planning for Our Future Selves." *Daedalus* 135.1: 20-31.

Harrington, Charlene, et al. 2012. "Medicaid Home- and Community-Based Services: Impact of the Affordable Care Act." *Journal of Aging & Social Policy* 24.2: 169-87.

Harris, J. Gordon. 1987. *God and the Elderly: Biblical Perspectives on Aging*. Philadelphia: Fortress Press.

Hauerwas, Stanley, Carole Bailey Stoneking, Keith G. Meador, and David Cloutier, eds. 2003. *Growing Old in Christ*. Grand Rapids, MI: William B. Eerdmans Publishing Company.

Hauerwas, Stanley, and Laura Yordy. 2003. "Captured in Time: Friendship and Aging." In *Growing Old in Christ*, edited by Stanley Hauerwas et al., 169-84. Grand Rapids, MI: William B. Eerdmans Publishing Company.

Hawes, Catherine, et al. 2012. "Nursing Homes and the Affordable Care Act: A Cease Fire in the Ongoing Struggle over Quality Reform." *Journal of Aging & Social Policy* 24.2: 206-20.

Hays, Richard B., and Judith C. Hays. 2003. "The Christian Practice of Growing Old: The Witness of Scripture." In *Growing Old in Christ*, edited by Stanley Hauerwas et al., 3-18. Grand Rapids, MI: William B. Eerdmans Publishing Company.

"Health Reform GPS." Robert Wood Johnson Foundation and Hirsh Health, Law, and Policy Program of George Washington University. http://www.healthreformgps.org.

Hebert, L.E., et al. 2003. "Alzheimer Disease in the US Population: Prevalence Estimates Using the 2000 Census." *Archives of Neurology* 60: 1110-22.

Hendricks, Howard G. 2000. "Rethinking Retirement." *Bibliotheca Sacra* 157: 131-40.

Heschel, Abraham Joshua. 1972. "To Grow in Wisdom." In *The Insecurity of Freedom: Essays on Human Existence*, 70-84. New York: Schocken Books.

Hinze, Christine Firer. 2005. "Commentary on *Quadagesimo anno* (after Forty Years)." In *Modern Catholic Social Teaching: Commentaries and Interpretations*, edited by Kenneth R. Himes, 151-74. Washington, DC: Georgetown University Press.

Hollenbach, David. 2002. *The Common Good and Christian Social Ethics.* New York: Cambridge University Press.

———. 2005. "Commentary on *Gaudium et spes* (Pastoral Constitution on the Church in the Modern World)." In *Modern Catholic Social Teaching: Commentaries and Interpretations*, edited by Kenneth R. Himes, 266-91. Washington, DC: Georgetown University Press.

"Home." Gray Panthers, Age and Youth in Action. http://www.gray panthers.org.

"Home Help: The Gestures of Friendship." Friendship with the Poor, The Community of Sant'Egidio. http://www.santegidio.org.

"Home Help: What We Do." Friendship with the Poor, The Community of Sant'Egidio. http://www.santegidio.org.

"House Promotes Green Houses." 2007. *McKnight's Long-Term Care News*: 21. *General OneFile*. Available online.

Houser, Ari. 2007. "Nursing Homes." AARP Public Policy Institute. http://www.aarp.org.

Hume, Cameron. 1994. *Ending Mozambique's War.* Washington, DC: U.S. Institute of Peace Press.

"Implications of an Ageing Society." United Nations Programme on Ageing. http://www.un.org.

"Interviews: Leon Kass, M.D." 2006. *Frontline: Living Old.* PBS online. http://www.pbs.org.

Jacoby, Susan. 2010. "Real Life among the Old Old." *New York Times,* December 30, 2010. http://www.nytimes.com.

John Paul II. 1982. "Message du Pape Jean-Paul II aux participants à l'Assemblée Mondiale sur le problème du vieillissement de la population." The Papal Archive, The Vatican. http://www.vatican.va.

———. 1984. *Insegnamenti di Giovanni Paolo II,* VII/1. Vatican City: Libreria editrice vaticana.

———. 1988. "Christifideles Laici." The Papal Archive, The Vatican. http://www.vatican.va.

———. 1998. "Message to Thirteenth International Conference 'The Church and the Elderly.'" Catholic Health Association of the United States. http://www.chausa.org.

———. 1999a. "1999 Letter to the Elderly from Pope John Paul II." United States Conference of Catholic Bishops. http://www.usccb.org.

———. 1999b. "Understanding and Respect for the Elderly." Catholic Health Association of the United States. http://www.chausa.org.

———. 2002. "Letter of John Paul II to the President of the Second World Assembly on Ageing." The Papal Archive, The Vatican. http://www.vatican.va.

———. 2005. "Message of His Holiness John Paul II for Lent 2005." The Papal Archive, The Vatican. http://www.vatican.va.

Johnson, Luke Timothy. 2004. "Making Connections: The Material Expression of Friendship in the New Testament." *Interpretation* 58.2: 158-71.

Johnson, Nicholas, Phil Oliff, and Erica Williams. 2010. "An Update on State Budget Cuts: At Least 46 States Have Imposed Cuts That Hurt Vulnerable Residents and the Economy." Center on Budget and Policy Priorities. http://www.cbpp.org.

Johnston, Laura E. 2008. "Signposts for an Ethic of Peacemaking: Reading Gaudium et Spes in Light of Yves Congar and The Community of Sant'Egidio." PhD diss., Boston College.

Jones, Susan Pendleton, and L. Gregory Jones. 2003. "Worship, the Eucharist, Baptism, and Aging." In *Growing Old in Christ*, edited by Stanley Hauerwas et al., 185-201. Grand Rapids, MI: William B. Eerdmans Publishing Company.

Jones, W. Paul. 1986. "Theology and Aging in the 21st Century." *Journal of Religion and Aging* 3.1-2: 17-32.

Jung, Patricia Beattie. 2003. "Differences among the Elderly: Who Is on the Road to Bremen?" In *Growing Old in Christ*, edited by Stanley Hauerwas et al., 112-28. Grand Rapids, MI: William B. Eerdmans Publishing Company.

Kalb, Claudia, and Vanessa Juarez. 2005. "Aging: Small Is Beautiful; The Newest Thing in End-of-Life Care: Residences That Look—and Feel—Like the House You've Lived in All Your Life." *Newsweek*, August 1, 2005, 46. *General OneFile*. Available online.

Kane, Rosalie A., Terry Y. Lum, Lois J. Cutler, Howard B. Degenholtz, and Tzy-Chyi Yu. 2007. "Resident Outcomes in Small-House Nursing Homes: A Longitudinal Evaluation of the Initial Green House Program." *Journal of the American Geriatrics Society*: 832-39.

Kassner, Enid, Susan Reinhard, Wendy Fox-Grage, Ari Houser, Jean Accius. 2008. "A Balancing Act: State Long-Term Care Reform." AARP Public Policy Institute. http://assets.aarp.org.

Keane, Bill. 2004. "Building the New Culture of Aging—One Leader at a Time: Bill Keane, MS, MBA, Director of Special Programs, Mather LifeWays, Interviews Bill Thomas, MD, Founder of The Eden Alternative and The Green House Project." *Nursing Homes* 53.8: 44ff. *General OneFile*. Available online.

Kimble, Melvin. 2001. "Beyond the Biomedical Paradigm: Generating a Spiritual Vision of Ageing." *Journal of Religious Gerontology* 12.3.4: 31-41.

Kimble, Melvin A., and Susan H. McFadden, eds. 2003. *Aging, Spirituality, and Religion: A Handbook, Volume 2*. Minneapolis: Fortress Press.

Kivnick, Helen. 1993. "Everyday Mental Health." *Generations* 17.1: 13-20.

Klapp, Dee Ann. 2003. "Biblical Foundations for a Practical Theology of Aging." *Journal of Religious Gerontology* 15.1-2: 69-85.

Kleinman, Arthur. 2010. "On Caregiving." *Harvard Magazine*: 25-29.

Knierim, Rolf. 1981. "Age and Aging in the Old Testament." In *Ministry with the Aging*, edited by William M. Clements, 21-36. San Francisco: Harper & Row Publishers.

Krisberg, Kim. 2004. "APHA Aging Task Force Tackles Work Force Issues, Recruitment." *The Nation's Health*, September 2004: 2.

————. 2005. "Public Health Work Force Not Prepared for Aging Population." *Nation's Health* 35.4: 1, 20-21.

Kristoff, Nicholas D. 2005. "The Greediest Generation." *New York Times*, May 1, 2005. http://www.nytimes.com.

Krugman, Paul. 2010. "Attacking Social Security." *New York Times*, August 15, 2010. http://www.nytimes.com.

Lagnado, Lucette. 2008. "Rising Challenger Takes on Elder-Care System." *Wall Street Journal Eastern Edition*, June 24, 2008, A1. *General OneFile*. Available online.

LaPorte, Jean. 1981. "The Elderly in the Life and Thought of the Early Church." In *Ministry with the Aging*, edited by William M. Clements, 37-55. San Francisco: Harper & Row Publishers.

LaPorte, Meg. 2010. "Culture Change Goes Mainstream." *Provider*. http://www.ahcancal.org.

"The Latest on Medicare and Social Security." 2010. *New York Times*, August 9, 2010. http://www.nytimes.com.

Lebacqz, Karen. 1986. *Six Theories of Justice*. Minneapolis: Augsburg Publishing House.

Leland, John. 2010. "Cuts in Home Care Put Elderly and Disabled at Risk." *New York Times*, July 20, 2010. http://www.nytimes.com.

"Living Arrangements 85+." 2006. *Frontline: Living Old*. PBS online. http://www.pbs.org.

"Loan Debt and Salary Statistics." The American Geriatrics Society. http://www.americangeriatrics.org.

"The 'Long Live the Elderly' Movement." Friendship with the Poor, The Community of Sant'Egidio. http://www.santegidio.org.

"Long Live the Elderly: A New Model of Welfare, Good and Sustainable." Friendship with the Poor, The Community of Sant'Egidio. http://www.santegidio.org.

Long, Stephen D. 2003. "The Language of Death: Theology and Economics in Conflict." In *Growing Old in Christ*, edited by Stanley Hauerwas et al., 129-50. Grand Rapids, MI: William B. Eerdmans Publishing Company.

"Long Term Care." AARP Public Policy Institute. http://www.aarp.org.

"Long-Term Care Insurance: Do You Need It?" Legal and Insurance, AARP. http://www.aarp.org.

"Long-Term Care Insurance Tax-Deductibility Rules." American Association for Long-Term Care Insurance. http://www.aaltci.org.

Lum, Terry Y., Rosalie A. Kane, Lois J. Cutler, and Tzy-Chyi Yu. 2008. "Effects of Green House Nursing Homes on Residents' Families." *Health Care Financing Review* 30.2: 35ff. *General OneFile*. Available online.

Lysaught, M. Therese. 2003. "Memory, Funerals, and the Communion of Saints: Growing Old and Practices of Remembering." In *Growing Old in Christ*, edited by Stanley Hauerwas et al., 267-301. Grand Rapids, MI: William B. Eerdmans Publishing Company.

MacKinlay, Elizabeth. 2001. "Ageing and Isolation: Is the Issue Social Isolation or Is It Lack of Meaning in Life?" *Journal of Religious Gerontology* 12.3-4: 89-99.

Madison, Anna-Marie, and Brenda F. McGadney. 2000. "Collaboration of Churches and Service Providers: Meeting the Needs of Older African Americans." *Journal of Religious Gerontology* 11.1: 23-37.

Mancinelli, Paolo. 2010. Personal interview. November 7, 2010.

Martin-Achard, Robert. 1991. "Biblical Perspective on Aging: 'Abraham was old . . . and the Lord had blessed him' (Gen. 24.1)." *Concilium* 3: 31-38.

May, William F. 1986. "The Virtues and Vices of the Elderly." In *What Does It Mean to Grow Old?: Reflections from the Humanities*, edited by Thomas R. Cole and Sally A. Gadow, 41-61. Durham, NC: Duke University Press.

McCarthy, David Matzko. 2003. "Generational Conflict: Continuity and Change." In *Growing Old in Christ*, edited by Stanley Hauerwas et al., 226-46. Grand Rapids, MI: William B. Eerdmans Publishing Company.

McKee, Patrick, ed. 1982. *Philosophical Foundations of Gerontology*. New York: Human Sciences Press.

McKenny, Gerald. 2010. *The Analogy of Grace: Karl Barth's Moral Theology*. New York: Oxford University Press.

McNamara, Marie Aquinas. 1964. *Friends and Friendship for Saint Augustine*. Staten Island, NY: Alba House.

"The Meaning of Old Age." Friendship with the Poor, The Community of Sant'Egidio. http://www.santegidio.org.

Meeks, Wayne. 1993. *The Origins of Christian Morality: The First Two Centuries.* New Haven: Yale University Press.

Meilaender, Gilbert. 1981. *Friendship: A Study in Theological Ethics.* Notre Dame, IN: University of Notre Dame Press.

Meiners, Mark R. 2012. "Partnership Long-Term Care Insurance: Lessons For CLASS Program Development." *Journal of Aging & Social Policy* 24.2: 152-68.

Miller, Edward Alan. 2012. "The Affordable Care Act and Long-Term Care: Comprehensive Reform or Just Tinkering around the Edges?" *Journal of Aging & Social Policy* 24.2: 101-17.

Mills, Eugene S. 1993. *The Story of Elderhostel.* Hanover, NH: University of New Hampshire Press.

Minda, Julie. 2010. "Small House Long-Term Care Facilities Make Residents Feel at Home." *Catholic Health World* 26.6. http://www.chausa.org.

"Mission and Vision." The Green House Project. http://www.the green-houseproject.org.

Moody, Harry R. 1988. *Abundance of Life: Human Development Policies for an Aging Society.* New York: Columbia University Press.

————. 1992. *Ethics in an Aging Society.* Baltimore: Johns Hopkins University Press, 1992.

————. 1993. "Overview: What Is Critical Gerontology and Why Is It Important?" In *Voices and Visions of Aging: Toward a Critical Gerontology,* edited by T. Cole et al., xv-xli. New York: Springer Publishing Company, 1993.

————. 1998. "Why Dignity in Old Age Matters." *Journal of Gerontological Social Work* 29:2/3 (1998): 13-38.

————. 2002. "The Changing Meaning of Aging." In *Challenges of the Third Age,* edited by Robert S. Weiss and Scott A. Bass, 41-54. New York: Oxford University Press, 2002.

Moos, Bob. 2006. "Close to Home: 'Green Houses' Are an Alternative to Nursing Facilities." *State News:* 15ff. *General OneFile.* Available online.

Moses, Sarah. 2007. "A Just Society for the Elderly: The Importance of Justice as Participation." *Notre Dame Journal of Law, Ethics, and Public Policy* 21.2: 335-62.

Moses, Stephen. 2007. "The Brave New World of Long-Term Care." *Notre Dame Journal of Law, Ethics, & Public Policy* 21.2: 561-70.

Muller, David. 2006. "Parents & Children." *Frontline: Living Old.* PBS online. http://www.pbs.org.

Netting, F. Ellen. 1995. "Congregation-Sponsored Housing." In *Aging, Spirituality, and Religion: A Handbook,* edited by Melvin Kimble, Susan McFadden, James W. Ellor, and James J. Seeber, 335-49. Minneapolis: Fortress Press.

"A New Image of Aging." Shepherd Centers of America. http://www.shepherdcenters.org.

The New Oxford Annotated Bible with Apocrypha [New Revised Standard Version], edited by Bruce M. Metzger and Roland E. Murphy. New York: Oxford University Press, 1991.

Nursing Home Data Compendium 2013 Edition. 2013. Centers for Medicare and Medicaid Services, Department of Health and Human Services. http://www.cms.gov.

Nussbaum, Martha. 1992. "Human Functioning and Social Justice: In Defense of Aristotelian Essentialsm." *Political Theory* 20.2: 202-46.

————. 2006. *Frontiers of Justice: Disability, Nationality, Species Membership* (The Tanner Lectures on Human Values). Cambridge, MA: Belknap Press of Harvard University Press.

"Our 10 Principles." The Eden Alternative. http://www.edenalt.org.

Outka, Gene. 1972. *Agape: An Ethical Analysis.* New Haven: Yale University Press.

"Parents & Children." 2006. *Frontline: Living Old.* PBS online. http://www.pbs.org.

Parkin, Scott. 2000. "Welcome to the Green House." *Nursing Homes* 49.12: 27. *General OneFile.* Available online.

Partridge, Linda. 2006. "Of Worms, Mice & Men: Altering Rates of Aging." *Daedalus* 135.1: 40-47.

Paul VI. 1998. "Octogesima adveniens." In *Catholic Social Thought: The Documentary Heritage,* edited by David J. O'Brien and Thomas A. Shannon, 263-86. Maryknoll, NY: Orbis Books.

Pear, Robert. 2011. "Health Law to Be Revised by Ending a Program." *New York Times,* October 14, 2011. http://www.nytimes.com.

————. 2014. "Gains Seen for Medicare, but Social Security Holding Steady." *New York Times,* July 28, 2014. http://www.nytimes.com.

Peck, Richard L. 2009. "Managing Alzheimer's in the Green House: It Starts with a Change of Role for the Administrator." *Long-Term Living*: 26ff. *General OneFile.* Available online.

Pinches, Charles. 2003. "The Virtues of Aging." In *Growing Old in Christ*, edited by Stanley Hauerwas et al., 202-25. Grand Rapids, MI: William B. Eerdmans Publishing Company.

Polivka, Larry. 1998. "The Science and Ethics of Long-Term Care." *Generations* 22.3: 21-25.

Pontifical Council for the Laity. 1998. "The Dignity of Older People and Their Mission in the Church and in the World." Pontifical Council for the Laity, The Vatican. http://www.vatican.va.

———. "International Associations of the Faithful Directory." Pontifical Council for the Laity, The Vatican. http://www.vatican.va.

"Population Statistics." 2006. *Frontline: Living Old*. PBS online. http://www.pbs.org.

"The Poverty of the Elderly." Friendship with the Poor, The Community of Sant'Egidio. http://www.santegidio.org.

"President Signs Health Reform Legislation; Reform Enhances Elder Care." 2010. The American Geriatrics Society. http://www.americangeriatrics.org.

President's Council on Bioethics. 2005. *Taking Care: Ethical Caregiving in Our Aging Society*. Washington, DC: President's Council on Bioethics.

"The Principles of Geriatric Care, Fact Sheet." The American Geriatrics Society. http://www.americangeriatrics.org.

Probst, Janice, Jong-Deuk Baek, and Sarah Laditka. 2010. "The Relationship between Workplace Environment and Job Satisfaction among Nursing Assistants: Findings from a National Survey." *Journal of the American Medical Directors Association* 11.4: 246-52.

"Projected Future Need for Geriatricians." 2010. The American Geriatrics Society. http://www.americangeriatrics.org.

Rabig, Judith, William Thomas, Rosalie A. Kane, Lois J. Cutler, and Steve McAlilly. 2006. "Radical Redesign of Nursing Homes: Applying the Green House Concept in Tupelo, Mississippi." *The Gerontologist* 46.4: 533-39.

"Reform Overview." HealthReform GPS, George Wasthington University and the Robert Wood Johnson Foundation. http://www.healthreformgps.org.

"Reforming the Medicare Payment System: Geriatricians are Disproportionately Affected." The American Geriatrics Society. http://www.americangeriatrics.org.

"Regulation and Legislation." The Green House Project. http://www. thegreenhouseproject.org.

"Respect for Self-Determination." Friendship with the Poor, The Community of Sant'Egidio. http://www.santegidio.org.

Riccardi, Andrea. 1998. "Promoting Democracy, Peace, and Solidarity." *Journal of Democracy* 9.4: 157-67.

———. 1999. *Sant'Egidio, Rome and the World*, translated by Peter Heinegg. London: St. Pauls.

———. 2002. "An Elderly Person as a Friend" (*Un anziano come amico*), translated by William Schenck. January 12, 2002. Lecture.

Ricoeur, Paul. 1992. *Oneself as Another*, translated by Kathleen Blamey. Chicago: University of Chicago Press.

Riley, Matilda White, Robert L. Kahn, and Anne Foner. 1994. "Introduction: The Mismatch between People and Structures." In *Age and Structural Lag*, edited by M. Riley et al., 1-6. New York: A Wiley Interscience Publication.

Rubenstein, Robert. 2002. "The Third Age." In *Challenges of the Third Age*, edited by R. Weiss and S. Bass, 29-40. New York: Oxford University Press.

"Ruth Sheets Adult Care Center." Edenton Street United Methodist Church. http://www.esumc.org.

Sapp, Stephen. 1987a. "An Alternative Christian View of Aging." *Journal of Religion & Aging* 4.1: 1-13.

———. 1987b. *Full of Years: Aging and the Elderly in the Bible and Today*. Nashville: Abingdon Press.

Sass, Steven, Alicia H. Munnell, and Andrew Eschtruth. 2009. *The Social Security Fix-It Book*. Boston: Center for Retirement Research at Boston College.

Schilling, Becky. 2009. "A Green House Movement: As Long-Term Care Facilities Implement Culture Change, Some Locations Are Turning to the Green House Model to Bring Person-Centric Care to Residents." *Food Service Director* 22.11: 22ff. *General OneFile*. Available online.

Schotsmans, Paul. 1991. "Life as Full Flowering: The Contributions of Older People to a Humane Civilization." *Concilium* 3: 46-57.

Schweiker, William. 2004. "On Religious Ethics." In *The Blackwell Companion to Religious Ethics*, edited by W. Schweiker, 1-15. Malden, MA: Blackwell Publishing.

Scott-Maxwell, Florida. 1968. *The Measure of My Days*. New York: Penguin.

"The Secret of an Alliance." Friendship with the Poor, The Community of Sant'Egidio. http://www.santegidio.org.

Seeber, James J. 2003. "Volunteer Ministries with Older Adults." In *Aging, Spirituality, and Religion, Volume 2*, edited by Melvin Kimble and Susan H. McFadden, 168-79. Minneapolis: Fortress Press.

Sharkey, Siobhan, Sandra Hudak, Susan Horn, Bobbie James, and Jessie Howes. 2011. "Frontline Caregiver Daily Practices: A Comparison Study of Traditional Nursing Homes and the Green House Project Sites." *Journal of the American Geriatrics Society* 59.1: 126-31.

Shaw, Jonathan. 2005. "The Aging Enigma: Scientists Probe the Genetic Basis of Longevity." *Harvard Magazine*: 46-53, 91.

Shuman, Joel James. 2003. "The Last Gift: The Elderly, the Church, and the Gift of a Good Death." In *Growing Old in Christ*, edited by Stanley Hauerwas et al., 151-68. Grand Rapids, MI: William B. Eerdmans Publishing Company.

Simmons, Henry C. 1998. "Spirituality and Community in the Last Stage of Life." *Journal of Gerontological Social Work* 29.3/4: 73-91.

Smyer, Michael A., ed. 1993. *Mental Health and Aging: Progress and Prospects*. New York: Springer Publishing Company.

Smyer, Michael A., and Sara H. Qualls. 1999. *Aging and Mental Health*. Malden, MA: Blackwell Publishers.

Span, Paula. 2010a. "Details on the Class Act, Pt. 2." In *The New Old Age, New York Times*, March 3, 2010. http://newoldage.blogs.nytimes.com.

———. 2010b. "States Cut Aid to the Homebound." In *The New Old Age, New York Times*, July 22, 2010. http://newoldage.blogs.nytimes.com.

Squillace, Marie R., Kevin J. Mahoney, Dawn M. Loughlin, Lori Simon-Rusinowitz, and Sharon M. Desmond. 2002. "An Exploratory Study of Personal Assistance Service Choice and Decision-Making among Persons with Disabilities and Surrogate Representatives." *Journal of Mental Health and Aging* 8.3: 225-40.

"Statistics about Alzheimer's Disease." 2007. Alzheimer's Association. http://www.alz.org.

Stoneking, Carole B. 2003. "Modernity: The Social Construction of Aging." In *Growing Old in Christ*, edited by Stanley Hauerwas et al.,

63-89. Grand Rapids, MI: William B. Eerdmans Publishing Company.

"Supporters." The Green House Project. http://www.thegreenhouse project.org.

Tarkan, Laurie. 2011. "A Nursing Home Shrinks until It Feels Like a Home." *New York Times*, November 1, 2011, A5.

Thane, Pat. 2000. "The History of Aging in the West." In *Handbook of the Humanities and Aging*, 2nd ed., edited by T. Cole, R. Kastenbaum and R. Ray, 3-24. New York: Springer Publishing Company.

Thiemann, Ron. 1991, *Constructing a Public Theology: The Church in a Pluralistic Age*. Louisville, KY: Westminster/John Knox Press.

———. 1996. *Religion in Public Life: A Dilemma for Democracy*. Washington, DC: Georgetown University Press.

Thomas, William H. 1996. *Life Worth Living: How Someone You Love Can Still Enjoy Life in a Nursing Home*. Acton, MA: VanderWyk & Burnham.

———. 2004. *What Are Old People For? How Elders Will Save the World*. Acton, MA: VanderWyk & Burnham.

Thompson, Jean E. 1986. "Life Care Ministry: The Church as Part of the Elderly Support Network." *Journal of Religion and Aging* 2.3: 65-76.

Thornton, James E., and Earl R. Winkler, eds. 1988. *Ethics and Aging: The Right to Live, the Right to Die*. Vancouver: University of British Columbia Press.

"Towards a Society for All Ages." Ageing: Social Policy and Development Division, United Nations Department of Economic and Social Affairs. http://www.un.org.

"Traceway Breaks Ground. (Strictly Business)." 2002. *Mississippi Business Journal*, September 9, 2002, 8. *General OneFile*. Available online.

Trible, Phyllis, and Letty Mandeville Russell. 2006. *Hagar, Sarah, and Their Children: Jewish, Christian, and Muslim Perspectives*. Louisville, KY: Westminster John Knox.

Tubbesing, Carl, and Joy Johnson Wilson. 2006. "A New Medicaid." *State Legislatures* 32.4: 20-21.

"U.N. Offers Action Plan for a World Aging Rapidly." 2002. *New York Times*, April 14, 2002, A4.

United Nations Department of Economic and Social Affairs, Population Division, Expert Meeting on World Population in 2300. 2003. *World Population in 2300*. http://www.un.org.

"United Nations Principles for Older Persons." United Nations Programme on Ageing. http://www.un.org.

"United States: Community of Sant'Egidio." Community of Sant'
Egidio, United States. http://www.santegidiousa.org.

United States Conference of Catholic Bishops. 1998. "Economic Justice for All." In *Catholic Social Thought: The Documentary Heritage*,
edited by David J. O'Brien and Thomas A. Shannon, 572-680. Maryknoll, NY: Orbis Books.

———. 1999. "Blessings of Age: A Pastoral Message on Growing Older
within the Faith Community." http://www.nccbuscc.org.

Universal Declaration of Human Rights (1948). 1998. In *Religion and
Human Rights: Basic Documents*, edited by T. Stahnke and J. Martin,
57-60. New York: Center for the Study of Human Rights, Columbia
University.

Urbina, Ian. 2010. "Earthquake's Burdens Weigh Heavily on Haiti's
Elderly." *New York Times, March* 12, 2010: A4.

Verhey, Allen. 1996. "Scripture and Ethics: Practices, Performances, and
Prescriptions." In *Christian Ethics: Problems and Prospects*, edited by
Lisa Sowle Cahill and James F. Childress, 18-44. Cleveland, OH:
Pilgrim Press, 1996.

———. 2002. *Remembering Jesus: Christian Community, Scripture, and
the Moral Life*. Grand Rapids, MI: Wm. B. Eerdmans Publishing Co.

Volzer, Robert. 2003. "Home Is Where the 'Hearth' Is." *Long Term Living*
47: 47-48.

Wadell, Paul J. 1989. *Friendship and the Moral Life*. Notre Dame, IN: University of Notre Dame Press.

———. 2002. *Becoming Friends: Worship, Justice, and the Practice of
Christian Friendship*. Grand Rapids, MI: Brazos Press.

"'We Love You': The Elderly of the Home-Community of Via Fontei-
ana Send a Message against Intolerance, for a Friendly and Solidal
Neighbourhood." 2009. The Community of Sant'Egidio. http://
www.santegidio.org.

Wallace, Nicole. 2006. "Dignity by Design." *Chronicle of Philanthropy*
18.16: 10-18.

Weiss, Robert S., and Scott A. Bass. 2002. "Introduction." *Challenges of
the Third Age*, edited by R. Weiss and S. Bass. New York: Oxford University Press.

Weissert, William G. 2012. "A 10-Foot Rope for a 50-Yard Drop: The CLASS Act in the Patient Protection and Affordable Care Act." *Journal of Aging & Social Policy* 24.2: 136-51.

Werner, Carrie A. 2011. "The Older Population: 2010." *2010 Census Briefs*. U.S. Census Bureau. http://www.census.gov.

"What Needs to Change." 2006. *Frontline: Living Old*. PBS online. http://www.pbs.org.

White, Carolinne. 1992. *Christian Friendship in the Fourth Century*. New York: Cambridge University Press.

Wiener, Joshua M. 2010. "Long-Term Care: Getting on the Agenda and Knowing What to Propose." *Medical Care Research & Review* 67.S4: 126S-40S.

———. 2012. "The CLASS Act: Is It Dead or Just Sleeping?" *Journal of Aging & Social Policy* 24.2: 118-35.

Williams, Rowan. 2012. "The Gifts Reserved for Age: Perceptions of the Elderly." In *Faith in the Public Square*, 243-51. New York: Bloomsbury.

Williamson, John B., and Diane M. Watts-Roy. 1999. "Framing the Generational Equity Debate." In *The Generational Equity Debate*, edited by J. Williamson, D. Watts-Roy, and E. Kingson, 3-37. New York: Columbia University Press.

Williamson, Julie E. 2003. "Study Underway to Measure Green House Outcomes." *McKnight's Long-Term Care News* 24.12: 17. *General OneFile*. Available online.

———. 2006. "Doubting Thomas. (Profile) (William H. Thomas)." *McKnight's Long-Term Care News*: 54. *General OneFile*. Available online.

Wilson, Chris. 2006. "The Century Ahead." *Daedalus* 135.1: 5-8.

Wimberly, Anne E. Streaty. 2003. "Congregational Care in the Lives of Black Older Adults." In *Aging, Spirituality, and Religion: A Handbook, Volume 2*, edited by Melvin A. Kimble and Susan H. McFadden, 101-20. Minneapolis: Fortress Press.

Wolicka, Elzieta. 1981. "Participation in Community: Wojtyla's Social Anthropology." *Communio* 8: 108-18.

Yang, Y. Tony, and Gilbert Gimm. 2013. "Caring for Elder Parents: A Comparative Evaluation of Family Leave Laws." *Journal of Law, Medicine & Ethics*. 41.2: 501-13.

Index